At Focus on the Family, I have the privilege of working with Dr. Greg and Erin Smalley on a regular basis. When it comes to marriage and relationships, they know their stuff! And they have assembled an amazing team of like-minded Christian marriage experts for this practical and readable volume. Trust me, if you're planning to get married, you need to read this book first. You and your spouse-to-be will be so glad you did.

JIM DALY
President of Focus on the Family

Marriage is a glorious but sometimes difficult journey for a man and a woman. I am thankful Greg wrote this book, and I believe it will become a trusted guide for couples who want a solid foundation for their relationship.

BRADY BOYD
Pastor of New Life Church and author of *Addicted to Busy*

Wow, what a treasure trove! All the best premarital wisdom from all my favorite marriage leaders. Every engaged couple should schedule a short break from auditioning DJs for their reception and read this during that time. It will be the best possible investment they can make.

SHAUNTI FELDHAHN
Social researcher and bestselling author of *For Women Only* and *For Men Only*

Striking the perfect balance between practical, instructional, inspirational, and spiritual advice, *Ready to Wed* will immediately take its place as one of the most important and valuable resources available for Christian couples who want to start their marriage off right. Highly recommended.

GARY THOMAS
Author of *Sacred Marriage* and *A Lifelong Love*

Ready to Wed

12 Ways to Start a Marriage You'll Love

Dr. Greg & Erin Smalley

General Editors

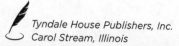

Tyndale House Publishers, Inc.
Carol Stream, Illinois

Library of Congress Cataloging-in-Publication Data
Ready to wed : 12 ways to start a marriage you will love / General Editors, Dr. Greg and Erin Smalley.
      pages cm
  Includes bibliographical references and index.
  ISBN 978-1-62405-406-8 (alk. paper)
  1. Marriage—Religious aspects—Christianity. I. Smalley, Greg, editor. II. Smalley, Erin, editor.
  BV835.R425 2015
  248.8´44--dc23   2014046637

Printed in the United States of America

22   20   19   18   17   16
 8   7   6   5   4   3

CONTENTS

INTRODUCTION

Dr. Greg Smalley and Erin Smalley

PLANNING FOR "THE DAY" or for a lifetime?

This question was written with big cursive lettering on a booth display that Erin and I (Greg) used at bridal fairs to advertise our premarital seminars. It was always so much fun to watch not only the prospective brides but also their mothers walk by and testify in their most sassy voices, "Mm-hmm!"

You see, rarely did we get any brides to stop at our booth. Each bride was so busy planning for her special day—the dress, the cake, the venue, the photographer, the honeymoon—she hardly gave much thought to planning for her future marriage. Sadly, only about 35 to 40 percent of engaged couples will receive quality premarital education.[1] And by quality, we mean at least eight to ten hours of instruction from someone who has been equipped to do so. This is so unfortunate because the premarital research is so strong. Note these remarkable statistics:

- You're 30 percent less likely to get divorced if you get some sort of premarital training before you marry.[2]

- Eighty percent of the couples who received premarital training stayed together.[3]

- Couples who participate in premarital programs experience a 30 percent increase in marital satisfaction over those who don't participate.[4]

The moms who were walking around with their daughters at the bridal fair understood this, and that's why the majority of the tickets we sold were to the mothers as gifts to their daughters and future sons-in-law.

But you're different! We're certain you're also thinking of your future with your fiancé(e)—especially since you are reading this book. That's why we're thrilled that in the midst of all you have going on, you're also spending time working on your relationship. It's so exciting that you're taking time to participate in Focus on the Family's *Ready to Wed* experience. Our desire is to help you grow a strong marriage relationship that will last a lifetime.

Growing a Strong Marriage

Over the years, I (Greg) have been blessed to officiate at several wedding ceremonies. But I'll never forget my first. Erin and I did premarital counseling with this one couple during their engagement period. As I thought about what I would say to them during the ceremony, I decided that I wanted to give them a creative picture of how to build a strong marriage relationship. I had sat through one too many wedding ceremonies where I could barely keep my eyes open during the teaching portion. So I developed what I thought was a powerful analogy of a strong marriage, using the bride's wedding bouquet. The key point I wanted to make was that it takes time and care to mature seeds (where their marriage was starting out) into a beautiful bouquet (a strong marriage). I thought I was so clever!

To construct my "amazing" analogy, I needed to know the types of flowers the bride had chosen for her bridal bouquet. After asking around, I discovered that she would be carrying calla lilies. So I went out in search of a packet of seeds to present to this young, anxious couple during my teaching, only to find out that calla lilies grow from bulbs. Good to know! Since bulbs obviously weren't going to work, I bought generic flower seeds instead and planned on telling the couple that they represented the bride's beautiful bouquet.

So there we were. A beautiful Missouri summer day—hot and humid but very pretty. The bride and groom were anxious with anticipation as they finally reached the day they were to become man and wife. The sanctuary was packed with their special guests, and my precious wife and kids were in the audience both to witness the union and to support me while I officiated.

I began the ceremony by holding up the bride's beautiful wedding bouquet. The audience let out several *oohs* and *aahs* as I explained that this bouquet was an image of the couple's ideal relationship—the marriage they'd always dreamed of. I then held up the package of seeds for the bride and groom to hold, clarifying that this was where their marriage was starting. I wanted them to understand that it would take time and effort to "mature" their relationship from a package of seeds to a bouquet of beautiful flowers. Then I went on to explain that the key was to use the right nutrients and care to begin growing their relationship seeds.

I was on a roll, and everything was going perfectly until I came to the last point of my brilliant analogy. I had already laid the groundwork for growing the seeds using water, sunshine, and proper pruning, and I related each of these aspects to a particular relationship skill (communication, spiritual connection, and conflict management). However, because I don't have a green thumb, and I know virtually nothing about growing flowers, I quickly ran out of gardening analogies to use for my last relationship point: spending time together. Unfortunately, the only thing I could think of was fertilizer.

I was almost done and was feeling rather proud of myself. But for some reason, the mood of the audience changed suddenly when I said, "Much like fertilizer helps calla lilies grow strong and healthy, if you want a strong marriage, you need to spend at least twenty minutes each day fertilizing each other."

The crowd broke out into roaring laughter. I had no idea why they were all laughing, so I looked at my wife, Erin—you know, my "helpmate"—for some type of clue, but she, too, had tears streaming down her face from laughing so hard. As I tried to recover by rambling on about something else, the groom leaned in and said, "If you would finish your point, I could get on with fertilizing my bride!"

I about died. I had never thought about my words from that perspective and very quickly learned why everyone was laughing at me. I did accomplish what I set out to do, though: No one was bored. And I made a point about the importance of spending time together (or fertilizing) that will never be forgotten!

Now back to you and your relationship with your future spouse. Like the couple in my illustration, you are starting out your marriage as a packet of seeds. As you picture your wedding bouquet, realize that growing your relationship will also take time, effort, and some important skills and tools that you'll learn throughout this book.

We've assembled an amazing lineup of marriage experts to help you grow the seeds of your relationship. We hope the time and effort you put into this experience will sprout your marriage and the advice you find in this book will act like Miracle-Gro in your relationship. We're confident that once you complete the *Ready to Wed* experience, your relationship will grow twice as big and will bloom with more vibrant colors!

So here are four steps to help you make the most out of the *Ready to Wed* experience and grow a marriage more beautiful than your wedding:

Step 1: Take the Couple Checkup. This is the best online relationship assessment available. By taking the Couple Checkup, you'll identify your unique relationship strengths and potential growth areas. The assessment is organized to match the chapter themes in the book, so it's a wonderful companion experience, and the results will help you focus on what's most necessary for your relationship. Refer to appendix A for more information on why this assessment is such an important part of your premarital training. Go to *www.FocusOnTheFamily.com/ReadyToWed* to take the assessment and receive your customized report.

Step 2: Find a mentor couple. You and your fiancé(e) will gain so much by reading this book together; however, we highly recommend that you go through *Ready to Wed* with a mentor couple as well. A mentor couple is a relatively happy (but not perfect), more experienced couple who will help you successfully navigate your journey to the altar and thrive during your first year of marriage. This is exactly why King Solomon wrote, "Where there is no guidance, a people falls, but in an abundance of counselors there is safety" (Proverbs 11:14, ESV). Go to *www .FocusOnTheFamily.com/ReadyToWed* for some ideas and tips on how to find a mentor couple.

Step 3: Complete the discussion questions. Be sure to answer the discussion questions and complete the activity points at the end of every chapter. These activities are designed to help you apply the key concepts you'll read throughout the book.

Step 4: Use the Ready to Wed *app.* This companion app provides the opportunity to have some fun with each other as you walk through your engagement journey. You'll find helpful questions to ask each other, games, quizzes, videos, Q&As, and other insights to strengthen your relationship while you're preparing for a marriage you'll love. Go to *www.FocusOnTheFamily.com/ReadyToWed* to download the app.

We applaud you for taking the time to prepare for the journey of marriage. We know that you have a lot on your plate right now as you plan for your wedding. What an amazing day that's going to be! But remember, your wedding is only *one* day; your relationship will last a lifetime. Thus, we strongly encourage you to avoid rushing through this experience—like one more thing to cross off your prewedding checklist. Take your time. Try to read only one chapter per week so that you have plenty of time to discuss these important topics and work through the discussion questions and activities together. Savor these moments of discussion.

Dig deep as you share with each other. Be real and honest and vulnerable with each other and your mentor couple. And get ready to experience love and commitment on a whole new level. If you happen to come across topics or issues that seem to cause concern or red flags, enlist the help of a pastor or counselor. You can call Focus on the Family at any time using our toll-free number (1-800-A-FAMILY). We have licensed counselors standing by who can help or can give you a referral for a counselor in your area. This is a free service, so don't hesitate to call us. The time you spend now preparing for your marriage will pay out dividends in the long run.

But before we jump into talking about skills and tools, we need to lay the proper foundation. As the Chinese philosopher Lao Tzu said, "A journey of a thousand miles begins with a single step." We believe that the first step in your journey toward the marital relationship you've always dreamed of is to understand God's true design for marriage.

CHAPTER 1

GOD'S DESIGN FOR MARRIAGE

Dr. Greg Smalley and Erin Smalley

GOD IS THE CREATOR OF MARRIAGE—it was His idea from the very beginning. Listen to how Eugene Peterson, author of *The Message*, paraphrases this truth:

> GOD, not you, made marriage. His Spirit inhabits even the smallest details of marriage. And what does he want from marriage? Children of God, that's what. So guard the spirit of marriage within you. Don't cheat on your spouse.
>
> "I hate divorce," says the GOD of Israel. GOD-of-the-Angel-Armies says, "I hate the violent dismembering of the 'one flesh' of marriage." So watch yourselves. Don't let your guard down.
> MALACHI 2:15–16, MSG

God is so passionate about marriage that He gave it a very important place throughout the Bible. The Scriptures *begin* with a marriage: "It is not good for the man to be alone. I will make a helper suitable for him" (Genesis 2:18). Then right in the *middle* of the Bible is a remarkable and very provocative book: the Song of Songs. It's a love story—passionate, provocatively physical, something that makes good Christians blush—between two lovers, a husband and wife. Finally God's Word *ends* with a very different but even more important wedding: the marriage of Christ to His imperfect but redeemed bride, the church, "the wife of the Lamb" (Revelation 21:9).

Scripture also records Jesus performing His first miracle at a wedding (John 2:1–11). And the metaphor of a bride and groom is used to describe the relationship between God and Israel—"I will make you my wife forever." (Hosea 2:19, NLT)—as well as Christ and the church. The apostle Paul wrote about this in Ephesians 5:31–32:

> A man shall leave his father and mother and hold fast to his wife,
> and the two shall become one flesh. This mystery is profound,
> and I am saying that it refers to Christ and the church.

When God said, "I hate divorce," in Malachi 2:16, we wonder if His words were less about His feelings toward divorce than they were about His love for marriage. Authors John and Stasi Eldredge, in their book *Love and War*, explain God's passion for marriage:

> When through the prophet Malachi the Lord God of Israel says,
> "I hate divorce," we hear it with a shudder. But it ought to be
> with a surge of hope—the passion conveyed in those three
> words reveals how deeply he *loves* marriage, how strong his
> vested interests are in its success.[1]

So if God is that passionate about marriage and has given it such a prominent place throughout the Scriptures, it's vital that we begin this *Ready to Wed* journey with a clear understanding of the true purpose of marriage.

At this point, some of you might be thinking, *Who cares? What difference does it make if I understand the true purpose of marriage or not? We're already engaged, and we're about to be married. We need to acquire new tools and learn new skills!*

Certainly tools and skills are important, and we're going to give you plenty as you read through the pages of this book. However, if you don't first understand how something is supposed to work, you might misuse it and end up frustrated, or worse.

I (Greg) learned this lesson the hard way on our honeymoon. On the night before Erin and I married, my mother surprised me with a special gift. She had carefully wrapped a small box and told me that it was something for our honeymoon night. Actually, her exact words were, "I got you something." This was the extent of her explanation.

After Erin and I checked into our hotel room that first night, she disappeared into the bathroom. As I nervously waited for my bride, I found the present that my mom had given me. I'd totally forgotten that I'd put it in my suitcase. As I unwrapped the box, I found a tiny pair of black underwear. And when I say "tiny," I mean extremely little—like a thong but much, much smaller. You get the picture.

I held this tiny black thong to the light, and I could literally see right through it. However, it looked so massively uncomfortable, and I wasn't even sure that I could wear the stupid thing. As I tried it on, I thought to myself, *Will seeing me in this minuscule patch of cloth really be something that my wife will find thrilling? I can't possibly believe that she would think this is sexy.*

Luckily I decided to go with my gut on this one, and I hid it away in my suitcase. Actually, to be honest, it was the fear of my wife seeing my gut squeezed around that microscopic thong that made me chicken out!

The next night, however, I showed Erin the underwear and asked her why my mother would have bought me something like that to wear.

"Would this have been sexy?" I innocently asked my wife.

I'll never forget Erin's reaction. She instantly started laughing at me.

I thought, *If this is all it takes to get her laughing, praise God I didn't wear the thong!*

I'm certain Erin must have realized that I was confused, so my wife, in her most tender and compassionate voice, said, "I think your mom gave you the lingerie to give to me."

All I could say was, "What? Oh! I'm an idiot."

As we said before, if you don't know how something works or what it's for, you'll end up either making a fool of yourself or misusing it and potentially causing frustration and heartache. We want to help you clearly understand how marriage is supposed to work, and we want to show you God's true purpose for marriage so you can avoid making some devastating mistakes.

Have you thought about *why* you're getting married? We're sure that your first response will probably be, "We're in love." That's usually what couples say when we ask that question. But let's dig a little deeper. Many couples enter marriage with a host of romanticized ideas about love and marriage. With great excitement they anticipate a spouse who will be all they ever dreamed of in a mate.

Here are some of the reasons for getting married that we've heard from engaged couples over the years as we've guided them through pre-marital counseling:

- To marry their soul mate
- To signify a lifelong commitment
- To find companionship—"I'm marrying my best friend so I won't be lonely anymore."
- To get their emotional needs met
- To raise kids and have a family
- To take the next logical step in the relationship—"It's what you do."
- Because they share common values and interests
- To fulfill sexual needs and desires

- Because of the amazing attraction and chemistry
- To become whole or complete as individuals
- To make a public declaration of their love
- For financial security (tax benefits, higher earning potential, better health care)
- To have the safety of a legal contract
- To find happiness

But we have to tell you, if any of these reasons describe the purpose of your upcoming marriage, then you could be in trouble. *Big* trouble! If seeking happiness or finding a soul mate is your objective, then you're setting yourself up for many years of hurt and frustration. Why? The real question is, What happens when you are *not* happy? What will an absence of happiness mean for your relationship? We can predict the questions couples begin to ask themselves, because we've heard them time and again:

- Did I marry the wrong person?
- Is something wrong with me or with my spouse?
- Is my true soul mate still out there somewhere?
- If I'm not happy with this person, then shouldn't I look for someone who will make me happy?

Shortly after the wedding, most of us begin to see faults in our spouses and "chinks in the armor" that we overlooked before the ceremony. Or we simply become disappointed.

Our future spouses *will* let us down. We suddenly realize that our new spouses need some serious work. In fact, it appears that they are far from being able to fully meet our needs. We begin to see that—horrors—instead of being sold out to *our* ideas of marriage, our spouses entered into the union with their own goals, along with their own lists of needs and expectations.

You know what happens then, don't you? Our goal of happiness or finding our soul mate shifts from marrying the right person to changing our spouses into the people we want them to be. We buy into the myth that if our spouses could change one or two key things, our marriages would be great. This is where the real trouble starts for many couples and leads them down a very dark path toward unhappiness, frustration, and disconnection. We love how author Reb Bradley, in *Help for the Struggling Marriage*, describes this truth:

> Considering that 20th century America places such emphasis on building marriages [with] the right romantic "chemistry," it should be no surprise that many [couples] are easily disappointed in their marriages. What we have come to believe to be right romantic "chemistry" is actually nothing more than "self-centered" love. Most people are romantically drawn to those who *gratify* them, so [they] marry with expectations of being fulfilled by their mate. That type of love is not true selfless love, but is self-centered, basing its attraction on personal gratification. It says, "I love you for what you do for me. I am drawn to you for how you make me feel. I know I am in love with you, because I need you so much." Needing someone is not evidence of a selfless, giving love for them— contrarily, it is evidence that you want them for the emotional fulfillment you will receive from them. It is a reasonable estimate to suggest that 98% of all Christian marriages today are based on this dangerous form of self-serving love. Is it a surprise that so many are unhappy in marriage?[2]

Isn't it interesting, however, that God never mentions *any* of these goals in the Bible? Nowhere does He talk about happiness, the search for a soul mate, chemistry, kids, security, comfort, companionship, sex, or even love as the "true" purpose for marriage.

God created marriage with something far more wonderful in mind than simply a place where we can get our needs met and find happiness. God uses marriage to accomplish a very important goal: to help us become like Christ. The apostle Paul clearly understood this: "Those God foreknew he also predestined to be conformed to the likeness of his Son" (Romans 8:29). If you miss out on *this* understanding, your marriage is destined for pain and frustration. But if you "get it"—especially now as you prepare to walk down the aisle—then you'll be far ahead of the rest of the pack.

Listen to how Tim and Kathy Keller explain the true purpose of marriage in their book *The Meaning of Marriage*:

> When looking for a marriage partner, each must be able to look inside the other and see what God is doing, and be excited about being part of the process of liberating the emerging "new you." . . . This is by no means a naïve, romanticized approach— rather it is brutally realistic. In this view of marriage, each person says to the other, "I see all your flaws, imperfections, weaknesses, dependencies. But underneath them all I see growing the person God wants you to be." . . . The goal is to see something absolutely ravishing that God is making of the beloved. You see even now flashes of glory. You want to help your spouse become the person God wants him or her to be. . . . What keeps the marriage going is your commitment to your spouse's holiness.[3]

How Do You Know?

As you prepare to get married, rather than asking yourself, "How will my needs be met?" ask, "How will my life show evidence of Christ's character?" Marriage is not the answer. It never was designed to meet our needs. Christ is the answer. In God's infinite wisdom, He knows that our greatest relational needs will be met as we become more like His Son. As with everything else He created, God wants to use marriage to direct us toward Himself. God uses the challenges and the joys of marriage to help shape and mold us into the image of Jesus—and that's been His goal from the very beginning:

> Then God said, "Let us make man in our image, in our
> likeness, and let them rule over the fish of the sea and the birds
> of the air, over the livestock, over all the earth, and over all the
> creatures that move along the ground."

> So God created man in his own image,
>   in the image of God he created him;
>   male and female he created them.
>
> GENESIS 1:26–27

This seems so simple: A great marriage is the outcome of becoming Christlike. So the real question is, How do we know if we are becoming like Jesus? The good news is that Christ Himself gives us the answer in John 13:34–35:

> A new command I give you: Love one another. As I have loved
> you, so you must love one another. By this all men will know
> that you are my disciples, if you love one another.

As you both become Christlike, the evidence is your ability to love each other as Christ loves you. That's what this book is really about: *helping you love your future spouse as Christ loves you.* This is exactly what the apostle Paul wrote: "Each one of you also must love his wife as he loves himself, and the wife must respect her husband" (Ephesians 5:33).

We hope this makes sense. God's paramount goal for your upcoming marriage is not your mutual happiness. It really isn't! That will surely come, if you cooperate with God's real purpose for your marriage. But in fact He wants so much more than mere happiness for you. He wants joy, significance, spiritual power, and a compelling attractiveness that turns people's heads. In other words, He wants to use your marriage to help you and others become more like His Son.

If Erin and I had known, going into marriage, that it wasn't intended to be the answer to all of our problems and the antidote to all of our fears and weaknesses and deficits, we both would have saved ourselves a lot of pain and matured a lot faster than we did. It helps enormously just to know that God *designed* marriage—with its joys and its trials, its ups and its downs, its good times and its bad times—to help us to grow to be more like Christ. If you realize ahead of time that the process won't always be pain-free and easy (and that it's not supposed to be), then when the rough times come, they won't feel quite so threatening. Especially since God will use your marriage struggles and challenges to benefit you spiritually and to grow your Christian character.

Knowing the true purpose of marriage also helps to vastly increase your chances of creating a satisfying and fulfilling relationship as a couple. And it has the power to change even "bad" things, the things that otherwise could threaten your marriage, into things that will actually make it stronger, better, and more solid. We want to end this section with a great summary of Gary Thomas's book *Sacred Marriage: What If God Designed Marriage to Make Us Holy More Than to Make Us Happy?*:

> Marriage is even more than a sacred covenant. If our hearts are attuned to what God is teaching us, our marriage relationship can help us learn sacrificial love, forgiveness, servanthood, and perseverance. Marriage is a sacred tool that helps us grow spiritually in ways nothing else can. . . .
>
> If I focus on changing myself rather than trying to change my spouse, I find I must depend on God and in that process I will find deep fulfillment. . . .
>
> We must be clear about why we married and why we should stay faithful in that marriage. A worldly point of view promotes staying married only if our desires and "needs" are being fulfilled. But from God's perspective, we are to maintain

our marriage because doing so brings glory to God and points others to Him. What a drastic difference![4]

Now that we've laid the proper foundation and you understand God's true design for marriage, let's talk about the tools and skills you're going to learn as you read this book.

Twelve Ways to Grow a Strong Marriage

The good news is, you are just beginning to grow the "seeds" of your marriage, and you get to decide what you want your "bouquet" to grow into. What should you focus on to set your marriage up for success? After many years of working with couples, studying the Scriptures, and investigating the scientific research, we have isolated twelve essential behaviors needed to help you grow your relationship into a thriving marriage. These twelve behaviors are divided into two main parts in this book.

The first part is about learning how to proactively invest in your fiancé(e) and marriage. French author André Maurois wrote, "A successful marriage is an edifice that must be rebuilt every day." He was right on the mark. Marriage is a lifelong process that we must commit ourselves to again and again. Every day we have to *decide* to love our spouses and invest in our marriages. In part 1 are six key chapters on the following topics to help you proactively invest in your marriage:

1. *Leaving and cleaving.* A thriving couple puts into practice Genesis 2:24: "For this reason a man will leave his father and mother and be united to his wife." They *leave* their dependency on Mom and Dad, the single lifestyle, and personal issues and learn how to *cleave* and unite with their new spouse.

2. *Making a lifelong commitment.* A thriving couple understands that *divorce is not an option* and that marriage is a *lifelong adventure*. They have the same attitude toward each other as God has toward us: "I have loved you with an everlasting love" (Jeremiah 31:3).

3. *Honoring each other.* A thriving couple intentionally honors each other. They seek to "be devoted to one another in . . . love [and] honor one another above [themselves]" (Romans 12:10). They recognize that the key to keeping their hearts open to each other is to view one another as a priceless treasure, "for where your treasure is, there your heart will be also" (Matthew 6:21).

4. *Sharing spiritual intimacy.* A thriving couple has a deep, shared faith. They consciously regard Christ as the bedrock of their relationship. Their relationship is "built on the foundation of the apostles and prophets, with Christ Jesus himself as the chief cornerstone" (Ephesians 2:20), and together they daily pursue an intimate relationship with Christ.

5. *Engaging in mutually satisfying physical intimacy.* A thriving couple regularly celebrates their marriage with passionate sexual intimacy, joining together to "become one flesh" (Genesis 2:24). They regard sex not as a chore or an obligation but as a delightful dance in which each spouse puts the other's needs and interests ahead of his or her own.

6. *Fostering positive communication.* A thriving couple knows that communication is the lifeblood of a vibrant relationship. They spend time every day in conversation to *know* each other and to be *known* by their partner, recognizing that one day they "shall know fully, even as [they are] fully known" (1 Corinthians 13:12).

The second part of the book focuses on healthy ways to manage conflict. When two fallen, inherently selfish people marry, they are bound to experience moments of disagreement, hurt, frustration, and irritation. It's inevitable! Instead of trying to eliminate conflict or avoid arguments, the key is to face our disagreements and learn how to use conflict as a doorway into the deepest levels of intimacy and connection. The chapters in part 2 are designed with exactly that goal in mind.

7. *Valuing differences.* A thriving couple realizes that God created men and women differently—and that's a very good thing! Genesis tells us that "God saw all that he had made, and it was very good" (1:31). A thriving couple understands that their differences (gender, personality, family of origin, etc.) can cause conflict, but they're never the problem; instead, it's attempting to manage these differences that creates many of the challenges they face in their marriage.

8. *Creating realistic expectations.* A thriving couple realizes that they have many expectations—things they want, hope, wish, and expect will happen in their marriage. However, unclear or unrealistic expectations cause many challenges within a marriage. Therefore, a thriving couple spends regular time talking through what they expect and finding win-win solutions for unrealistic expectations. The apostle Paul knew the secret to a win-win approach to expectations: "Each of you should look not only to your own interests, but also to the interests of others" (Philippians 2:4).

9. *Practicing healthy conflict management.* A thriving couple recognizes that *conflict is inevitable.* They know that the secret of their success lies in the way they *manage* conflict, and they embrace the concept that God uses this bumping and jarring to cause them to grow—"As iron sharpens iron, so one [person] sharpens another" (Proverbs 27:17). Instead of avoiding conflict, they believe that healthy conflict is the doorway to intimacy and deeper connection.

10. *Sharing responsibility as a team.* A thriving couple finds ways to resolve the issue of male and female roles *between themselves.* They hammer out a plan that preserves fairness and equity in the way they divide household tasks and responsibilities. They try to outserve each other every day, and they strive to

be unified, to "bear one another's burdens" (Galatians 6:2, ESV), and to function as a *team*. Their goal is to "have unity of mind, sympathy, brotherly love, a tender heart, and a humble mind" (1 Peter 3:8).

11. *Pursuing financial peace and harmony.* A thriving couple understands that the number one conflict in marriage is money, and that "the love of money is a root of all kinds of evil" (1 Timothy 6:10). They take time to understand their different money personalities and how to make financial decisions as a team.

12. *Coping with stress and crises.* A thriving couple expects that they will face challenges and painful trials in the course of their marriage. The Scriptures make this fact clear: "Dear friends, don't be surprised at the fiery trials you are going through, as if something strange were happening to you" (1 Peter 4:12, NLT). They learn how to manage the stress and challenges that are inevitable, especially during their first year of marriage.

During your engagement, and in the first months of your marriage, you are "seeding" behaviors, patterns, and habits into your relationship. We believe that these twelve healthy behaviors are the best way to equip and prepare yourselves for a thriving marriage.

We're thrilled that you've invited Focus on the Family and some of the nation's best relationship experts on your marriage journey with you. We're excited to continue supporting you and encouraging you through all the seasons of life to come in your marriage and family.

DR. GREG SMALLEY is the vice president of marriage and family formation at Focus on the Family. Greg earned his doctorate at the Rosemead School of Psychology at Biola University and a counseling degree from Denver Seminary. He is the author of thirteen books, including *The DNA of Relationships*, *The Wholehearted Marriage*, *Fight Your Way to a Better Marriage*, and *The Date Night Challenge*.

ERIN SMALLEY is a program manager at Focus on the Family. She is a registered nurse (labor and delivery) and earned her master's degree in clinical psychology from Evangel University. Erin is the coauthor of several books, including *Before You Plan Your Wedding, Plan Your Marriage, Grown-Up Girlfriends,* and *The Wholehearted Wife.* Greg and Erin have led marriage seminars around the world and trained pastors, professionals, and lay leaders on how to effectively work with married and engaged couples. They've been married for more than twenty-three years and are the proud parents of three daughters and one son.

Ready to Talk

Here are some questions the two of you can discuss. Share as honestly as you can; it's good practice for when you're married!

1. When you hear that God's purpose for marriage is to help you become more like Christ, how do you feel? Why?

   - Fortunate
   - Contemplative
   - Doubtful
   - Worried
   - Eager to get started
   - Excited

   How do you *hope* to feel about it by the time you finish this book?

2. This chapter lists a lot of reasons why couples want to get married. Which of the following are closest to yours?

   - I've found my soul mate.
   - I want to signify a lifelong commitment.

- I want companionship—I'm marrying my best friend so I won't be lonely anymore.

- I want to get my emotional needs met.

- I want to raise kids and have a family.

- I want to take the next logical step in our relationship—it's what you do.

- We share common values and interests.

- I want to fulfill my sexual needs and desires.

- We have amazing attraction and chemistry.

- I want to be whole or complete as an individual.

- I want to make a public declaration of our love.

- I'm looking for financial security (tax benefits, higher earning potential, etc.).

- I'd like the safety of a legal contract.

- I want to find happiness.

Having read the chapter, did you change any of your reasons for desiring to get married? Why or why not?

3. Pick one of the twelve traits of a thriving marriage listed in this chapter. Have you seen this trait in anyone else's marriage? If so, what did it look like? What do you think it might look like in yours? What would you like to learn about it between now and your wedding day?

Ready to Try

Choose a project that takes extra patience such as:

- Find a recipe for a three-course meal (on Pinterest, in a recipe book, or online) and together go through the process of planning, shopping, and preparing the meal.

- Plan a day to do a service project at a homeless shelter or a retirement community. Or volunteer to babysit someone's children for the day.
- Find a crafting project together that you can make to use at your wedding ceremony, reception, or in your new home (a centerpiece or decorative item). Come up with an idea, plan out its steps, shop for supplies, and carry out the project together.

Follow up by discussing the experience. Were there some tense moments, frustrations, and disagreements? When did you have to watch your words? How can experiences like these sand off rough edges and help you develop Christ-like traits? How can you get the most out of these times after marriage?

PART 1

PROACTIVELY INVESTING IN YOUR MARRIAGE

CHAPTER 2

LEAVING YOUR PARENTS AND CLEAVING TO YOUR SPOUSE

Ted Cunningham

THE GIVING OF THE BRIDE is my favorite part of the wedding ceremony. Everyone is in position, and all eyes are on the bride as she gracefully strolls down the aisle with her dad. After a brief welcome, I ask, "Who gives this woman to be married to this man?"

"Her mother and I" is the usual answer.

I then ask Dad to turn, face his daughter, and speak a blessing over her. At the rehearsal the night before, I prep Dad by encouraging him to take his time at this moment, "We are not in a hurry, and you will not have a microphone. This is a special moment between you and your daughter."

Without exception, every dad whimpers and cries his way through the entire blessing. Gathered guests hear every sniffle. Family and friends who hadn't planned to cry reach for tissues.

After Dad blesses his daughter with spoken words of high value, he turns and speaks a blessing over the groom. Then Dad gives his daughter's hand to the groom, steps back, and takes a seat. This is called "cutting the strings." This intentional and strategic separation of parent and child is the key to initiating the bond between husband and wife.

I love when a mom comes up to me at a wedding and says, "I don't feel like I'm losing a daughter today; I feel like I'm gaining a son."

My rebuttal is always the same: "Nope, you're losing a daughter." My use of hyperbole is necessary to drive home the point that Mom and Dad need to back off and allow the new marriage to flourish. Meddling and enmeshment will erode the forever bond.

My daughter, Corynn, is convinced that she's never leaving home. At seven years of age, she made up her mind that Mom and Dad take such good care of her, she'll just stay with us forever. But she knows I'll have none of that. Parenting with the end in mind means I'm daily preparing her to leave home.

One of the hardest questions Corynn has ever asked me is, "Dad, who do you love more, me or Mom?"

Ouch! Naturally my first response to a question like that is to act as if I didn't hear the question, or I squint my eyes as though I didn't understand it. She has me wrapped around her little finger.

"I love your mommy and you both," I then say gently, "but God wants me to love Mommy in a different way. Your mommy and I are together for life. We will be together until one of us goes to heaven or Jesus returns. But you, Corynn, will not be with us forever. You will one day leave our home and start a family of your own."

Corynn is quick to reply, "I want to be with you and Mommy forever."

"You can't be with us forever, Corynn," I say.

As tears form in her eyes, she glares at me and says, "I am going to college online and staying home forever. You can't make me leave."

While I must admit I like the sound of that from a tuition standpoint, I need her to know that separation from Mom and Dad is actually a sign of health and maturity. Leaving home as an adult should be a top goal for every parent and child!

Part of me wants her to stay home, but my assignment is to prepare Corynn for adulthood. I won't be with her for three-quarters of her life, but God gave me this time on the front end to invest in her and help form the beliefs of her heart.

Genesis 2:24 says, "For this reason a man will leave his father and mother and be united to his wife, and they will become one flesh." These words were first written about a couple in the garden of Eden who had no biological parents. One must wonder if God was instructing Adam and Eve on how to raise their children rather than teaching them about their own marriage. We have no record of the conversation, but I wonder when Adam and Eve first taught the "leave and cleave" of marriage to Cain and Abel. I'm thinking earlier rather than later.

Marriage is a priority relationship that trumps your relationship with your parents. When you see the word *leave*, you may think you need to move a thousand miles away from Mom and Dad. While there are some cases where that is beneficial, it isn't necessary. The focus of this text is not *geographical*. Most couples live in close proximity to their parents and move away later in life. The focus of this text is *relational* and *emotional* leaving.

"Leaving" is the idea that no relationship, apart from your relationship with God, is more important than your marriage. Your spouse, not your parent, is your new priority relationship. To leave Mom and Dad means to forsake, depart from, leave behind, and abandon your family of origin.

The emphasis of Genesis 2:24 is a young man or woman leaving his or her family of origin and immediately entering into marriage. However, today that isn't always the case. Young people are leaving home and living single for longer periods of time. There is now a gap between leaving and cleaving.

Scripturally and historically, there are two life phases: *child* and *adult*. The apostle Paul explained this transition when he wrote, "When I was a child, I talked like a child, I thought like a child, I reasoned like a child. When I became a man, I put childish ways behind me" (1 Corinthians 13:11).

Traditionally, going from child to adult meant

- Leaving home
- Completing an apprenticeship or formal education
- Finding employment
- Getting married
- Starting a family

In generations past, these five adulthood milestones happened quickly, if not simultaneously. There was no prolonged track for entering adulthood. You left home prepared for the responsibility of work, spouse, and the world. Parents sent children out as adults, not on a journey to become adults.

I love sharing the story of my wife's grandparents Lloyd and Lorraine Freitag. Lloyd came home from World War II and met a sweet redhead working in a diner. They dated for an entire week before Lloyd asked her, "Are we going to get serious about this relationship, or what?" He knew he wanted to spend the rest of his life with Lorraine. In September of 2011, they celebrated their sixty-fifth wedding anniversary before Lloyd went home to be with the Lord in June of 2012. Lloyd and Lorraine were part of what Tom Brokaw called "the greatest generation." World wars and the Great Depression forced them to embrace responsibility more than privilege.

Leave Your Adolescence Behind

Marriage and adolescence don't mix well. Adolescence starts in the early teen years and, for some people, continues on into their thirties and forties. *Prolonged adolescence* is defined as "too much privilege, not enough responsibility." The truth is that marriages struggle when husband, wife, or both live with too much privilege and not enough responsibility.

Leaving home and cleaving to your spouse means prioritizing your spouse above nights out with friends, hours in front of the television or video games, and excessive participation in hobbies or sporting activities. As a pastor I've seen this play out one of two ways: (1) A spouse is never able to break free from the single lifestyle from the get-go, or (2) the marriage starts out with oneness, but later, one or both spouses feel as if they missed out on something, and they revert to the single lifestyle. In either case, prolonged adolescence fosters the single lifestyle over oneness in marriage.

Becoming an adult means leaving home, making wise adult decisions, and taking responsibility for the outcome of those decisions. In my opinion, parents often wait too long to teach their kids to be adults, and as a result, intentionally or unintentionally, they're prolonging their children's journeys into adulthood.

Is some of this making you nervous? If so, don't stress out. There's hope! Even if you grew up in a home where Mom and Dad handed you privilege and withheld responsibility, you can still do something about it. You can *choose* to prioritize responsibility over privilege. You can begin to see privilege as something you gain after a season of responsibility. This is a choice you can and must make. Your marriage depends on it.

I want my children to learn maturity at an early age. My wife, Amy, and I define *maturity* in our home as "knowing I will not be with Mom and Dad forever and planning accordingly." We believe that separation from parents is good and healthy. Good parenting recognizes the blessing that every child needs to one day be released into a new journey with Christ and his or her mate. Our children need to be encouraged and filled with confidence that they will one day make capable adult decisions on their own.

For you, that time is now. You're about to embark on a new journey together. Marriage is exciting, fun, wonderful, and, at times, challenging. Leaving and cleaving is part of your new journey, and deciding now to do it well will only make your marriage stronger.

Leave Home Financially

Leaving your family of origin requires severing your dependence on what your parents can provide. Let's get really honest for a moment. If you make thirty or forty thousand dollars a year and you're married with children, you cannot afford to keep up with the latest trends in technology. It's too expensive. Your parents may have paid for your iPhone, iPad, and Mac while you were in college, but those days are over.

Modern entitlement makes us want in a few years what our parents spent a lifetime accumulating. Leaving home financially is tough. When your parents have always handed you all of your vacations, food, school, cars, insurance, and spending money, it makes it quite difficult to lower your expectations and tastes to match your current income.

Because of the lavish lifestyles many children enjoy today, young couples have a tendency to become slaves to debt early in marriage, and it follows them throughout their entire married lives. Avoid borrowing and asking your parents for money. Scripture says, "The rich rule over the poor, and the borrower is servant to the lender" (Proverbs 22:7). Borrowing money from your parents is expensive. The relational and emotional interest is high. You will pay on it for years.

Years ago, a young married man in his twenties sat in my office and told me, "I'm sick and tired of my parents treating me like a little kid. They're always telling me what to do and meddling in my business."

I could tell by his clothes, technology, and the Starbucks cup in his hand that he was living large, so I asked him, "Have you ever asked your parents for money since you've been married?"

He looked at me with disdain as though I had asked a ridiculous question. Come to find out, his mom still purchased his clothes, and his cell phone was still on his parents' plan!

"How many hours a week are you working?" I asked.

"They cut my hours at work, and I'm down to twenty hours a week," he said.

My response? "In your twenties, you should be working as many jobs as necessary to get forty hours a week, and if that doesn't pay the bills, you'll need to work more than forty hours a week. You have the energy and the time. Make it happen."

Here is the simplest equation I know for leaving home financially: Hard work plus moderate spending equals a content new marriage. In other words, produce more than you consume (see chapter 12 on finances). You may be cringing right about now, or maybe you've been taking care of yourself for years. Let me encourage you that together, you can do this! The two of you are in love and have decided to begin your lives as a married couple. Making it on your own might take some sacrifices and adjustments to your lifestyle expectations, but it's worth it. You can do this!

Leave Home Relationally and Emotionally

A few years ago, a loving mom confronted me at her son's wedding. "How dare you tell my boy he can't call me," she shouted during the preceremony photo session. The photographer stood ready for an action shot.

"I think you misunderstood what I told your son," I gently responded. "I told your son to limit his calls to you and definitely do not call every day."

This infuriated the mother. "What's wrong with a son loving his mom?" she asked. Did you catch that? She used extreme exaggeration to make a point. That's called hyperbole. Her equation was love equals a phone call every day.

This brief conversation forced me to adjust the wedding message. I usually spend half the message on leaving and the other half on cleaving. Not this time. I went 75 percent on leaving and 25 percent on cleaving. We walked on eggshells for a few moments, but Mom eventually came around. To this day, the bride still thanks me for that message.

While parents can be a source of support and encouragement, you must not allow them to be a controlling factor in your marriage. When your relationship with your parents becomes enmeshed, you begin to take responsibility for their feelings and actions. You begin making decisions, scheduling activities, raising your children, joining a certain denominational church, and choosing a lifelong career path based on your parents' desires and expectations. Leaving your parents relationally and emotionally means you leave and abandon their expectations for your life. You begin making decisions with your spouse in mind, not your parents.

Whether you're young and this is your first marriage, or you're remarrying, a healthy relationship with clear boundaries is possible with your parents. Part of my premarital counseling with couples always includes the following six keys for promoting oneness in marriage while fostering healthy relationships with parents.

1. *Prioritize your future spouse over your parents.* Leaving your family of origin starts with understanding the proper bond between parent and child. The bond between a husband and a wife is stronger than the bond between a parent and a child. Your mom and dad love you and want to be involved in your life. The question becomes, "How much should they be involved?" Your spouse-to-be needs to be the first go-to person for all decision making, parenting plans, personal struggles, and conflict resolution.

2. *When in conflict, don't seek your parents as allies.* When you fight with your future spouse, give yourself a time-out and be alone with the Lord. You don't need to call your mom or dad. Healthy parents know how to advocate for the marriage, not just their son or daughter. However, some parents may choose to side with their child and make statements like these:

"Honey, your dad and I just want you to be happy."
"You deserve better."
"No one should have to put up with that."
"It's not your fault."
"You've tried everything to make it work."
"He's not going to change."

These are not helpful responses.

3. *Never compare your future spouse to a parent.* She's not your mom. He's not your dad. This seems obvious, but couples often overlook that fact. Unspoken expectations over meal preparations, car maintenance, and household chores can grate on a spouse over time. Never compare the strengths of your parents to the weaknesses of your spouse.

4. *Don't take responsibility for your parents' emotions, words, or actions.* The bond you have with your parents becomes unhealthy when you

start making decisions and moving forward in your marriage with these questions in the back of your mind: *How will Mom and Dad feel about this? What will Dad say if he knows we plan to buy this car? How will Mom react if we decide to relocate with your company?* You can love, honor, and bless your parents without taking responsibility for their hearts.

Identify and take responsibility for the messages in your mind and heart. Your parents contributed to those messages, but you are 100 percent responsible for your own heart, not theirs. You did not choose your family of origin. They influenced who you are today, but they do not define you, and you are not responsible for them.

5. *Forgive your parents.* Leave home with an open and free heart. If you leave home with unresolved anger in your heart toward a parent, it will resurface in your marriage. The question is not if but when.

You cannot change your parents, but you can forgive them. You cannot relive your childhood and change your mom and dad. You have zero responsibility for the way you were raised. But you can choose to take 100 percent responsibility for your own heart and decide what to do with the hurt and the past.

Release the hurt caused by your parents. Turn the past over to the Lord; you will then be able to *live at peace with everyone.* You will no longer be held hostage or powerless in life. You will change once you begin to resolve your anger. You can choose to live the rest of your days as a victim of your past, or you can choose to embrace personal responsibility and be an example for generations to come. "Forgive as the Lord forgave you" (Colossians 3:13).

6. *Stop obeying your parents, but never stop honoring them.* When we're young and living at home, we're commanded to obey our parents. Ephesians 6:1–3 says,

> Children, obey your parents in the Lord, for this is right. "Honor your father and mother"—which is the first commandment with a promise—"that it may go well with you and that you may enjoy long life on the earth."

As adults, we don't obey our parents. We no longer call them to find out what our next move in life should be. We no longer ask them for permission to take a vacation or a trip. Obedience ends, but honor never does.

God takes honor so seriously that He gives strong words to those who would dishonor their parents:

> Children who mistreat their father or chase away their mother
> are an embarrassment and a public disgrace.

PROVERBS 19:26, NLT

> The eye that mocks a father,
> that scorns obedience to a mother,
> will be pecked out by the ravens of the valley,
> will be eaten by the vultures.

PROVERBS 30:17

Honor your parents by calling home and thanking them for a life lesson they taught you as a kid. Since you have left home financially, pay for their meal the next time you eat out with them. I know what you're thinking, *They have way more money than I do, so it makes more sense that they pay!* That's not the point. Pay to show honor. Instead of buying your mom another sweater or your dad another ratchet set for a birthday, write them a blessing and share it with family and friends at the next family holiday.

The Blessing and Separation

Solomon didn't wear a royal crown to his wedding, even though he was king. Instead, he wore a crown his mother gave him as a sign of her blessing:

> Come out, you daughters of Zion,
> and look at King Solomon wearing the crown,

the crown with which his mother crowned him
on the day of his wedding,
    the day his heart rejoiced.

SONG OF SONGS 3:11

At your wedding and in your marriage, you want the crown of your parents' blessing because it recognizes and honors their role in your life. They raised you, fed you, schooled you, and clothed you, and you must honor their hard work. While they need to acknowledge your rite of passage into adulthood and marriage, you need to praise them for their investment in you. You left home and are now starting your own.

However, the crown of blessing isn't always possible. If your parents don't bless your marriage, you still need to esteem them as highly valuable. Hear me on this: *You can honor them without agreeing with them.* Your skill in doing so will help you as a spouse. You'll spend much of your married life honoring your spouse even though you don't always agree with him or her. Loving and honoring a difficult parent or spouse models the way Jesus loves and forgives us.

I've seen my share of difficult parents. In my seventeen years as a pastor, only one dad has rebelled against giving away the bride at a wedding. We were on schedule, and everyone was in place. Dad walked his daughter down the aisle and stopped at the front, and the groom stepped beside him. I welcomed family and friends, prayed, and then asked, "Who gives this woman to be married to this man?" Dad was silent.

Thinking he didn't hear me, I repeated the question, "Who gives this woman to be married to this man?" Dad remained silent.

With a deeper voice and greater strength, I asked a third and final time, "Who gives this woman to be married to this man?"

Dad answered, "I will not give her, but I will share her." With that I declared the wedding over.

A startled groom looked at me with eyes that said, "This has to happen!"

I told him, "We can't go on until Dad gives you his daughter."

Finally Dad submitted to the authority of the church and relinquished his daughter.

Your parents can't share you with your spouse. Things have to change. But let me reassure you that leaving your parents and cleaving to your spouse does not mean abandoning your relationship with your parents or isolating yourself with your new spouse! It simply means that you've made the wise decision to put your marriage right under your relationship with God—where it belongs. When you and your parents choose to separate, your marriage will thrive!

TED CUNNINGHAM is the founding pastor of Woodland Hills Family Church. He enjoys being married to his wife, Amy. They live in Branson, Missouri, with their two children, Corynn and Carson. He is the author of *The Power of Home, Fun Loving You, Trophy Child*, and *Young and in Love*, and coauthor of four books with Dr. Gary Smalley, including *The Language of Sex* and *From Anger to Intimacy*. Ted is a regular guest on *Focus on the Family, Life Today*, and Moody Radio. He is a graduate of Liberty University and Dallas Theological Seminary.

Ready to Talk

1. Discuss the following statements based on the chapter. Do the two of you agree with them? Do you agree with each other about them? If not, what kind of conversation—with a mentor, pastor, or counselor, perhaps—would help you work through your differences?

   • Your spouse, not your parent, is your new priority relationship.

   • Leaving home and cleaving to your spouse means prioritizing your spouse above nights out with friends, hours in front of the television or video games, and excessive participation in hobbies or sporting activities.

   • Avoid borrowing and asking your parents for money.

- Leaving your parents relationally and emotionally means you leave and abandon their expectations for your life.
- When in conflict, don't seek your parents as allies.

2. Where are you in the leaving-and-cleaving process? Do you feel your family ties weakening? In what ways are you and your spouse-to-be starting to cleave to each other? Are you going too far in one direction? How can you help each other find the right balance?

3. Discuss how you can intentionally bless your parents as you prepare to "leave" the season of childhood and enter into adulthood with your marriage. Will you do something at the wedding ceremony or reception? Or will you do something prior to your actual wedding day? Discuss what you will do and say. Remember, this will be done in order to thank them and bless them for all they have done for you as you leave one season and begin another.

Ready to Try

Think about all of your most important relationships, and find pictures representing those relationships. Plan a time where you and your fiancé(e) can discuss taking a leave of absence. Discuss what this will look like practically. How will you communicate to your parents, siblings, and friends that you need time to cleave to your spouse? How long will your leave of absence be? What boundaries will need to be placed? What will this uniquely look like for you and your new spouse?

CHAPTER 3

THE POWER OF COMMITMENT

Scott Stanley, PhD

To have and to hold from this day forward,
for better or for worse, for richer, for poorer,
in sickness and in health, to love and to cherish;
and I promise to be faithful to you,
forsaking all others, until death do us part.
—TRADITIONAL WEDDING VOW

THE BIG DAY FINALLY ARRIVED. The wedding had been carefully planned, and everything was going smoothly—except that Lisa didn't feel so smooth inside. As her mother helped her straighten her veil, Lisa whispered, "What if I'm not making the right choice?"

Her parents divorced when Lisa was seven. She remembered the pain of their separation as if it were yesterday. That event and the preceding years of turmoil left her skeptical that any marriage could really work—at least over many years.

Her mother tried to comfort her: "Honey, you don't have to worry; you can always come back home if things don't work out with Steven." To her mother's surprise, Lisa burst into sobs. She didn't want to hear that there was a lifeboat, that she could go home if she needed to.

Through her tears, Lisa said to her mother, "Mom, thank you for trying to reassure me. But I desperately want to know that it's really possible for this to work, that it's not a fairy tale. I'm so afraid that Steven and I don't have what it takes, but I want our marriage to last all my life. Am I being realistic?"

Lisa's mother gave her a reassuring hug and then told her that things could be different for her and Steven. She gave Lisa all the reassurance she was hoping for. Lisa managed a smile, but in the back of her mind, she still agonized: *Do we know how to live out a commitment over many years?*

Commitment may not seem like the sexiest topic when it comes to marriage. In fact, sex is the sexiest topic. But commitment is the root of what it takes to build and maintain a truly lasting, happy life together.

The Foundation for Being Deeply Connected

What do you desire most in your marriage? Consider this passage from Genesis about Adam and Eve. It's the same core passage on marriage that both Jesus Christ and the apostle Paul referred to in their major teachings about marriage (Matthew 19 and Ephesians 5):

> Therefore a man shall leave his father and his mother and hold
> fast to his wife, and they shall become one flesh. And the man
> and his wife were both naked and were not ashamed.
> GENESIS 2:24–25, ESV

What does being *naked and not ashamed* mean to you? I think this means that Adam and Eve felt completely accepted and loved. They had a deep emotional safety. I think this reflects the desire most of us have—to be accepted at the deepest level of our being. This is the type of love you can give to each other in marriage.

Notice that the deep intimacy described in Genesis is founded on the commitment implied in the earlier phrases. For starters, when you get married, your commitment implies that you must leave some things behind. In the passage it says that "a man shall leave his father and his mother." The full meaning of this passage is easier to appreciate if you bear in mind that the Bible promotes a very high level of respect for parents.

This passage also portrays *permanence*. The word for "hold fast" used in the original Hebrew is *dabaq*, which means "to adhere" or "to stick." This is more than being stuck together. It's sticking together in a deep, freely chosen commitment. Joining together in commitment is not to entrap the two of you but to free you for intimacy and connection. Only in the *safety* of a secure commitment is it reasonable to be naked and unashamed. The loss of freedom that comes with the boundaries of commitment in marriage actually creates new opportunities for a profound level of freedom within those boundaries.

Two Kinds of Commitment

What are the ways in which commitment is expressed in the course of a life together? Consider these two statements:

"Mary sure is committed to that project."

"Bob committed to that project; he can't back out now."

The first statement reflects commitment as *dedication*, and the second reflects commitment as *constraint*. *Dedication* implies an internal state of devotion to a person or project. *Constraint* entails a sense of obligation. It refers to factors that would exact a cost or consequence if the present course were abandoned. While dedication is a force drawing you forward, constraint is a force pushing you from behind.

According to research, couples who maintain and act on dedication are happier, more connected, and more open with each other. That's because dedicated partners show their commitment in these very specific ways:

- They make their partner and marriage a high priority.
- They protect their relationship from attraction to others.
- They sacrifice for each other without resentment.

- They make decisions as a team.
- They invest of themselves in building a future together—they have a long-term view.
- They dream together and create specific plans for the future.

Those who lose dedication and have only constraints will either be together but miserable or come apart. Maintaining the type of dedication that keeps a marriage strong and growing means consistently making choices that protect your marriage. That means consistently doing the things in the previous list.

Making a Choice to Give Up Other Choices

Every aspect of commitment revolves around the issue of choice. Commitment fundamentally requires making a choice to give up other choices. That's stating it simply, but couples who thrive rather than merely survive are those who consistently make the right choices throughout life. Those choices confirm your commitment, protect what you have built so far, and allow you to build toward the future.

It's choice that really makes commitment so powerful, giving you the ability to do things, daily and weekly, that go a long way toward creating a happy future in your marriage. But beware. You can't make and keep commitments if you're unwilling to make choices. Meditate for a moment on this simple verse from the wise King Solomon: "He who observes the wind will not sow, and he who regards the clouds will not reap" (Ecclesiastes 11:4, ESV).

To use Solomon's expression, we've become a society of wind watchers. Wind watchers never plant, because the conditions just don't seem right. They never bring in the crop, because it looks like it might rain. Wind watchers enter marriage with a "maybe I do" commitment, not a fully expressed commitment that clearly says "I do." Our "maybe I do" culture encourages us to hedge our bets and protect ourselves rather than take any risks. But "maybe I do" won't get you where your soul longs to be.

Jason and Laura: Working It Out

Jason and Laura each learned some of the most crucial lessons about commitment before they even met. Those lessons came back to being important in their marriage.

"I Signed Up for Adventure!"

Jason was eighteen and fresh out of high school. His life was ahead of him. Up late one night surfing the TV channels, not certain where he wanted his life to take him, he found the answer in a US Marine Corps commercial: "Be one of the few and the proud." He thought to himself, *Those guys look strong. They look proud. I bet they have an exciting life.*

After a few weeks, Jason finally got up his nerve and talked to the recruiter, who, as recruiters do, painted a pretty positive picture of service in the Marine Corps. Jason signed up on the spot. Though basic training turned out to be pretty tedious, combat training proved to be more exciting. Jason thought he had found what he was looking for.

When he completed his training, Jason got his orders and shipped out to an island in the Indian Ocean that he had never heard of. *No big deal,* he thought. *This is an adventure.* Six weeks later, he was doing guard duty on a wharf for navy supply ships. It was not exciting work. It was not an adventure. It was pure, hot drudgery. *I may be one of the few,* he thought, *but I'm not so proud at the moment. I did not sign up for this!*

Most of us don't talk to a recruiter before we get married. However, like Jason entering the Marine Corps, many of us start out in marriage with unrealistic expectations, or we pay attention only to the really wonderful-sounding stuff. When Jason signed up for the Marines, he was filled with a sense of dedication. I say a "sense" because his dedication was really more like *potential* dedication. But his initial dedication carried him happily through the commitment of signing up, basic training, and combat training.

However, what had been enough to see Jason through the early stages of joining the Marines wasn't enough to see him through the hard duties that carried no particular prospects for glory and adventure. His dedication began to drain away. He was still committed, but he was no longer a free man. He couldn't go to the staff sergeant and say, "Sir, this has been an interesting time so far, but I don't think I'm really into being a marine anymore." That would not be a good move.

Jason came to feel the full force of constraint. Though he did talk with the chaplain about his dilemma, he couldn't simply get up and walk away. Actually, he could, but the Marine Corps takes a rather dim view of doing so.

Jason started his commitment in the Marines with the force of dedication. It was his choice. Despite that, when he was faced with unmet and unrealistic expectations, deep disappointment set in. While he was no less constrained before his dedication left him, he wasn't very aware of his constraint until that moment. Once he became aware of it, he realized, *I can't leave, or I'll go to federal prison.* He felt trapped. And trapped he was. What was he to do?

In the end, Jason made it through his three-year commitment to the Marines. The awareness of his constraint led him to make the wise choice to embrace a more informed and more mature dedication. He realized that he had made the choice to join the Marines, so he would give it his best. It was a good attitude, and with that attitude, Jason's ability to handle assignments he didn't like got better—as did his future assignments. As he discovered, sometimes all of life hinges on a positive shift in perspective. To put it in terms a marine would love, when you hit the beach, you can sit there and get pinned down and shot up, or you can take the hill. Go for the hill. Go for the higher ground. Jason learned that the essence of commitment was about what you do when it's not so easy.

Committing to a Choice

When Laura graduated from high school, like Jason, she had no idea what she wanted to do for a career. But she did want to go to college.

After agonizing over the choice, she picked a university in another state. As it turned out, she loved the school she had chosen.

Close to the end of her sophomore year, Laura still had no idea what career she wanted to pursue. She had always enjoyed photography, but her parents had told her it would be hard to make a living as a photographer. So she decided to major in business, and perhaps become an accountant like her father. He seemed to like his work and was always very busy. The decision was hard, and Laura worried that she was always going to have trouble making decisions. But accounting it was.

At the start of her senior year, she met a classmate who had just done a wonderful summer internship as a photographer for a local magazine. Suddenly Laura was filled with doubts. When she dedicated herself to a career in accounting, she put aside her interest in photography. Now that interest was back. But being close to graduation, she couldn't just start over. Laura took some time to think it through. The more she thought, the more she realized that she had made a choice she needed to stick with. It was the right thing to do on several levels.

Still, she felt a sense of loss. *I could have become a magazine or newspaper photographer,* she thought. *I won't be able to do that now.* But she also realized that being a photographer might not be the right career for the kind of life she wanted. For instance, she might have to travel a lot rather than be close to her family, and there might not be many magazines to work for where she wanted to live.

She also realized that she could still pursue her interest in photography. It just wouldn't be her career. She realized that all of life was a series of choices, and from time to time, she might feel grief about the "road not taken." Laura learned pretty early on that this was part of what it means to be truly committed to anything in life. Our culture encourages us to hang on to every option, but the committed life means making some choices among our options.

This fundamental essence of commitment—about choosing—is why it's crucial for two people who are marrying to each be clear about the choice they're making. Each should be freely and fully making the choice to give up other choices.

Déjà Vu

Jason did great in the Marine Corps but decided that it wasn't his life's work. After leaving the Marines at the age of twenty-two, he decided to go to college, where he studied computer science. It was there, in a computer lab, that Jason met Laura. He thought she was beautiful.

They fell deeply in love, and after they had dated for nine months, Jason asked Laura *the* question. She said yes. Seven months later, they walked down the aisle with a wealth of approving friends and family in attendance. It was a wonderful day.

Fast-forward six years after their wedding day. Laura was working for a large accounting firm and enjoyed her work. Jason was likewise doing fine, working on computer networks at a local company that took good care of its employees. All his colleagues liked him, and he was in line for a promotion.

Jason and Laura had a child named Kristi. She grew into an adorable three-year-old. Both Jason and Laura loved being parents. However, around this time, things weren't so great between Jason and Laura. Even before Kristi was born, it had grown harder to deal with their relationship than either Jason or Laura had imagined. Neither had very good skills for handling conflict, so many of their arguments ended up with her yelling and him pulling back into himself. The arguments could be about anything. They rarely went out or did anything fun, and their sexual relationship had cooled. They lost the sense of being friends, and neither was trying very hard any longer to meet the needs of the other.

Déjà vu struck them both. Laura remembered the day when it hit her that life was going to be a series of choices, with occasional grief attached. Now she realized that her choice of Jason was one that had grief attached. Similarly, it struck Jason that once again he was feeling a lot of constraint with waning dedication. He felt discouraged, thinking once again, *This isn't what I signed up for.*

How can Laura and Jason recapture and protect their dedication? How could they have prevented losing it? The answer is the same: To keep a marriage on track, or to recover what one has lost, both partners have to act on dedication. Laura and Jason had each learned this lesson before they ever met, but it was time to put it in action in their marriage. At times you have to remind yourself of what you have committed to, dig deeper, and act. Dedication is action.

Let's look at a few of the powerful ways you can act on dedication to make your marriage all it can be.

Yes and No: Living Out Your Commitment

You can understand a lot of the essence of dedication by thinking about the words *yes* and *no*. Yes and no have a lot to do with how we live out our priorities in life.

Knowing Rather Than "No-ing" Each Other

Rick and Margo met when he was twenty-seven and she was twenty-five. Both worked for the same software firm, he in development and she in sales. Margo was drawn to Rick's intelligence and drive, and he was very drawn to her outgoing personality, her way of approaching issues in life, her humor, and how comfortable he felt talking to her. While they dated, he made plenty of time to see her, even though the projects he was working on demanded tremendous amounts of time and energy. They married after a year.

Ten years and two kids later, Rick was indeed the star of the software-development team. But Margo never saw him. He came home late every night, rarely before eight. Margo had begun working part-time for the software company years earlier to spend more time with their children, but she felt as if she was raising them by herself.

Occasionally Margo confronted Rick about his absence. Each time he convinced her that his real priorities were her and the kids. She wanted to believe him.

When she asked him if he could attend their older child's school program, he answered, "No, honey, sorry. I have to finish my project, or I'll be in a real bind." When she asked him to sit down and talk with her before they went to sleep, he said, "No, I can't tonight. I'd love to, but I have this big presentation in the morning." He was "no-ing" her and not "knowing" her.

Margo understood the pressure Rick was under, but they'd gotten married to have a life together—that's what they both had wanted when they said "I do."

What Margo and Rick were experiencing in their marriage is common. These patterns don't doom a marriage. The key is doing something when you start to feel this happening to you.

Why do couples put their spouses last on their priority list? It may be because their partners have committed to them for life. If a couple believes that their spouse will be there for them, no matter what, then they may also feel that at times they don't have to try as hard.

In marriage we sometimes take advantage of the very commitment that forms the foundation of life together. You should resist letting this happen to you, but if (or when) it does, put your effort back in a lower gear and get the power of commitment working for you again. Later in the chapter, I'll list some practical tools to help you accomplish this.

"Yes Takes Too Much Time!"

Before my son Luke turned six, he uttered these profound words: "Yes takes too much time!" Luke arrived from the factory tuned to use the word *no*. I cite the following:

Dad: "Luke, you need to go brush your teeth, now."
Luke: "No."
Dad: "Luke, time for bed. Hop to it."
Luke: "No."

> *Dad*: "Luke, how about if we go and throw the football? You haven't been outside all day."
>
> *Luke*: "No."

You get the idea. One day I asked him to stop playing something and get ready for dinner. Surprise! He said, "No." I was in a pretty good mood and felt like kidding around some. This is like verbal tickling, and it went on a lot longer than what I capture here:

> *Dad*: "Luke, let me hear you say yes. You can do it. It sounds like this: Yeesssss."
>
> *Luke* (giggling): "No."
>
> *Dad* (playfully): "Oh, come on. You can do it. Let me hear you say yes."
>
> *Luke*: "No."
>
> *Dad*: "You are such a no boy. Let's try being a yes boy. It would be fun!"
>
> *Luke* (laughing): "No."
>
> *Dad*: "Yes, yes, yes!"
>
> *Luke* (on the ground in hysterics): "No, no, no!"
>
> *Dad* (not looking for a serious reply): "Luke, how come you say no all the time?"
>
> *Luke*: "Because yes takes too much time."

I instantly knew that Luke had just uttered something profound. He had the secret to preserving priorities in life: saying no more than saying yes.

Luke knows both his mind and his priorities, so when someone asks him to do something that's not on his list, he says no. He understood before age six this powerful idea that most of us spend our lives working out.

What are you saying yes to that means you're saying no more often to those you love most? Maybe you need to say no more often to requests that compete with the most important parts of your life—your future spouse and your families. Those are the people to whom you should be saying yes more than anyone else.

Think about Rick and Margo from earlier in the chapter. When they talked about priorities, Rick would sound reassuring because he really believed it when he said that things would get better. Rick's intended priorities were Margo and the kids. The problem was that his actual priorities were different.

In our fast-paced world, many people struggle with the difference between their intended priorities and their actual priorities. If this is you—or gets to be—you are far from alone. Spouses and children can handle the discrepancy for periods of time. Spouses can understand in part because of their faith in the future. But when what's on the back burner is rarely stirred or moved to the front, problems develop. You must move the stuff that matters most to the front burner.

Relationship Capital and Trust

My wife, Nancy, and I have had rough spots in our marriage over the years, but I trust her and her instincts deeply.

Nancy once confronted me in a way that highlights the intersection between trust and the long-term view of commitment. I had been in yet another period of working too much. Nancy thought I was looking particularly ragged (departing, no doubt, from my natural good looks and youthfulness!), and she was concerned. She found me in front of my computer one day (where else?) and took the opportunity to voice her concern. She said, and I quote, "You have to slow down because I'm the one that's going to be changing your diapers when you're old."

The way she expressed her concern was unusual, even kind of funny. I got my reaction right and didn't become defensive. One of the reasons for that is because she said what she said gently. I cannot tell you strongly enough how important that is when you confront your mate about something. I know gentleness doesn't always work, but it can be powerful, especially when you can clearly see the love and commitment in what's being said.

Here's what I heard: "Dear, I love you, and I'm going to be here for you all the way—until you or I fall apart—but I'm worried about how much you work. I'll be here for you when you're old and gray, but I want you to leave something for me!"

This is one of those moments in marriage where two mates fully realize that the whole deal is meant to be a long-term investment. That's the essence of the really good stuff.

Being Disciplined in Your Investing

Most people who develop true wealth have a strategy. Clearly I'm focused on marital wealth here. People who do best with their investments understand the long-term view and make commitments based on it. They invest *regularly*. If you talk to a financial adviser about how to do well in the stock market over time, he or she is likely to tell you about a strategy called dollar cost averaging, or DCA. With DCA, you decide how much you're going to invest in the market and invest that amount at regular intervals, whether the market is up or down, soaring or crashing. *You invest no matter what.*

Having a long-term view and a plan to accompany it keeps you from bailing out during short-term dips and losing what you invested.

What does DCA look like in marriage? Only you know the best investments for your marriage, but following are some of the more powerful investments for most marriages. If you don't carve out time for them, the investment can't be made and the benefit won't take place. Nothing will happen without the investment. Thriving couples proactively invest in each other and in their marriages. Here are some great ways to invest relationally:

- Leaving small notes of appreciation
- Doing something fun together

- Planning a special date (together or as a surprise for your partner)
- Working on a budget together
- Praying for your spouse and your marriage
- Resolving a conflict about money as a team
- Learning how to communicate better together (in a class, from a book, on the web, or however else you can)
- Planning a vacation together
- Going to church together
- Getting involved in some ministry together

Do you want a relationally rich and full life together? Regular investments like these will keep your marriage alive and thriving. Commitment requires action. You can't just sit back and reflect on it or wish you had it. Acting purposefully on your commitment from deep within your heart will accomplish the most in your marriage. It's your choice today and every day for the rest of your lives.

Exercise Your Commitment

Think about areas in your lives where you'll need to say no more often to something that will detract from your marriage so that you can say yes more fully to your future spouse. Come up with a way to remind yourselves of the importance of making your marriage a high priority.

Sit down together as a couple and identify types of investments that matter to your relationship. Start by listing, separately, things that are important to each of you. Put down whatever is important to you and whatever you think is important to your fiancé(e). Next, talk. You may discover some things that matter to one of you but not to the other. Take the time to talk through the kinds of investments you both believe are most important to keep making in your marriage, and commit to doing what it takes to have a marriage that thrives.

SCOTT STANLEY, PhD, has authored a number of popular books on marriage, including *A Lasting Promise* and *The Power of Commitment*. Portions of this chapter were excerpted from *The Power of Commitment*. He also writes a popular blog, *Sliding vs Deciding*, at SlidingvsDeciding .com. Scott is a research professor and codirector of the Center for Marital and Family Studies at the University of Denver. His research is internationally recognized, and he has published extensively in scientific journals on marriage and family. Core research interests include marital commitment, couple development, and the prevention of marital distress.

Ready to Talk

1. Remember Lisa from the start of the chapter? Which of the following statements comes closest to what you'd tell her? Why?

    • "You don't have to follow in your parents' footsteps."

    • "Just do the best you can."

    • "God won't let your marriage fail."

    • "Good point. Let's tell everybody to go home."

    • "If you have real commitment, you have what it takes."

    • Other _____

2. How are the statements in each of the following pairs different? How might the differences make a difference in your marriage?

    • "We're sticking together" versus "We're stuck with each other."

    • "I'm committed to this marriage" versus "I committed to this marriage, so I can't back out."

    • "Divorce is not an option" versus "I don't have any options."

    Why is it important to choose your words carefully when you talk about your commitment to each other?

3. How could having the viewpoint of a long-term investor help you see the following scenarios as temporary dips in the "stock market" of your marriage?

- One year after the wedding, you lose your job—which means you can't afford the "honeymoon" trip you never got to take.
- You feel a growing distance between you and your spouse that has been increasing for several years.
- Your spouse begins experiencing serious depression and isn't able to fully engage with you as in the past.
- Your spouse drops out of school prior to finishing his or her degree.
- As a couple you decide you are ready to start a family, and nothing happens for a year. After visiting the doctor, you learn that fertility is going to be an issue in your marriage.
- Your spouse develops a close relationship with an attractive colleague at work.

Which of these situations might be the hardest for you to cope with? How would you desire to respond? How would you want your spouse to respond? What would you do to show continued investment in the marriage?

Ready to Try

Take turns reading 1 Corinthians 13:4–8, 13. Pretend you've decided to write your own wedding vows and base them on this passage. How would you do it? Try writing your own individual versions. Then compare your vows with your spouse-to-be's version. See whether you can harmonize the two into a description of your commitment to each other.

CHAPTER 4

HONORING YOU ALL THE DAYS OF MY LIFE

Gary Smalley

AS YOU PREPARE TO BE JOINED together as husband and wife, you've probably given some thought to what you'll say to each other as you exchange vows. If not, don't admit this to anyone—especially to your future mother-in-law!

Over the years I've heard couples declare their love for each other in ways that brought tears to my eyes. I've listened to words that caused me to laugh out loud, and sadly, I've heard couples say things that made me shake my head in disbelief. But the wedding vow I'll never forget sounded like this: "I, Josh, take you, Brianna, to be my wife, to have and to hold from this day forward, for better or for worse, for richer, for poorer, in sickness and in health; from this day forward until death do us part."

Sounds perfectly wonderful, doesn't it? You can just imagine this beautiful bride standing there, gushing with sheer joy as her prince charming promised everlasting love. The only problem is that Josh wasn't standing next to Brianna—that was the name of his ex-girlfriend. True story. That's one wedding ceremony worth forgetting!

However, unlike Josh's vow, there's a very interesting phrase many couples use during the wedding ceremony that's worth a closer look. It goes something like this: "I will love and honor you all the days of my life."

Maybe you've chosen to use this very line to recite during your wedding vows. If so, you're about to unleash what I believe is the single most important concept for building a strong marital relationship.

What's the word? Let's go back to that common phrase *"I will love and honor you all the days of my life."* The word that has such a powerful impact on a marriage relationship isn't what most people guess—*love*. Although love is important, it's the other word I want to focus on. I want to show you the amazing power of the word *honor*.

Webster's dictionary defines *honor* as "having high respect; to confer distinction on; show high value." I define it as "a decision we make to see another person as a priceless treasure, recognizing their incredible worth and value."

When we choose to honor someone, it has a powerful effect on the relationship. Marriage expert Dr. John Gottman has said that "without honor, all the marriage skills one can learn won't work."[1] Dr. Scott Stanley notes that "honor is the fuel that keeps the life long marriage loving and functioning. If only a spark of respect or adoration remains, the spark can be turned into the flame in a few days."[2]

For me, the reason why honor is so important is because it's exactly what brought my wife and me together many years ago.

I can remember when Norma and I first met. I was sitting with a group of my friends at Cru (Campus Crusade for Christ) in Whittier, California, on a seemingly normal Friday night. All of a sudden, a girl walked in who, let's just say, caught my eye immediately. She was stunningly beautiful in a pink-colored sweater. All of the chairs in the room were full (I really hadn't moved chairs out of the room to manipulate this), so she had to sit on the floor *right in front of me*! This somewhat normal Friday night rapidly became quite exciting!

I gazed at her throughout the meeting, not sure if I could muster up enough confidence to talk to her. But that didn't stop me. After the meeting was over, I immediately tapped her on the shoulder and introduced myself. As we began talking, I felt myself drawn toward her witty personality. And her smile lit up the room!

I soon discovered that we both had a heart to be in full-time ministry. She shared that she was going on a missions trip to Mexico with her youth group, so I asked her for more information about the trip (which meant that she had to give me her phone number!). Within two weeks of that Cru meeting, I asked Norma out on our first date, and that led me to join her on the missions trip to Mexico.

We ended up dating for a year and enjoyed nonstop laughter whenever we were together. We often attended Cru events together. One night I took her to the Hollywood Bowl, and then as I took her home, I shared with her that I felt we should date other people. (What was I thinking?) For the next three years, we dated occasionally but not exclusively—and certainly never talked about marriage.

However, things changed rapidly when I heard from my youth director that Norma was dating another guy. I realized how much I cared for her, and I didn't want to lose her. I loved her and wanted her to be my wife.

As I tried to think of what would be the perfect place to pop the question, I realized that a youth retreat in Palm Springs was approaching. We would both be there, and it seemed like just the right venue, since our relationship had been built around our involvement in Cru. At that retreat later in the month, my friends helped me come up with the perfect romantic scenario to ask Norma to be my wife. Norma was somewhat surprised, seeing as how we had never really talked about marriage. But it turned out that she loved me as well, and she said yes. Four months later, we were walking down the aisle.

You might be wondering what my decision to propose had to do with honor? Everything. When I heard that Norma was dating that other guy, it made me think long and hard about our relationship. But more important, it caused me to think deeply about her as a person. It brought to life 1 Samuel 16:7: "The LORD does not look at the things man looks at. Man looks at the outward appearance, but the LORD looks at the heart." And the more I thought about her heart, the more I realized how amazing she was. Her beauty, her fun personality, her laughter, her heart for ministry, her devotion, her thoughtfulness, her integrity, her relationship with Christ, her selflessness, and her attention to details—all of these qualities pointed to one thing: *her incredible value*.

At that moment I understood how precious Norma was to me and how much I treasured and cherished her. It was honor that made me realize I wanted to spend the rest of my life with her as my wife. Fifty years later, I'd do it all again!

Do you see why honor must be a key part of the foundation you build to have a healthy marriage? I'm not exaggerating the fact that I can't think of another principle that can influence the overall temperature of your marriage relationship more than learning to honor your fiancé(e).

Creating a Marriage That Feels Like the Safest Place on Earth

Let me build a case for honor by talking about divorce for a moment. I know that the D word is the furthest thing from your minds right now, and that's a good thing. I'm not going to lament about the state of marriage in our country or throw any bleak statistics at you, so hang in there with me.

Let's focus on the only time Jesus talked about divorce. Look closely at what He said in Matthew 19:8: "Moses permitted you to divorce your wives because your hearts were hard. But it was not this way from the beginning." Basically, Jesus was saying that divorce happens when a heart becomes hardened. I like this explanation from best-selling author Max Lucado:

A hard heart ruins, not only your life, but [your marriage as well]. . . . Jesus identified the hard heart as the wrecking ball of a marriage. . . . When one or both people in a marriage [harden their hearts], they sign its death certificate.[3]

Why is a hardened heart so destructive to a marriage? It inhibits your ability to hear and understand God. It impedes your ability to recognize His voice and understand what He is saying. You're operating solely by your own understanding and perspective. And that's incredibly dangerous.

Author Doug Apple explains why:

When your heart is hard, it is not open to God. You do not want to listen to God. You don't want to hear His word. You don't want to know about His plan or His design. And you certainly don't want to listen to any correction. A hard heart toward God separates us from God. It separates us from His wisdom, which allows us to become ignorant. It separates us from His light, which puts us in darkness.[4]

Sadly, people with hardened hearts often ignore what God is saying about their relationship problems, and they usually disregard His will for their marriages as well. How does God respond? He gives them what they demand: "He has blinded their eyes and [hardened] their hearts, so they can neither see with their eyes, nor understand with their hearts" (John 12:40).

The bottom line is that you never want to harden your heart. I think this is exactly what Jesus meant in the last part of Matthew 19:8 when He said, "But it was not this way from the beginning." In other words, in the beginning of a relationship, a heart wasn't hard; it was open.

Don't miss the significance of the seemingly minor point Christ was making. This is one of the most important truths you could ever grasp about relationships: *If you want to have a great marriage, both of your hearts must stay open to each other.* To say that differently, to get whatever you want in your marriage—passion, fun, connection, communication, intimacy, sex, whatever—two hearts have to be open. These critical components of a healthy marriage won't happen when hearts are closed. And over time, a closed heart becomes hard.

Although you might not have ever heard it put this way, you may have heard people say things like "I've fallen out of love" or "I love him, but I'm not *in love* with him." Don't ever fall for those lines. They're simply not true. We don't "fall out of love"; instead, our hearts close and harden, and we don't *feel* love. But the issue is never love. God is love. First John 4:7–8 says it this way: "Dear friends, let us love one another, for love comes from God. Everyone who loves has been born of God and knows God. Whoever does not love does not know God, because God is love."

You and I don't create love; "we love because [God] loved us first" (1 John 4:19). God's love is always available. His love is like air; it's all around us. As the psalmist wrote, "The earth is filled with your love, O Lord" (Psalm 119:64). So when someone talks about not feeling love toward another person, what that person is really saying is that his or her heart is closed, or worse, hardened. As you marry, you'll face a daily battle to keep your heart open. I think this is why King Solomon warned, "Above all else, guard your heart, for it is the wellspring of life" (Proverbs 4:23). Guarding your heart means to guard it from closing and hardening.

Every day your heart is at war. You will face internal problems with your spouse, such as conflict, hurt feelings, frustration, and disappointment. But you'll also face external challenges, including health problems, the loss of a loved one, financial problems, a job loss, and busyness. You must learn how to keep your heart open in the midst of these internal and external challenges.

The key to an open heart in your marriage is what I call "emotional safety." In other words, one of your primary goals must be to create a marriage that feels like the safest place on earth. Why is this so important? It's all about creating an environment that allows two hearts to remain open. When you feel safe with your future spouse, your heart opens and connection happens. However, on the other hand, when you feel emotionally unsafe with your future spouse, your heart closes, and you'll disconnect and emotionally pull away.

Let me take a moment to summarize what I hope you're hearing me say: To have the type of marriage you've always dreamed of—a relationship teeming with passion, laughter, communication, fun, intimacy, and deep connection—two hearts must be open to each other. And the only way a heart will open is when it feels safe.

So to come full circle, honor is the foundation for creating a marriage that feels like the safest place on earth. Let me show you how this works.

Honor: The Foundation for Creating a Safe Marriage

I believe the master plan for building a foundation of honor and safety in your marriage begins with a very straightforward directive from the apostle Paul: "Let each one of you love his wife as himself" (Ephesians 5:33, ESV). Here, we are told to love our spouses as we love ourselves. Does this instruction sound familiar? Jesus said the same thing when He was asked about the greatest commandment: "Love your neighbor as yourself" (Matthew 22:39). So if loving ourselves is the answer to how we are to love our spouses, what does that look like practically speaking? What does it mean to love yourself? The good news is that we don't have to search very hard to find the answer.

Let's go back to the Ephesians 5 passage on marriage. In verses 28–29, it says,

> Husbands ought also to love their own wives as their own
> bodies. He who loves his own wife loves himself; for no one
> ever hated his own flesh, but nourishes and cherishes it, just
> as Christ also does the church. (NASB)

And we have a winner! There it is in plain English. Paul is telling us that since we *nourish* and *cherish* our own bodies, we should do that for our spouses. When we choose to regularly cherish and nourish each other, we build a solid foundation of honor and safety in our marriages.

Let's first look at the word *cherish*. This is a mind-set, a mentality, an attitude. To cherish your spouse-to-be means that you recognize his or her incredible value. Your fiancé(e) will feel safe to the extent that you keep in mind how valuable he or she is.

The secret to cherishing your future spouse is best illustrated by something that happened to me when I was speaking at a large marriage conference. A friend of mine in that town lent me an item he had recently purchased so that I could use it to make a point. What he had loaned me was actually an old, beat-up violin. Several of the strings were missing, and the one that was still there was actually hanging off, attached only to one end of the violin. There was little of the polish or brilliance one might see emanating from an instrument owned by a professional musician or played at a symphony.

I passed the violin around the audience so they could see it. It moved along pretty quickly from row to row. But when I pointed out that if they looked inside, they could see in faded but very genuine writing, the word *Stradivarius*, the room instantly came alive with *oohs* and *aahs*. All of a sudden, this out-of-shape violin took on a whole new level of significance. It was valuable! After all, a Stradivarius violin, made in the seventeenth or eighteenth century, is worth in the range of hundreds of thousands to millions of dollars. The violin passed through the audience slowly and carefully after that. Its value had been recognized. It was cherished. This is what honor conveys. It recognizes value and, in turn, cherishes and nourishes.

You have the opportunity each and every day you spend with your future spouse to choose to see how incredibly valuable he or she is. When someone truly knows that you deeply understand his or her value, that person will feel safe with you. Your hearts will open toward each other, and the connection desired in marriage will be established. But think about when you know someone doesn't honor you. Does your heart feel safe? No . . . you desire to get as far away from this person as you can.

Do you see the types of challenges this could cause in marriage because of the simple logistics of living in the same house, sleeping in the same bed, sharing a bathroom, and so on? The great news is this: Even if you forget how valuable your future spouse is, the Lord never does. You can turn to God's Word to see that he or she was made with His value:

You were made in My image.
PARAPHRASE OF GENESIS 1:27

[You are] fearfully and wonderfully made.
PSALM 139:14

You [are] my treasured possession.
EXODUS 19:5

You are my glorious inheritance.
PARAPHRASE OF EPHESIANS 1:18

You are precious and honored in my sight.
ISAIAH 43:4

Look at the birds of the air; they do not sow or reap or store away in barns, and yet your heavenly Father feeds them. Are you not much more valuable than they?
MATTHEW 6:26

A man's greatest treasure is his wife.
PARAPHRASE OF PROVERBS 18:22

> Marriage should be honored by all.
>
> HEBREWS 13:4

These verses are the epitome of honor. God desires for you to grasp your fiancé(e)'s value as well. However, let me be very honest with you. There are times when this can be a challenge for anyone in any relationship. Marriage seems to provide many opportunities to love and honor, but it also offers many occasions for dishonor. It's all in how we choose to see it.

I began doing something a few years into our marriage that I would recommend you do prior to walking down the aisle. Begin reflecting on the things that first drew you to your spouse-to-be—even differences. As I described earlier, I remembered Norma's witty personality and her smile that lit up a room, and soon I discovered that she had a great sense of humor. Think of all the things you admired about your fiancé(e) when you first started dating and other things you've discovered throughout your journey together. Think of physical characteristics, personality qualities, thinking patterns, faith, convictions, opinions, work ethic, sensitivity, gender differences, integrity, detail orientation, hospitality, an ability to lead, and so forth. Whatever you admire about your fiancé(e), write it down and keep this list handy. Let me explain why.

About five years ago, Norma and I were hosting my son Greg and his family for Thanksgiving at our home in Branson, Missouri. Norma and I both woke up in irritable moods that morning. Nothing specific was bothering us; we were just irritated and grumpy. Thanksgiving isn't necessarily the best day to be grumpy, since you're supposed to be thankful, right?

Honestly, the last thing we felt that day was overwhelming gratitude. We had a lot to do—prepare for the meal, set the table, and, of course, watch a little football intertwined with throwing the football in the backyard with Greg and my grandson, Garrison. We had to recreate in real action what we were seeing on television. So from my perspective, I was helping Norma in the kitchen between each exit to the backyard and each entrance into the living room to watch a few more minutes of the game.

After a few of these rotations, I could sense Norma's level of frustration increasing, and for whatever reason, I was already irritated with her. Soon things erupted, and my irritation took the plunge into "mad." I went into my office and slammed the door. I quickly entered into what I call my "tornado of thoughts" and could only find myself remembering things about Norma that irritated me. However, over the years, I had learned that there was something I could do to stop this tornado and start remembering how priceless Norma really is.

The Cherish List

As I sat in my office and stewed and perseverated, I decided to open up the Word document on my computer that always helps me remember what I love about Norma. After a few clicks, I opened the file, and there it was, clear as day—the list titled "Why Norma Is So Valuable." As I began reading the list, I wanted to delete about the first ten items that described how wonderful she is. But after a few more negative thoughts, I read further down the list and began to remember that I married a pretty amazing woman. Ephesians 5:29 closely resembles this process. We remember to cherish and value each other.

Here's a portion of my "Why Norma Is So Valuable" list:

1. She has a great sense of humor.
2. When she smiles, it lights up the room.
3. She can always think of the details I miss.
4. She loves me even when I do "dingbat" things.
5. She works enormously hard.
6. She has raised three wonderful kids with me.
7. She is passionate about simple things—like her birds.
8. She has supported me in ministry over the years.
9. She loves to see movies with me.
10. She is able to think things through at a level I need.

My list about what makes Norma so valuable could go on and on, and it does. But what about your list? What makes your spouse-to-be so incredibly valuable? I encourage you to start your list right now. The longer the list the better!

Take out a sheet of paper and list all of the reasons why your fiancé(e) is so valuable. For example, you might write down a character trait, a gender difference, a faith pattern, values, morals, spirituality, a role you appreciate (e.g., worker, friend, sibling, son or daughter), a personality characteristic, or how your fiancé(e) treats you.

Here are some words to prime the pump and get you thinking about your future spouse's value:

Humble

Brave

Values integrity

Courageous

Funny

Loyal

Caring

Unselfish

Generous

Self-confident

Respectful

Considerate

Creative

Independent

Intelligent

Honest

Adventurous

Hard-working

Fun-loving

Successful

Responsible

Helpful

Loves to dream

Happy

Is a natural leader

Gentle

Loving

Neat

Joyful

Cooperative

Curious

Determined

Energetic

Cheerful

Thoughtful

Calm

Mannerly

Be sure to keep this list nearby so you can periodically add to it. The longer your list becomes, the more reasons you'll have to remember just how much you cherish and honor your future spouse. Also, add to the list as you travel through the different seasons of your marriage journey—storms will come! There *will* be many different seasons, and you'll both continue changing, maturing, and growing (emotionally, spiritually, and yes, even physically). As things change, it's important to remember what drew you close to your fiancé(e).

And whatever you do, don't keep this amazing list to yourself. Share it with your fiancé(e). Let him (or her) know that you recognize his value, because some days, he may forget how priceless he is. Talk about creating safety. When this happens, not only will your fiancé(e) benefit, but you'll be positively impacted as well. Luke 12:34 explains why this is so powerful: "For where your treasure is, there your heart will be also." In other words, your heart will be open to what you value. One way to keep your heart open and your future spouse feeling safe with you is to focus on his or her value. This will not only encourage an attitude of honor, but it will cause you to treat your future spouse in honoring ways.

Nourish: Treating Each Other Like Treasures

"Love is a verb, not a noun. It is active. Love is not just feelings of passion and romance. It is behavior."[5] I love this Susan Forward quote. Understanding your mate's incredible value is the beginning of safety, but to create a marriage that feels like the safest place on earth, you must be able to express honor through action and behavior. This is exactly what 1 John 3:18 says: "Let us not love with words or tongue but with actions."

Now I can honestly say that while Norma and I were dating and engaged, it wasn't hard to remember to value her or even treat her like a treasure. But let me just say that after we were married and moved across the country to Minnesota, where I started working as a full-time youth pastor and attended graduate school, sometimes it was easy to forget that I married a gem. When I think back to the first time I met Norma, I knew she was a priceless treasure after one conversation. So how is it that less than two months into our marriage, it seemed I could forget that pretty easily?

This is actually fairly common when it comes to marriage. Not that you'll necessarily forget what a treasure you married, but as you settle into the stress and busyness of everyday life and start to discover things they do differently from you or things they do that irritate you, your attitude and behavior may begin to show that you don't think all of these once "cute" behaviors are so cute anymore. At times you may even forget how very valuable your spouse is, and your behavior may reflect it. So, what can you do to help you remember to treat each other like priceless treasures? I've found a statement (five little words, actually) that you can ask your fiancé(e) to complete that puts honor straight into action.

I Feel Loved When You . . .

First Peter 3:7 encourages spouses to live together "in an understanding way, showing honor" (ESV). One of the best and most practical ways to begin to nourish your future spouse and show honor is to understand what he or she needs from you to feel loved.

To nourish your fiancé(e)'s relational desires, you must realize that everyone's needs are different, based on personalities, interests, gender, backgrounds, and expectations. So before you can begin nourishing your future spouse, you have to know what he or she needs from you. You can't make an educated guess or treat your fiancé(e) the way you would like to be treated. The Golden Rule doesn't apply here! The problem is that your guess might be wide of the mark, or your "love language" might be extremely different from what your fiancé(e) needs or wants.

To give you an easy method for discovering your future spouse's love language, let me tell you about a time when my son Greg almost drove his truck and his wife into the mighty Mississippi River.

One day Greg and his wife, Erin, were driving from southwest Missouri to Nashville, Tennessee. Leading up to the trip, Erin had asked Greg to consult the American Automobile Association (AAA) about the best way to get to Nashville. As a guy, he resented her request and felt he could guide them better than AAA. Greg spent several hours diligently studying maps and found a great route, including a special shortcut that would save them hours.

As Greg stood back to bask in the glory of his accomplishment, Erin wasn't impressed. There was no praise or applause. To make matters worse, Erin begged Greg to call AAA so they could "verify" his route. The nerve! But Greg was not going to cave in and ask for directions—especially from AAA. At this point, much more was riding on their trip than simply getting there. Guys all around the world were counting on Greg to show his wife that as a man, he could find the way without any help.

Several hours into the trip, Greg was feeling great because his route was perfect. They were thirty-minutes ahead of AAA's schedule. Greg was king of the road. But just like that, disaster struck.

It was just starting to get dark, and the sunset was incredible. Erin and Greg were laughing and singing, and she had even stopped asking him if he knew where they were. Then all of a sudden, Erin said, "Did you see that sign? I swear it read 'dead end.'"

"Nice try," Greg joked. "You just can't admit that I was right and you were wrong."

"I'm serious," she begged. "I think this road is a dead end."

"This road does not end," Greg shot back. "Don't worry. Trust me!"

Have you ever uttered something you so wish you could take back? For Greg, "Don't worry. Trust me!" remains one of those statements I'm sure he'd give anything to have back.

Greg and Erin continued to drive for about one hour. Neither of them spoke a word as they waited for the truth to be revealed. The surrounding area gradually began to be less populated, until it transformed into cornfields as far as the eye could see. And then it happened.

Dead end!

Greg barely stopped the truck in time to avoid crashing into the rather large Dead End sign.

"That's impossible," he shouted in disbelief. "This wasn't on the map!"

The worst part was that Erin didn't have to say anything. She just sat there with that look of disdain, shaking her head from side to side. Next Greg did what any man would do in his situation. He got out of the truck to survey the area.

As Greg gazed down at the mighty Mississippi River, he could actually see the road form again on the other side.

"It's not my fault that the map didn't show that a bridge wasn't here!" Greg shouted back at the truck.

But as he reached to study the map, Erin quickly jerked it out of his hands. Greg didn't even try to get it back. He was defeated.

Driving back the way they had come, Erin and Greg didn't speak for quite some time. When Erin finally started to say something, Greg was certain she was going to give him a piece of her mind. And he deserved it, no doubt. But Erin didn't get frustrated or say "I told you so." What she did was actually the same thing you can do to begin to nourish your fiancé(e).

Erin spoke in a tender voice and said, "I read something very interesting the other day about marriage."

Greg just nodded and prayed that it wasn't something about a guy's unwillingness to ask for directions.

"Some expert said that a great way to better understand each other's love language is to have each person answer the statement 'I feel loved when you . . .' I say we give it a try."

Greg gulped and nodded, grateful to have escaped what could have been well-deserved wrath. "Why don't you go first."

"Well . . ." Erin smiled. "I feel loved when you ask AAA about our trip route."

Touché.

As you can see, I've got a very spirited daughter-in-law, and I love that about her.

The Nourish List

What about you? How would you answer the statement "I feel loved when you . . ."? Following are some ideas for both husbands- and wives-to-be to help prime the pump.

Husbands: "I feel loved when you . . ."

- Tell me you both love me *and* like me.
- Show interest in my interests and give me space to participate in them freely.
- Look for ways to laugh together.
- Focus on what I'm doing right instead of focusing so often on the negatives.
- Participate in the things I like to do—even if they're not interesting to you (such as watching football!).
- Give me thirty minutes to unwind after I get home from work.
- Compliment me often for what I do that you appreciate.
- Avoid bringing up problems when we go out on a date and have fun instead.
- Don't overcommit yourself. Leave time for me.
- Give me the benefit of the doubt when I hurt you.
- Give advice in a loving way—not in a nagging or belittling way.
- Share your feelings with me at appropriate times and keep it brief—I often feel "flooded" by too many words.
- Share what you appreciate about me in terms of what I do.
- Remember that I define intimacy as "doing" things together (e.g., having sex, watching a movie, playing Ping-Pong, taking a drive together, fishing, etc.).
- Initiate sex periodically. And respond more often.

- Sometimes let me enjoy my day off work without having to "work" at home.
- Don't expect me to read your mind.
- Pray for me.
- Graciously teach me how to demonstrate my love for you.

Wives: "I feel loved when you . . ."

- Help me feel safe—protected and shielded from physical, emotional, and spiritual attack.
- Start and end each day by praying together with me.
- Pursue me and show me that I'm your top priority.
- Help me feel beautiful in your eyes—that you're fascinated and captivated by my beauty and delight in who I am.
- Validate and care deeply about my heart, especially my emotions. Never forget that I won't care what you *know* until I know that you *care*.
- Show interest in my friends and give me time to be with them.
- Express interest in the things I'm passionate about and show it by your actions.
- Share responsibilities around the house (e.g., folding laundry, unloading the dishwasher, etc.) without looking for special recognition.
- Allow me to share my feelings and thoughts, and don't become defensive when I do.
- Be a good listener and make eye contact when I'm talking. Show me you value what I say.
- When we've been apart for a time and I ask how your day went, don't just say "fine"; actually give me details.
- Be the spiritual leader of our family.

- Surprise me with a card, flowers, or a little gift.
- Give me your undivided attention when I want to talk.
- Encourage me to relax and give me alone time to recharge.
- Continue to court me.
- Hold me close and vocally express your love and care for me when I'm hurt, discouraged, or burdened.
- Call, e-mail, or text me during the day just to say you're thinking of me.
- Show me affection without sexual intentions.

Throughout your marriage, be sure to update your nourish list periodically, and keep current with what each of you needs to feel loved. During each season of life (health problems, busyness, moving, job loss, raising kids, empty nest, etc.), you'll each need something different, and these needs can change in an instant. Stay current with each other!

As we all know, life can throw curveballs at us. As you and your fiancé(e) advance into married life, I want to encourage you to remember that you have a very important role to play in each other's lives. As each of you experiences different challenges and disappointments in your day-to-day life, remember that when your spouse walks through the front door each night, you are faced with a choice. You both have a lot of influence over the environment that you walk into. When the world has been hard all day, wouldn't it be great to come home to the safest place on earth? Or even the safest place you've experienced all day? When you walk through the front door, wouldn't it be nice to truly believe that you can share the deepest thoughts, feelings, needs, and dreams in your heart, and that your future spouse will really listen, understand, and validate you? This is really the essence of emotional safety—that your fiancé(e) understands your value and, in essence, honors you.

Here's what I really want you to remember: Apply the concept of honor now and forever. "Be devoted to one another in brotherly love; *give preference to one another in honor.*" (Romans 12:10, NASB, emphasis added). You are beginning a journey with the person you've chosen to spend the rest of your life with. Throughout the years of your journey, you won't always feel like you do right now, and that's okay. You'll encounter rough spots and challenges ahead, but through all the ups and downs, you can choose to see your spouse's value (cherish) and treat him or her in valuable ways (nourish). Remember what you feel right now and why you chose your fiancé(e) as your partner on this journey. Honor will go a long way in marriage—now and forever.

GARY SMALLEY is one of the country's best-known authors and speakers on relationships. He is the author and coauthor of fifty-two best-selling, award-winning books and videos that have reached more than twelve million people. In forty years Gary has spoken to more than two million people in live conferences, and he has appeared on national television networks and programs, including TBN, *The Oprah Winfrey Show*, *Fox & Friends*, *Larry King Live*, NBC's *Today* show, and *Life Today* with James Robison, as well as numerous national radio programs such as *The Sean Hannity Show*, *Focus on the Family*, Oliver North's show, and many more. Gary served as the president and founder of the Smalley Relationship Center, which has been providing research, relationship coaching, nationwide conferences, books, videos, and small-group curriculum for years. Gary and his wife, Norma, continue ministering to couples and live in Colorado Springs, Colorado. They've been married for more than fifty years.

Ready to Talk

1. Think about when you first saw your fiancé(e). What was it about him or her that you noticed? As you talked to him or her, what was it about the interaction that made you ask for/agree to a first date?

2. Song of Songs 4:1–3 and 5:10–16 reflect a groom's and bride's desire to honor each other. How would you rewrite these tributes to honor your spouse-to-be? Be sure to include some of your future mate's unique attributes, and use terms that make sense in today's culture. Then read your tributes to each other.

3. One key to a great marriage is keeping your heart open. When a heart feels safe, it is more likely to stay open. Take turns answering this statement: "I feel safe when you . . . ," and then share your answers with each other. The idea is to create a list of specific behaviors that help your fiancé(e) feel safe and, thus, keep his or her heart open to you. Choose one behavior off of your fiancé(e)'s list, and commit to carrying it out throughout your engagement.

Ready to Try

Make your own Cherish List about your spouse-to-be, like the one Gary made about Norma. Then get together with your fiancé(e) and share your lists with each other. Put the lists in a time capsule (perhaps a jar, jewelry box, or envelope) that you'll plan to open on your first anniversary—if not before. Look your list over whenever you have a hard time honoring each other. It will help remind you of the qualities that attracted you to your mate in the first place.

CHAPTER 5

SOUL MATES: BUILDING SPIRITUAL INTIMACY

Joe White

BETH WAS OVERJOYED when her boyfriend, Don, became a Christian. She'd told him she couldn't marry a non-Christian. But she didn't know what lay ahead.

Almost from the day he received Christ as his Savior, Don was talking to Beth—and anybody else who would listen—about Jesus and his new life. Don was so enthusiastic, in fact, that Beth wasn't sure what to do with him. He wanted to pray with her—out loud! That was something she'd never done with a man. He thought they ought to bow in prayer at meals, even in restaurants!

When Don finally convinced Beth to marry him, she was still concerned. She cringed at his desire to read the Bible together, much less pray. It was starting to drive her crazy.

Don didn't get it. Why wasn't Beth as thrilled as he was that they were both Christians? After all, the guys in his men's Bible-study group had all been applauding his spiritual growth.

When he asked her about it, she tried to explain that her personal devotional life always had been just that—personal. Did they have to pray *aloud* together *all the time*?

Another couple, Nick and Margaret, had a slightly different problem. A busy airline pilot, Nick found it tough to keep up with regular church attendance and personal prayer and Bible reading. Margaret, on the other hand, was devoted to those things. The fact that praying together was so important to her made Nick feel uneasy . . . then irritated.

In premarital counseling, the two of them met with a mentor couple. Nick complained that when it came to prayer, Margaret was setting the bar too high: "I feel awkward doing that with her. Is it really better than praying by yourself?"

Deep down, Nick felt that praying as a couple was something people did in "the olden days." What was the point of doing it now?[1]

When You're Not Exactly Soul Mates

There's a whole slew of Dons and Beths and Nicks and Margarets out there. Plenty of couples run smack into spiritual conflicts soon after—if not before—the wedding-reception DJ packs up the speakers and the photographer starts erasing the "red eye" from the group pictures. The bones of contention can pile up pretty quickly:

- "She sure isn't the Proverbs 31 woman!"
- "He's not even close to being a spiritual leader!"
- "I don't want to raise my kids in that kind of church!"
- "We should tithe *after* taxes, not before!"

Part of the problem is that many couples don't get around to talking about the details of their faith before they walk down the aisle. The result: conflicts that can leave more scars than an NFL championship game.

The good news is that there's a solution to this problem. It gets engaged couples and husbands and wives on the same page. It creates unity. It's a kind of intimacy a lot of future spouses forget—the spiritual kind.

The Goo Is Good

So what *is* spiritual intimacy? In marriage it's like epoxy, which has two parts. Part A is the goo, and the goo is good. The goo is the lovey, "feely," warm part of intimacy. It's the part of love that we all *love* to experience! But epoxy doesn't turn solid until you add part B. Part B is the hardening agent—in this case, the commitment to pleasing God together even when things are tough.

Spiritual intimacy is a strong, solidifying bond. Without it, marriage won't work the way it should. Realizing that you both need to have Christ in the center and actually *putting* Him there will create spiritual intimacy in your marriage, just as it adds intimacy with Him when He's the center of your personal lives.

If you figure this will involve things like prayer, going to church, serving, teaching spiritual truths to your children, and charitable giving, you're right. But that's not the whole story. It will also involve knowing your spouse's spiritual heart and mind better than anyone else, and vice versa—being intimately familiar with each other's questions, doubts, fears, bedrock convictions, priorities, and spiritual gifts. Creating this kind of closeness—and encouraging each other in your growth as Christians—is the foundation of spiritual intimacy.

Maybe you're thinking, *Man, that sounds hard. Is it really worth it?*

I can tell you from experience that it is.

For more than thirty years, I've had the indescribable privilege of being assigned a fifty-yard-line seat in a most amazing arena where talent, charm, and character have been displayed like no other place on earth. The players are male and female. The male team dresses in well-tailored tuxedo uniforms; the female team is adorned in exquisite evening gowns. The star of the show wears a pure, dazzling-white dress. Her beauty is beyond my ability to describe.

By now, I'm sure you've guessed that the event is a wedding. My fifty-yard-line seat is the spot between the bride and groom where I can place their hands together and invite them to say, "I do."

Almost all the weddings at which I've officiated feature a bride and groom from the staff of our Christian sports camp who met and fell in love there. The number of couples over the decades has become too large to keep up with. Even more amazing is that, at this writing, most of these couples are not only still married but are also very *happily* married.

So many marriages end in divorce, and a large percentage of those who stay married aren't truly happy. What makes the difference for those I've closely witnessed? It's found in these few simple verses of Scripture:

> If you have any encouragement from being united with Christ,
> if any comfort from his love, if any fellowship with the Spirit, if
> any tenderness and compassion, then make my joy complete
> by being like-minded, having the same love, being one in spirit
> and purpose. Do nothing out of selfish ambition or vain conceit,
> but in humility consider others better than yourselves. Each of
> you should look not only to your own interests, but also to the
> interests of others.
>
> PHILIPPIANS 2:1–4

United.
Fellowship.
Like-minded.
The same love.
One in spirit and purpose.

These people are on the same page. They're in harmony. They've found spiritual intimacy.

What difference does that make? I'll let Anne Graham Lotz, daughter of Billy Graham, answer that one. Here's what she told Focus on the Family:

If you have two Christlike people, each putting the other one first and each living to serve Christ and the other one, you are going to have a wonderful marriage and a wonderful relationship. That doesn't mean there aren't going to be hard times and trials and things that afflict everybody in a marriage. But you are going to be healthy because your relationship with God is healthy.

I can't argue with that. And after seeing it work for so many couples I've had the honor to join in marriage, I wouldn't even try.

Top Tools to Build Spiritual Intimacy

So spiritual intimacy can be a game changer in your marriage. But how do you build it? Based on my years of experience with my wife, Debbie-Jo, my observation of many other couples, and listening to some of the wisest marriage experts in the country, let me share with you what I've learned.

Intimacy Builder No. 1: Share Your Faith History

To know where you're going, you need to remember where you've been. In my case, that can be a painful experience.

My first wife abandoned me for the man who'd been my best friend in college. That left a pain in my heart that lasted a long time.

Both my first wife and my college friend are wonderful people. Although there's little doubt that initiating divorce is wrong in most circumstances, I've never blamed them, nor have I ever been bitter. I cried my eyes out for a few months. Yet during that horrible time, I fell completely in love with God for the first time. I learned to give Him my todays as well as my tomorrows.

God not only healed my broken heart, but He also brought Debbie-Jo to me. (In case I haven't told you, she is the greatest woman alive and the mom of my four kids.) God also gave me a passion for people who, like myself, find themselves at the bottom of an emotional canyon with no apparent way out.

I learned a lot in my brokenness before God. I can see Him at His best when I am at my worst. He is never closer than those times when I fall on my face.

That's not my whole faith history, of course, but it's an important part of it. If I hadn't shared my spiritual journey with Debbie-Jo, how would she truly know and understand where I'm coming from? And if she hadn't shared her spiritual journey with me, how would I know and understand her?

Start sharing your faith history with your spouse-to-be, if you haven't already. Talk about the role faith played in your growing-up years and what it means to you now. Have there been times when you've felt extremely close to God? Or times when you've wondered if your prayers went beyond the ceiling?

Some parts of your story may be happy or even funny. Others may be hard to talk about. But before you can write new chapters of your own as a couple, make sure you both understand what's come before.

Intimacy Builder No. 2: Start with Yourself

Make sure you're growing spiritually as an individual. One of the first steps toward spiritual intimacy is making sure your *own* relationship with God is in order. Not perfect, but alive and growing.

I used to cohost a radio program called *Life on the Edge LIVE!* One evening a young woman called in. She had this to say:

> Picture yourself driving a car. . . . You're driving down the highway, and you forgot to turn your lights on. But you can see because everyone else's lights are on, and they're going the same way. But what would happen if everyone else left the picture? [You'd be] lost too, because your lights aren't on. You've got to have that fire and that light inside of you from the Lord. It's got to be *genuine* and *yours*.

Do you have your spiritual headlights on? Or are you depending on others—maybe even your spouse—to show the way?

Dr. Juli Slattery put it this way in an interview with Focus on the Family:

> I think growing together starts with growing individually, because as God has a relationship with husband and wife together, He also has an intimate relationship with each of us. A couple that isn't individually spending time with God and praying to Him and striving to grow on their own is going to have a lot of difficulty coming together as one and growing. . . .
>
> Now, once both the husband and wife have a personal relationship with God that is growing and thriving, it's a wonderful thing to begin doing things together as a couple that enhance and express that.

And what if your personal relationship with God *isn't* growing and thriving? Talk about it honestly with each other and with your pastor or another mature believer you trust. You can work on this together, even before the wedding. You'll probably find it a lot more fulfilling than picking out invitations and registering for casserole dishes on the Internet!

Intimacy Builder No. 3: Be Patient with Differences in Spiritual Maturity

"Accept one another" (Romans 15:7) is a simple three-word phrase that's the best possible prescription for holding a marriage together. Acceptance is the strongest glue for relationships. No earthquake or tornado can compare to its power.

Debbie-Jo had a rocky childhood from contending with generations of family dysfunction. At first her emotional wounds didn't fit into my pious formula for "the perfect wife." Yet we have a blast together these days because I've learned to accept her just as she is and thank God for giving me far more than I deserve!

One or both of you might feel inadequate at first when it comes to blending your spiritual lives. You might feel as though you haven't reached the same "level"—maybe one of you is a new Christian. Just start where you are and remember to give each other grace along the way.

Intimacy Builder No. 4: Value Your Relationship More than Winning

Jason and Tyra are newlyweds. Jason *knows* that God doesn't want worshipers to raise their hands in the air or play electric guitars on the sanctuary platform. Tyra *knows* the exact opposite. Tyra also *knows* that God doesn't want husbands to play video games with the words *evil* or *theft* in the title. Jason *knows* that's nonsense.

The result of all this *knowing* is a lot of sharp words and cold stares.

There's nothing like arguing to prove how spiritual you are. It's kind of like hiring the Goodyear Blimp to pull a banner across the sky that says, LOOK HOW HUMBLE I AM! Yet many couples can't resist the urge to set each other straight, even if it means their relationship takes a kidney punch.

Dr. Paul Reisser and Teri Reisser, a very smart couple (he's a pediatrician; she's a counselor) came up with this advice:

Here's a hot tip: Most couples get into trouble when they're discussing issues because they're more committed to winning than to actually understanding the other person's point of view, let alone giving it credence. Thus it is vitally important that you and your spouse feel heard, understood, and respected when there is a difference of opinion regarding spiritual values. Not only does this prevent discord and anger—which is what Scripture would ask of us, by the way—but from a practical standpoint you're more likely to succeed at wooing, rather than arguing, the other person to your viewpoint.[2]

Your spouse isn't the enemy. And you're not the spirituality police. The same goes for husbands who aim to "convict" their wives. Want to get closer? Don't push your spouse away, hoping to score one more point.

Intimacy Builder No. 5: Pray Together

It amazes me how many married couples never pray together outside of saying grace at meals. Nothing builds spiritual intimacy like praying together. It doesn't have to be hard or embarrassing; you're talking to a loving heavenly Father who wants to be a close friend. So at least once a day, make time to pray together.

One of my favorite things is sitting next to Debbie-Jo at night and reading the Bible with her. Then I hold her hand and ask how I can pray for her needs. The intimacy and bonding it brings to our relationship is indescribable.

Such a simple question! "Honey, how can I pray for you?" Once, during one of the craziest weeks of my life, I asked her this, and she said with a playful smile, "Pray for yourself! You're nuts!" (She was probably right!)

Good times, bad times, busy times, and peaceful times—taking each other's needs seriously and praying about them together is a key to open hearts and richness in a relationship.

You may find time to do this first thing in the morning, in the evening after dinner, or at bedtime—whatever works for you as a couple. But carve out time to pray together. If you make this a habit early in your marriage, it can make all the difference in setting the tone for your relationship. By doing this, you're saying to each other, "Your spiritual growth is important to me. Our spiritual growth as a couple is a priority."

During this prayer time, besides praying for each other, praise God and give thanks. Make requests. When issues arise or decisions need to be made, pray together to find resolution. Avoid using prayer to preach at each other—a sure way to chill spiritual intimacy.

Like two of the spouses mentioned at the beginning of this chapter, many husbands and wives feel awkward about praying together. To some it feels artificial or phony or forced—or just embarrassing. My friends (and in-laws) Gary and Barb Rosberg know all about that. Their experience shows how praying together can go from scary territory to a safe haven. Here's how Gary tells it (as told to Focus on the Family):

Barb and I first met on a blind date. She had just come to Christ and invited me to a Bible study. I had just become a Christian and had never been to a Bible study. . . . This girl starts praying, and then a guy starts praying, and then another guy starts praying. . . . We were all in a circle, and we were supposed to close our eyes and pray. But I remember my eyes were as big as saucers, and I was thinking, *I am not going to pray.* . . . I remember thinking, *What is the deal with this? How do you do this?*

[Afterward] we sat for two hours in the parking lot behind the frat house. . . . I thought there should be a minister in there or somebody to lead this thing. And I said, "How do you pray?"

Barb looked at me and said, "Gary, just talk to God. Just talk." So I took her hand and I bowed my head and I just said, "Dear Lord, I want to know you like Barb knows you." I remember she looked up, and she had this little tear coming down her cheek, and she leaned over and kissed me. I remember *pray and kiss, pray and kiss.* . . .

I began going to spiritual intimacy seminars. . . . I think what became clear to us at that time was that if a relationship was going to have any kind of legs to it, if [we] were going to sustain a relationship, it would have to be a relationship of three—with [both] husband and wife . . . submitting to Christ and allowing Christ to be in the midst of that. . . .

Praying together allows us to grow spiritually together. . . . We have learned to do conversational prayer. So we will hold each other's hand, and I will kind of pray a sentence, and she will pray a sentence and [then] I'll pray a sentence.

Barb adds one more reason to pray together:

> You know how hard it is to be mad at your mate and have to
> pray together? [The Bible] says that if you are praying to the
> Lord and you are angry with someone, leave your sacrifice to
> the Lord and make it right with that other person. This is so
> true in marriage. . . . We are connecting to Jesus Christ so that
> we can walk in oneness . . . because God loves it when we live
> together in harmony.

Intimacy Builder No. 6: Read the Bible and Devotional Books Together

One of the best ways to grow closer spiritually is to read God's Word together. Maybe this doesn't sound terribly original. But that's because it's so true.

What you read is up to you. Chances are the two of you won't be drawn to the same Scripture at the same time. Some couples take turns picking which books of the Bible to read. I tend to choose easy reads, like Luke. Debbie-Jo likes to dig deep into God's Word and His plans, so she picks books like Ezekiel! I usually let her decide what we read together and honor her by reading aloud to her in the evening.

Author Tricia Goyer and her husband, John, take a more laid-back approach:

> About seven years ago John and I started reading the Bible
> together before he leaves for work. We're reading through the
> Bible, but we don't try to stick to a plan. We tried that and it
> just stressed us out!
>
> Instead, we keep a bookmark in the Bible and pick up where
> we left off last time. We each take a turn reading a chapter out
> loud if we have time. If not, we split a chapter and each read half.
> We don't stress if we can't get it in, but we enjoy it when we do. It
> also gives us great topics of conversation throughout the day.[3]

As you read, don't get hung up on which spouse is more intellectual or "deeper." This isn't a competition. It's a time to learn and grow closer to God together, sharing questions and insights as you talk about what you've read.

For variety, try reading a couple's devotional together. For a change of pace, read the day's passage separately and then come together to talk it over. Choose a devotional book that sparks interest in both of you. One possibility is *The Best Year of Your Marriage* by Jim and Jean Daly and the counselors at Focus on the Family. It even has a year's worth of relationship-building activities you can do together. Some couples I know get daily devotionals on their smartphones or via e-mail. Over dinner they ask each other what they thought about the reading and how they might apply the ideas.

As Debbie-Jo and I read the Bible and Bible-based books together, we often receive guidance and answers we've been needing. Proverbs 16:9 says, "In his heart a man plans his course, but the LORD determines his steps." One way He does that is by getting us on the same page—literally.

Intimacy Builder No. 7: Learn from Church, Small Groups, and Mentors

Will just showing up at church boost your spiritual intimacy? Nope. Merely watching the Olympics won't get you a gold medal either. But one of the most practical ways to grow together spiritually is to be truly connected to a life-giving church.

Find one where you both feel comfortable; this might mean visiting several and asking for recommendations from people you know. Don't expect perfection, but find a place where you feel challenged and inspired. And make friends! Building relationships with other Christians can help yours, too.

Consider joining a small group or Sunday school class. These can provide creative ways to study the Bible together and learn how it applies to married life, helping you stay accountable in your walk with God.

Some of your best spiritual conversations may take place in your car on the way home from a small-group meeting.

That's what Lana and Ian discovered. Because of a job opportunity, they relocated to a new state not long after marrying. Finding themselves without friends or family nearby, both were eager to find people to "do life with." After visiting several churches in their new town, they settled on one they both liked and joined a small group for young married couples.

Now Lana says, "That group of couples became our second family. We prayed for each other and studied Scripture together, but we also just spent time together—like conversations over dinner and activities on the weekends. They brought meals when our first baby was born. Even now, we consider those people to be our lifelong friends. I had no idea how much having a Christian community of friends would mean to both me and Ian. That was a season of spiritual growth for us."

Once you've found a community of believers, consider taking things to the next level—by connecting with a mentor couple. If you're not sure what mentors are, think Obi-Wan Kenobi and Luke Skywalker—or Charles Xavier and the X-Men. They teach, especially by example.

Learning from other believers—whether through a congregation, class, or mentor—takes a little humility. But when it comes to building spiritual intimacy, it's hard to beat.

Intimacy Builder No. 8: Serve Together

Service doesn't just benefit those you're serving. It can do wonders for your spiritual intimacy, too. Has your own Christian life been less than exciting? You can start today to change things for the better.

One newlywed couple I know was struggling to connect. Spiritual growth was important to these two, but they seemed to be on different tracks. They needed to figure out how to live out their journey together.

Karen had a heart for others, and Mike had the gift of service; he loved to help people in hands-on ways. They discovered that doing acts of service as a couple was a great way to grow together spiritually. At Christmastime they visited nursing homes and ministered to the elderly. During the summer they volunteered at the local rescue mission and served side by side in the soup kitchen. They connected with a community children's home to provide supplies that some of the kids needed—and in the process connected with each other.

What will work best for you? Engage in some fun brainstorming. You might even come up with something really original—as my friends Will and Cindy did. Every year in December, they save all their Christmas cards and put them in a basket. They keep the basket on a shelf next to the dining-room table. Each night at dinner, they select a card and pray for the person or people who sent it.

"Dear God, help Johnny in his dental practice in Oregon."

"Lord, comfort Ted and Ginger as they make their move from Boise."

It didn't take long for word to get out concerning Will and Cindy's basket. Now people send them cards throughout the year just so they can be on the prayer list!

Intimacy Builder No. 9: Review Each Day for Signs of God's Blessing

Counting your blessings may not be a new idea, but it's a classic. Blessings give us a chance to thank God and cheer each other on. They can be an opportunity to make spiritual strides as we celebrate God's love and power.

It's harder, though, when blessings are in disguise. The fine art of seeing Romans 8:28—the truth that God ultimately works everything together "for the good of those who love him"—is a huge challenge in some situations. Every couple will go through pain and brokenness, especially in today's tragic world. Every spouse needs to know that all those things *do* work together for good when God gets His hands on them.

How can you turn your traumas into opportunities for spiritual growth? I've found it helpful to use a word picture with my family, that of stained-glass windows. None of God's "paintings" are on canvas.

They're all made of thousands of broken pieces, skillfully picked up and dusted off and soldered together into magnificent murals. The broken pieces are made of our hurts and hard times. With my family I've used examples of my own hurts, and theirs, to show how God is slowly making stained-glass windows of our lives.

Using this word picture with your mate may not be easy. It can take lots of asking "What's wrong?" and "How do you feel?" and "What are you doing about it?" questions, not to mention hours of warmth and empathy and unconditional love.

When your hearts break—when the job or the pregnancy or the friendship is lost—you can use the word picture carefully. You can sit down with your mate and say, "God makes stained-glass windows. Let's look at ours."

At night before you go to sleep, start thinking of how God blessed you throughout the day. Once you're married, share a blessing or two with your spouse at bedtime. Doing this helps you both maintain a positive perspective and also gives you an opportunity to share unique details about your day.

Intimacy Builder No. 10: Be Biblical (and Humble) About Spiritual Leadership

When I asked my son Brady if he knew how he felt about spiritual intimacy in marriage, he said, "Yes." Then he hesitated. Finally he went on to say that he knew how important it is in marriage, but he also realized that "no one is more intimidating to lead spiritually than your wife."

I agree wholeheartedly! Debbie-Jo is one of the most amazing and brilliant women I know. She's smarter than I am and spiritually deeper as well. The idea of leading her is definitely intimidating! Where do I even start?

Scary as the concept may be, God says that the man is to lead his wife (1 Corinthians 11:3). Still, it takes time, patience, and humility to work out exactly what that means in your marriage. Taking a wrong turn in this area can actually *undo* spiritual intimacy.

Take James and Jennifer, for instance. They'd been married for only a few months, but Jennifer was beginning to feel frustrated. It seemed to her that since the wedding, James rarely asked her opinion anymore on matters of faith. Often when she shared her feelings, hurts, or fears with him, he tended to dismiss her feelings and simply quoted Bible verses to her.

While James did have an impressive knowledge of the Bible, his inability to be open, transparent, and loving in this area hindered his effectiveness as a spiritual leader. Rather than sharing spiritual closeness with her husband, Jennifer ended up wanting to pull away.

How can you avoid that trap? You might try the approach Dr. Juli Slattery took (as shared with Focus on the Family):

When my husband and I first got married, I sat back and wondered how it was going to feel to really trust his leadership. In some ways I was the more natural leader. . . . So I struggled with, *How can I respect his leadership?* . . .

I had a wise counselor who sat down with me one day and said, "Juli, you approach things like, 'ABCD all the way to Z.' Your husband approaches things like, 'Start with a little bit of D and do a little bit of M and a little bit of O and P,' and it drives you crazy. But you have to remember he is always going to get to Z too; you are going to end up at the same place. You just need to learn to trust."

I also learned that there are areas of leadership, strength, and maturity that Mike had that I was not recognizing. He is a man of great faith, just really trusting God where I felt like, *I need to get it done right now on my own and trust my own strength.* . . .

No matter whom you are married to, there are character qualities, even if you think you are stronger, that you can get behind and begin to encourage your husband to lead physically, spiritually, and emotionally in ways that you never thought of before.

Plan ahead to deal with this issue respectfully, lovingly, and humbly. Let God's design draw you nearer to each other, not further apart.

The Most Lasting Bond of All

How will building spiritual intimacy make a difference in your marriage? Prioritizing your faith will only make your marriage stronger. When times get rough (and they will), you'll have a solid foundation of faith to help you weather the storm together. When it's hard to keep your commitment to one another, or when you're not feeling that "loving feeling," your mutual commitment to Christ can remind you why you signed on for the long haul—and why it's worth it to stay.

JOE WHITE is president of Kanakuk Kamps and founder of Kids Across America. He is also the author of more than twenty books and speaks across the country for Men at the Cross/Wildfire Weekend, After Dark, Pure Excitement, NFL chapels, and *Focus on the Family* radio. Dr. James Dobson says, "Joe White knows more about teenagers than anyone in North America." Joe and his wife, Debbie-Jo, are the parents of four grown children and the grandparents of eleven. The Whites reside in Branson, Missouri.

Ready to Talk

1. How would you define spiritual intimacy? Which of the following fit your perspective best?

    • Being soul mates

    • A vague term that must legally be included in every Christian book about marriage

    • Something that only missionaries and pastors experience, not the average Christian couple

    • Agreeing to the same doctrine and theology

    • Holding hands and praying regularly

• The closeness of sharing a desire to please God

• Other _____

How do you think your childhood, friends, family, and church, along with TV, social media, and the culture, have influenced the way you view this subject?

2. A shared spiritual relationship is a journey that you are starting now as an engaged couple. Which of the Intimacy Builders within the chapter would be most helpful as you seek to take your spiritual relationship to the next level?

3. How would you rank the following in order of importance? If the two of you rank the items differently, try to explain your choices. Then take each person's number one suggestion and talk about how you'll work on it during the first six months after the wedding.

• Praying together

• Reading the Bible together

• Learning to make decisions together prayerfully

• Attending church and a small group together

• Reviewing each day for signs of blessing

• Serving together

Ready to Try

Do you attend church together? If not, visit one this week. If you already go to church together, attend according to your usual schedule. In either case, stop by a coffee shop or café after services and talk about your preferences in a church home. Do you like the church you attend? If not, what do you look for in a church community? If you could wave a magic wand to create your most perfect church, what would it look like? Talk about your experiences with church attendance. Did you go to church with your family as a child? Was faith an important part of your home life? If not, what role do you hope faith will play in your marriage? How do you feel about devotional reading? Praying together? Mentorship? Service opportunities? Choose at least two of the ideas from this chapter that you'd like to carry out in married life.

CHAPTER 6

ONE FLESH: SEXUAL INTIMACY IN MARRIAGE

Juli Slattery, PhD

ON YOUR WEDDING DAY, you'll receive lots of gifts, but none of them will come close to the beauty of the gift of sex. Sexual intimacy in marriage is a gift that keeps on giving. It can create vulnerability between husband and wife that makes every other relationship pale in comparison. The hormones released through regular sexual activity do everything from making you feel in love to lowering your blood pressure and helping you sleep better. Sex is also mysteriously spiritual, as the apostle Paul explained in Ephesians 5:31–32, painting a picture of God's infinite love for you. Not to mention that sex is a lot of fun and feels great! The problem is that the gift of sex usually isn't immediately appreciated but may take years to fully unwrap.

If you want a good laugh, get a conversation started about honeymoon horror stories. Almost every married person you meet will have one. I've heard tales of vomiting and sunburn for an entire week in

Mexico, flat tires, a flooded hotel room, missed airplanes, and mistaking toothpaste for K-Y Jelly (ouch!). Perhaps the worst was when friends of the groom decided to play a prank and hid under the bridal chamber bed all night. *Not* funny. I think I would have been scarred for life!

Mike and I could add to the tales of newlywed woes. Our wedding night started out with a bellman who wouldn't leave our hotel room. He spent fifteen minutes showing Mike how to work the TV (like he would be watching TV!). Then the bellman couldn't find the champagne that was part of the honeymoon package and came knocking on our door to present it to us about forty minutes later. Superb timing!

We then drove to a cabin in Tennessee with hardwood floors and no bed. Mike bought an air mattress that ended up having a not-so-slow leak. There were some other more personal challenges on the honeymoon that could have devastated us early on. I wish I could tell you that things got drastically better right after the honeymoon, but they didn't. Along with some good times, our first few years of marriage were filled with challenges in the bedroom.

Before we talk more about challenges, let me encourage you: Things got better. A *lot* better! Sex is meant to be a beautiful part of your marriage. It truly is a gift. There may be challenges at first (as I can attest to!), but hang in there. Intimacy in marriage can be all you hope it will be. Throughout this chapter, we'll talk a little about common problems and what it takes to have the love life you want.

Looking Ahead

As you look forward to your honeymoon and beyond, are you excited or filled with trepidation? You may be wondering, *Is sex a great blessing, or will it be a huge disappointment?* Honestly, it may initially be both. Intimacy in marriage can be all you hope it will be, but it may not be so immediately.

A honeymoon is like opening a brand-new set of Legos. When a child gets Legos, he certainly doesn't expect to find the finished model in the box. The whole point of Legos is to build. The picture on the box is simply to reflect what the pieces are designed to eventually create. The same is true of sex. When you get married, you open the set of Legos. From that moment on, it's going to take time, patience, and dedication to become expert builders. Along the way, you'll run into roadblocks in the building process.

The most normal thing about sexual intimacy is to encounter challenges along the way. Here are some common ones:

- Trouble with arousal or climax
- One of you wanting sex more often than the other
- Feelings of rejection when your spouse turns you down
- Unfulfilling sex because of porn, masturbation, or fantasy
- Inability to have intercourse because of physical pain
- Guilt because of past sexual partners
- Feelings of inadequacy as a lover
- Severe body-image issues
- Medical barriers
- Flashbacks from sexual trauma
- Secrets that you know you could never confess to your new spouse

Here's the good news: *Every sexual challenge can be a pathway to deeper intimacy and, ultimately, greater sex.* Nineteen years into marriage, I'm actually thankful for the intimacy struggles Mike and I have been through. Why? Because through them, we learned how to love each other.

What If You've Already Opened the Box of Legos?

Realistically, many Christian couples have had sex together before their honeymoon. If you fall into this category, you probably have an additional layer of confusion about sex. On the one hand, you are supposed to be excited about having sex within a marriage covenant that God blesses. On the other hand, you may be experiencing other emotions, such as guilt, knowing that God created the gift of sexual intimacy for you to enjoy after you make a public covenant.

I want to take a moment and speak to you as your sister in Christ. I want you to hear my heart and know that I have your very best interest in mind. I'm not trying to judge you, shame you, or criticize you. Instead, I'd like to speak truth into you and your relationship. If you and your fiancé(e) are having sex before marriage, you should consider some important truths. First, the fact that you're getting married soon doesn't mean that God overlooks the fact that you are currently choosing to violate His expressed will for you. Many Scripture verses, including 1 Corinthians 6:18–20, tell us to stay away from sexually immoral choices.

Second, God takes sin seriously, and He wants us to as well. The plain fact is that He doesn't excuse an unmarried couple sleeping together because "everyone is doing it" or just because they love each other.

Unconfessed sin is a heavy burden that can dampen the enthusiasm of your sexual relationship in marriage. God says to confess your sin honestly, and He will forgive and cleanse you (see 1 John 1:9). If you and your future spouse have been sexually intimate, ask God together to forgive and cleanse you. Be encouraged that God will freely forgive you, and He wants your marriage to thrive! He wants you to live with integrity when it comes to your sexuality.

You might say, "What's the use of not living together or sleeping together now? We're getting married in a few months!" I think it makes a big difference to God. You're choosing to yield this important part of your lives to Him. Yes, it will cost you something, but God will honor that choice. What does this look like? You might need to limit the time you spend alone with each other. Respect each other enough to find ways to avoid having sex until marriage.

If you're already living together, I strongly recommend you both come up with a plan for how you can live separately until the wedding. Could one of you stay with your parents or a roommate? While this may seem inconvenient, I promise it's the right thing to do, and it's worth it. Decide together to start your marriage off by honoring God with your sexuality. Set the foundation for your future family by choosing to follow God's biblical plan for your marriage. Commit to abstaining from sex until your wedding night. Why does it matter? Because you want to begin your marriage journey by honoring the Lord and asking for His unrestrained blessing. I can assure you that I've never met a couple who regretted making these adjustments to honor God. Although it may be inconvenient, it's worth it!

Love Isn't Proven to Be Love Until It's Difficult to Give

Any husband or wife can show love when love comes easily. Any spouse can be a responsive lover when all his or her needs are being met. Jesus said that even pagans know how to love when someone is being nice to them (see Matthew 5:43–48). This kind of love is really self-love. It is based on your appreciation for how your future spouse treats you. God wants you to learn how to make a different kind of love, and He may just use sex to teach you this important lesson.

The form of love God calls you to learn has very little to do with how you feel or how you are being treated. It's a love that is absolutely committed to the well-being of the other person—no matter what. You won't know if you have this kind of love for your future spouse until love becomes difficult to give. When you run into disagreements in the bedroom (and believe me, you will!), will you resort to selfishness, or will you strive to understand and meet the needs of your spouse?

I recently talked with one young wife who was frustrated that she is always the one who initiates sex. Often when she does, her husband says, "Not tonight." She's riddled with questions about how she looks and her inability to please her husband. Finally her husband admitted that he prefers to masturbate because "it's just easier than having sex." Although his statement sounds harsh, it's a common conclusion for men and women to reach but never speak out loud. Who wants to risk the possibility of rejection or the humiliation of failing as a lover? And why invest all of the work and effort of pleasing another person when you can quickly and effortlessly please yourself?

What will your love look like when you've been rejected? Shamed? Misunderstood? Ignored? The challenges of sexual intimacy are certain to bring out all of these experiences at one point or another. You may be able to negotiate the budget, the thermostat, work schedules, and whose family to go to for Christmas, but sexual conflict cuts right to the core. For example, if one of you is still using porn or flirting with a coworker, or if either of you had many sexual partners in the past, you'll need to talk through these discoveries. These will be tremendous tests of your love and will reveal places in your hearts you never knew existed.

Each of these challenges will either destroy or build a foundation of love, largely depending upon how you respond to them. The couples I know who are most in love have been married for many, many years. They've weathered storms that required true forgiveness, humility, patience, and honesty. Together they've walked through things like infertility, cancer, grief, sexual-abuse recovery, and even infidelity. The very things that should have torn them apart ended up gluing them closer together.

I remember the lowest point of our honeymoon. Sex was creating tension and conflict between us. I was in tears, and my husband was frustrated. His anger flared briefly. I felt ashamed and humiliated. I wanted to be anywhere but in an isolated cabin all alone with *him*!

God, did I make a mistake by marrying Mike? I prayed. *I'm so lonely!*

I looked up from my tears to see my new husband sitting on the couch reading his Bible. After about twenty minutes of reading, he put his arm around me and said something like, "Juli, I love you so much. This is just the beginning of our lives together. We're going to work through this."

My despondency immediately turned to hope. The man I just wished I hadn't married was now my white knight.

How Mike and I responded to those early disappointments became the foundation of the love that we've continued to build upon. Sometimes he's the one selflessly accepting my limitations. Other times I'm the one graciously extending forgiveness or stretching out of my comfort zone to learn to love him sexually. The very things that threatened to sour our love ended up fortifying it.

Sex Is the Greatest Test of (and Laboratory for) True Love

Do you find it ironic that while sex is touted to be a dynamic force of unity between a couple, it can also be a source of conflict? If God designed sexual intimacy to bond a man and wife together, why do so many couples cite sexual issues as a main reason for splitting up? Why did God create men and women so differently? It almost seems as though we're set up for sexual incompatibility and conflict. Let me encourage you as you look forward to your wedding and beyond: I believe that God will use sexual differences to test and refine your love for your spouse.

Nothing will drastically reveal selfishness and fear like sexual challenges between you and your spouse. After a few months (or maybe a few days) of marriage, you'll realize that you don't always want sex when your spouse wants it. Your thoughts will probably go like this: *Why should I have to give him/her my body whenever demanded? I'm not some object with an on-off switch.*

If you're the one who initiated sex, only to be rejected, maybe you had thoughts like this: *Seriously? We are married! I thought part of getting married was never having to be rejected again. This is just humiliating!*

And if you can agree to have sex at the same time, that certainly doesn't guarantee marital bliss. You might find yourselves arguing over foreplay or talking too much or not enough. You might say things like "Why don't you kiss me anymore?" "I don't like to be touched there!" "Can't we do something different for once?" Or your spouse might mysteriously shut down in the middle of the act.

Every time a challenge like this presents itself, your love will be tested. You're not getting what you deserve. You're not being treated with respect. He doesn't understand how you feel. She has no clue how to meet your needs. You may begin to doubt that you're in love at all! After all, love could never be so disappointing and painful. Or could it?

How Will You Respond to the Challenges You Face?

You must determine now what kind of lover you will be. How will you respond to the inevitable disappointments and discouragements of sexual love? Will the challenges prove that you're quick to hold a grudge or eager to forgive? Defensive or humble? Selfish or sacrificial? Demanding or sensitive?

The conflicts and disappointments you'll encounter in marriage will have little to do with whether or not you married the wrong person. More likely they'll reveal whether you're willing for God to make you a great lover.

The best marital advice I can give you is to determine to *be a team* in sexual intimacy, no matter what. God has given you sex not just for pleasure and procreation but also to glue you together in profound ways. Sexual oneness isn't just about naked bodies touching; it eventually demands that your love is tested and shared with vulnerability and ultimate intimacy.

Here are four practical suggestions for nurturing sexual intimacy in your marriage. These qualities are true of every great team and all great lovers:

1. *Great teams communicate with each other.* Talking about sexual intimacy can be a challenge. To start with, what words do you use to describe sexual acts, desires, and the sexual parts of the body? The words you like might be offensive to your future husband or wife. Or maybe you just feel awkward talking about the whole topic.

Sexual conversations can quickly escalate into raw conflict. Why? Because sexuality is so core to who each of you is as a person. It's humiliating to admit to a porn struggle. It's embarrassing to ask your spouse for more sex and devastating to hear that you aren't meeting your husband or wife's sexual needs. Sexual conflict usually taps into issues of shame, control, body image, trust, masculinity, and femininity. A lot of couples choose not to venture into this emotional landmine, so they just avoid the topic.

It doesn't take a psychologist to figure out that you can't solve problems together if you don't communicate. You can't learn to please each other if the very topic is off limits. So how do you learn to talk about sex together? I have two tried-and-true suggestions for you:

- *Let someone else start the conversation.* When Mike and I encountered this roadblock, we used things like books, marriage seminars, and radio broadcasts to bring up the topics that we didn't know how to address. When authors like Cliff and Joyce Penner explained a common problem, I could just say, "I feel like they just described me." These outside resources gave us the permission and the words to start the conversation.

- *Make sexual conversations safe.* I can think of at least a handful of times when I hurt Mike with insensitive words on this topic. Sometimes it was a flippant remark; other times my cutting words came out of my own hurt. Be aware that your future spouse is probably very sensitive about sexual issues, just like you are. Ask questions and listen. His or her perspective will be very different from yours, so don't assume anything. If you have a "complaint" about your sexual relationship after you marry, share it with grace, remembering that you are both just learning how to love each other.

2. *Great teams have solid coaching.* If talking about sex with your future spouse is difficult, admitting a sexually related problem to a doctor, therapist, or pastor may feel even harder. Yet that's exactly what might be required to get through challenges like a sexual addiction, physical problems, infertility, or healing from sexual abuse.

I've seen couples stop having sex at all because the husband or wife was too embarrassed to get help. A great sexual relationship will require you to fight through barriers. At times this will mean admitting that you'll need help. Getting married, establishing a sexual relationship with your spouse, and even having children can trigger wounds and memories of sexual trauma for both men and women. It will be very difficult to move forward in intimacy in marriage without addressing past trauma.

As a psychologist, I've had the privilege of working with many marriages through difficulties related to intimacy. I have the greatest respect for a young man or woman who is willing to ask for help and engage in the healing process. If you have sexual trauma in your past or think you have a sexual addiction, please don't try to convince yourself that your wounds will go away. The great news is that God is the healer, even of sexual pain. His truth can set you free from lies, His peace can calm your anxiety, His forgiveness can cleanse the darkest sin, and His love can be a healing balm over violation and betrayal.

How do you know whom to ask for help? It might sound cliché, but the best place to start is to ask the Lord for wisdom and healing. Very few Christian couples ever pray together about their sexual relationship. Has it ever dawned on you that God cares about your sexual intimacy? He does. He created it and He blesses it. He is also able to provide the wisdom and direction you need through His Word, His Spirit, and the advice of wise counselors and experts.

Remember that sexual topics are often morally laden. Some "sex experts" offer immoral and destructive advice. When I was in my doctoral program, I took classes on human sexuality that encouraged married couples to do everything from visiting strip clubs together to divorcing if they were "sexually incompatible." Be sure that any books you read or advice you take comes from someone who recognizes God as the creator of sex and the ultimate source for how it should work.

3. *Great teams never confuse a teammate for the opponent.* Sexual temptation is nothing new. Just read Proverbs, which was written thousands of years ago, and you'll see that even then, young men were strongly warned to avoid the deception of an alluring harlot. Though elicit sex could always be found thousands of years ago, now it is *actively pursuing* us—whether we're male or female, married or single.

Almost every young man and many young women will enter marriage with some history of exposure to pornography or erotica (often the female version of porn). Because of its widespread use, visual and written porn are often just accepted as facts of modern-day life. But just because something is accepted as normal doesn't mean it isn't also dangerous.

One of Satan's most successful strategies is to turn husbands and wives against one another. He constantly attempts to destroy, demolish, and distort married sex. Not only will he use sexual temptation to water down your sexual intimacy, he will try to use the battle to divide you. Battling sexual temptation is difficult enough, but it becomes impossible when you are fighting each other instead of clearly identifying the true enemy.

If either of you struggles with sexual temptation, you must begin to see this as your problem *as a couple.* I don't mean that you should take responsibility for your fiancé(e)'s purity. However, when sexual sin and temptation hits one of you, it impacts both of you. Satan will use pornography, inappropriate emotional attachments, and other forms of temptation to further divide you if he can define your spouse-to-be as "the problem" or "the enemy." As long as you are fighting each other, you cannot stand together.

Standing together starts with humility and empathy. As Jesus taught, we cannot lovingly confront another person's sin until we've brought our own failings before God and sought His grace. You might not know what it's like to struggle with sexual temptation, but you do know what it's like to have a "besetting sin." Maybe yours is gossip, dishonesty, bitterness, pride, or coveting. Once you're married, if you encounter sexual sin in your marriage, confront your spouse with the humility and awareness of your own weaknesses rather than feeding shame with a self-righteous spirit of judgment.

Empathy doesn't mean that you ignore the problem, but that you strive together in God's strength to honor Him. The thing I love about this is it turns Satan's strategies against him. Instead of letting Satan divide you, you and your future spouse will become more united than ever as you fight together for your marriage. Indeed, God can "[work all things] together for the good of those who love God and are called according to his purpose" (Romans 8:28, NLT).

4. *Great teams play offense and defense.* If you're a sports fan, you know the importance of a great offense and defense. No team can win the Super Bowl, the World Series, an NBA championship, or the World Cup without both. The same will be true in your marriage. For your love life to flourish and go the distance, you'll have to work together to build offensive and defensive strategies.

A lot of the information you get from Christian sources emphasizes defense. Many sermons and books teach about the importance of purity in marriage, setting up hedges against affairs, and battling temptation. Building boundaries and safeguards to keep your marriage bed pure is extremely important. You'll need to talk about things like whether to keep old flames as Facebook friends and what boundaries to have with opposite-sex coworkers. What is currently an innocent connection now may become a source of temptation when things in your marriage get difficult. As hard as it may be to imagine today, you will face sexual temptation at some point in your marriage. Start preparing for it now.

Just as important as playing defense in your marriage, you'll need to work together to learn how to "score" (yes, the pun is intended)! As they say in sports, "The best defense is a great offense." This definitely applies to marital sexuality. A couple who has a mutually satisfying, exciting sex life is far less open to temptation than a couple who doesn't.

How do you plan for an exciting sex life in marriage? First by realizing that you have permission to do so. A lot of Christians have a hard time erasing all of the "thou shalt not" messages. Even though you might intellectually know it's okay to have sex once you're married, you may still feel restrained or guilty for being *too* sexual. Are Christians really supposed to get carried away with sexual pleasure in the marriage bed? The answer is yes! If you don't believe me, take a look at the Song of Songs. Both Solomon and his bride were very free with their bodies and their words and were absolutely taken with sexual pleasure. And God said this was good!

John Piper encourages married couples to offensively battle Satan by pleasing each other in bed:

A married couple gives a severe blow to the head of that ancient serpent when they aim to give as much sexual satisfaction to each other as possible. Is it not a mark of amazing grace that on top of all the pleasure that the sexual side of marriage brings, it also proves to be a fearsome weapon against our ancient foe?[1]

There is nothing spiritual about settling for a mediocre sex life. Yes, there will be seasons of marriage in which sex might be difficult or may not be a high priority. But God's desire for you is that you work toward experiencing the greatest sexual delight in one another. As you look forward to marriage, take some time to talk together about what steps you think God would have you take to lay the foundation for intimacy that will last a lifetime.

Building a great sex life over the years will take intentionality, time, and effort. But trust me, it's well worth the effort, and it's a whole lot more fun than just playing defense!

I'm so glad that the greatest sex isn't on your honeymoon (or before you're married), as some might have led you to believe. If you stay committed to "making love" after the honeymoon, your sexual journey will get sweeter and sweeter with time. Once you're married, don't neglect this important part of your marriage. With a little effort and patience, the depth of intimacy you can achieve will be indescribable.

DR. JULI SLATTERY is a widely known clinical psychologist, author, speaker, and broadcast media professional. She cofounded Authentic Intimacy, a women's media ministry focusing on intimacy in marriage and intimacy with Christ. Juli's books include *Passion Pursuit* (coauthored with Linda Dillow), *Pulling Back the Shades* (coauthored with Dannah Gresh), *Finding the Hero in Your Husband*, *No More Headaches*, *Beyond the Masquerade*, and *Guilt-Free Motherhood*. Juli and her husband, Mike, have been married for more than nineteen years.

Ready to Talk

1. On a scale of 1 to 10 (10 is the highest), how awkward does it feel to discuss sex at this point in your relationship? Why? What limits would you like to place on this discussion? What subjects from this chapter would you most like to talk about?

2. The author shared about her honeymoon and how things didn't necessarily go as planned. Take some time to talk about your expectations for your honeymoon and, specifically, the wedding night. After hearing what each of you are thinking and expecting, discuss what you could do to avoid misunderstandings, unrealistic expectations, and embarrassments—and how you'll deal with things if and when they don't go perfectly. We recommend seeking accountability or help from a mentor or counselor if you and your fiancé(e) are struggling with past sexual experiences, pornography, or current sexual activity. Or call Focus on the Family at 1-800-A-FAMILY for one free counseling session and a referral to a Christian counselor in your area.

3. After reading the chapter, which of the following statements do you most identify with?

   • "I want the wedding to get here faster."
   • "I feel guilty because we've already gone too far sexually."
   • "I'm afraid I'm going to make some really embarrassing mistakes."
   • "I feel better because the author was so honest about her own marriage."
   • Other _____

   This might be a good time to pray for each other, keeping your answers in mind.

Ready to Try

Remember what the first chapter of this book had to say about sex? Thriving couples "regard sex not as a chore or an obligation but as a delightful dance in which each spouse puts the other's needs and interests ahead of his or her own" (see Philippians 2:4). To help you start thinking and talking about the need to put each other's interests before your own (sexually and otherwise), try the following. Whether or not you're planning to dance at your reception, sign up together for dance lessons, or if you don't have an option like this, watch some instructional videos online. Have fun practicing your ideal "first dance." Talk about how much better the dance works if you pay attention to your partner's needs and responses. Consider pledging to take the same approach to your sexual relationship when you're married.

CHAPTER 7

COMMUNICATION:
THE LANGUAGE OF LOVE

Joshua Straub, PhD

MY LOVELY WIFE, CHRISTI, is Canadian. So was our wedding.

If you've ever been to a Canadian wedding, you understand the reception north of the border tends to be more elaborate than its American counterpart—often full of skits, family speeches, dancing, and games that keep everybody laughing and crying, frequently at the same time.

In the months prior to the wedding, Christi's mom put together a lifelong video of the two of us for our reception. As dinner ended, our attention turned to the video screen, where we saw footage of Christi at three years of age. It was an image I'll never forget—this innocent, precious little girl sitting in the bathtub with her mom by her side. Christi was splashing water and singing without a care in the world, "And so I thank the Lord for giving me the things I need, the sun and the rain and the apple seed. The Lord is good to me" (the "Johnny Appleseed" song; otherwise known as "The Lord Is Good to Me").

Only two weeks later, on the last night of our honeymoon in the romantic ambience of a dimly lit Mexican restaurant, we somehow found ourselves in the middle of the biggest argument of our relationship to date. As I sat across from Christi, defending my perspective, I noticed her eyes well up with tears. I knew at that moment our honeymoon was over.

Poor Communication Personified

As I tried my best to "fix" the situation and redeem the evening, I knew I was fighting a losing battle. Then, without warning and in the heat of the argument, I saw through Christi's tears that precious video of her singing in the bathtub as a little girl. My defenses suddenly diminished. That innocent little girl was now my wife, and it was my duty to fight for her, not with her.

Christi and I settled the issue that evening, albeit temporarily. We came to realize over the next few months that our problem wasn't conflict resolution but poor communication. Poor communication is when you hide your negative feelings from your future spouse or act out aggressively or defensively toward him or her.

The argument Christi and I had that evening was about my desire to continue leading a ministry she neither felt a part of nor felt was *ours* together. Never mind that Christi had already left *her* church family and community to get involved in *mine*. Now she was concerned (to say it nicely) that I wanted to continue leading a ministry (voluntarily) that would keep me away from her Friday nights and Sunday mornings. Her idea of doing ministry together looked different from mine. And I didn't see it. So I did what any young, oblivious husband would do. I continued leading that ministry.

I was partially blinded by my own expectations, something we all must check at the premarital door. Before Christi and I were married, my ideal spouse was somebody who enjoyed doing ministry *with me*. I was too self-centered to admit these subconscious thoughts and realize it would involve doing ministry *together*, to include Christi's passions as much as mine. Her heart was still back at her old church. Yet she sacrificed that to join me, despite believing that once we got married, I would step down and do something else that involved her, too.

The situation we encountered early in our marriage was eventually resolved, but not without a few months of unspoken expectations, hidden negative feelings, and defensive attitudes clouding our communication.

A Bittersweet Ending

No matter what the issue(s)—expectations about doing ministry together, relating to in-laws, raising children, or simply "administrating" the marriage—at some point, usually early in marriage, the honeymoon phase ends. Unfortunately, some marriages never recover after this blissful and naive love has been shattered.

In fact, John Gottman, one of the most renowned marital researchers over the past three decades, found that in 70 percent of "miserable marriages," something happened that forced the relationship to shift in one direction or the other. Whether an affair or a decision to divorce forced the relationship in one direction, or a transformation of heart and commitment to do whatever it took to save the marriage forced it in the opposite direction, either way, change happened.[1]

To me, the most disturbing finding was that 30 percent of miserable marriages continued as sad, depressed relationships, primarily because couples clung to their deep religious beliefs that the marriage covenant must remain intact.[2] I find it sad that people stay in sad marriages. Don't get me wrong; I believe in the sanctity of marriage. But I also believe in intentionally seeking to love, communicate, and dream with our spouses. If the latter isn't happening, it's time to make some changes.

Perhaps that's why Solomon said, "The tongue has the power of life and death" (Proverbs 18:21). A miserable marriage is one in which communication carries a condescending tone or doesn't happen at all.

The end of the honeymoon phase in a marriage is a very critical moment that can actually lead a couple toward deeper love and understanding. It's an opportunity to move beyond the superficial naïveté of believing that God most assuredly designed you to be together because you both love spaghetti. Though your love for spaghetti may be what brought you together, it won't keep you together.

Experiencing marriage as an everyday honeymoon isn't an event; it's a way of life. And it begins by speaking life into the life of your future spouse using proactive communication.

What Is Proactive Communication?

Simply put, proactive communication is when you intentionally seek *to know your future spouse and to be known*. First, it involves remaining intentional, each day, about understanding the underlying motivations of your fiancé(e) (knowing) as he or she communicates with you. Second, it means communicating in a manner that seeks to honor your fiancé(e)'s heart as you reveal your own desires (being known). This builds deeper trust in the relationship.

To experience an everyday honeymoon in marriage requires emotional safety on the part of both spouses. If you aren't safe with each other, you won't be able to communicate the deepest parts of who you are so that you can be known. Likewise, you won't feel safe enough to have the confidence or wherewithal to know the heart of your spouse. The purpose of proactive communication—to know your future spouse and be known—requires safety.

When Christi and I went on our honeymoon, we packed our suitcases full of items intended to build our relationship. We included books on marriage. We packed clothes and accessories to go kayaking in the ocean, play tennis, go snorkeling, and do yoga. We packed for activities we loved doing together. Just like most couples in the honeymoon phase, we were proactive about connecting at a deeper level.

But for many couples, when the honeymoon phase ends, and expectations about the relationship haven't been met, all too often they begin packing another suitcase.

Before we delve deeper into how proactive communication works, let's first explore why and how communication changes in a marriage.

When the Honeymoon Ends

Couples stop communicating from the heart for a number of reasons. Yet one key factor is at the root of them all: intimacy. Psychologist David Burns defines *intimacy* as "the willingness to endure the negative feelings you get when you get close to another individual."[3]

We aren't willing to endure much angst in our culture today. The production of Tylenol and other over-the-counter painkillers is a thriving industry for one reason: Pain hurts. So do negative feelings. When my wife, Christi, says or does something that offends or hurts me, the hardest task is to talk about it.

As you prepare for marriage, it's important to understand why communication breaks down and what you can do about it when it does. Following are the top five reasons for communication breakdowns in most marriages.

Reason No. 1: Gender Differences

The communication differences between men and women make it challenging from the very beginning. Perhaps you've seen the video clip titled *It's Not About the Nail.*[4] The guy in the video tries to fix the issue (a literal nail stuck in the woman's forehead); she just wants him to listen while she talks about the literal nail stuck in her forehead.

When it comes to communicating, consider the following gender differences:[5]

Men:

• The goal of talking is purposeful action.

• He might see little need to speak unless there's a specific purpose:

> *A point to make*
> *A problem to solve*
> *A decision to make*

- He tends to focus on facts and seeks immediate resolutions (i.e., communication is used to get to the root of the dilemma as efficiently as possible).
- Action (or implementing a solution) is often the conversational goal.
- He doesn't always like to make eye contact when talking (e.g., he may prefer walking side by side to talk).
- He speaks, on average, around 12,500 words a day.

Women:
- The goal of talking is intimacy and connection.
- She sees conversation as an act of sharing, a way of releasing negative feelings, and an opportunity to increase intimacy with her husband.
- She communicates to "discover" how she is feeling and what she wants to say.
- She desires more extensive discussion about problems, sharing feelings and finding common experiences.
- She loves to look deeply into her man's eyes when talking.
- She speaks, on average, around 25,000 words a day.

Reason No. 2: Busyness

I know this may sound crazy at this stage in your relationship, but busyness happens in marriage. In fact, some studies show that the average couple spends less than four minutes in meaningful conversation per day.[6] Consider that many young couples get married when both are finishing college or graduate degrees and are also working full-time jobs. This pattern of busyness and staying afloat sets the precedent for the marriage. Conversations are filled with such phrases as "Well, once we have kids, it will slow down," or "Once I finish school, we can have more time together."

But this type of thinking is naive. The patterns you set today will determine the trajectory of your relationship. If you're not intentional now, busyness will be a great excuse to avoid talking about negative feelings (i.e., intimacy).

Reason No. 3: Business Meetings

A far more sinister reason for communication breakdown is that married couples can "administrate" their relationships almost to death. They can often get caught in a destructive pattern in which they spend their limited couple time talking about work, the budget, kids, chores, household responsibilities, schedules, to-do lists, and so on. Thus, conversations become very "transactional"—like doing business with each other. Certainly couples need to talk about managing the household, but they cannot allow "business meetings" to dominate their conversations.

The problem is that over time, couples become conditioned to avoid engaging in conversation with each other, since it's not very fun or safe. Business meetings can often lead to arguments and negative feelings, and over time, couples become conditioned to believe that talking will inevitably lead to conflict and disconnection. Thus, they stop talking. Or worse, they get so self-focused and caught up in their own expectations that they begin to make negative comparisons.

My inability to hear Christi's passion for ministry caused arguments during the first few months of our marriage. I started comparing myself to my friends, and I compared Christi negatively to my friends' wives. When I saw how these wives loved doing ministry with their husbands, I wondered, *Why doesn't my wife love to do ministry with me?*

Negative comparisons can range from seemingly harmless statements like "I wish my husband . . ." or "I wish my wife would have this or do this more" all the way to wishing a spouse was someone completely different. A lack of proactive communication can set us up for negative comparisons and a lack of intimacy.

Reason No. 4: External Stressors

Earlier in the book we read that "a man shall leave his father and his mother and hold fast to his wife" (Genesis 2:24, ESV). Sons in ancient Israel didn't move away; they stayed close to home and inherited their fathers' land. However, they "left" in the sense of putting their wives' welfare before that of their parents. The kinship between a husband and wife creates obligations that override the duty to one's parents.

In fact, when Jesus discussed marriage and divorce in Matthew 19, He used this passage in Genesis to emphasize that a husband and wife's primary human priority is to each other. Why? Because it reflects their relationship to Jesus Himself.

Yet for many marriages, including my own, in-laws are often the cause of the biggest communication breakdowns. Take, for instance, a couple I recently counseled, whose wedding I officiated. He just graduated college and accepted a job four hours from her family. Needless to say, her parents, in a very subtle yet manipulative way, made sure to let him know of their displeasure for taking their little girl away from them. Those parents also nearly caused the wedding not to take place when they put doubts in their daughter's mind about whether her fiancé was even the "right one."

Add work pressures and school demands, in addition to kids later on, and the external stressors in a marriage can lead to exhaustion and a lack of desire to even want to connect.

Reason No. 5: Internal Stressors

My wife, Christi, gives a talk titled "Tomorrow Never Comes." In it she describes the idea that all we have is today. When we think, *I'll deal with this tomorrow*, we lie to ourselves and establish a pattern of pushing off what needs to be done on the only day we have—today.

Over time, disagreements and conflicts can add up in a relationship. Secret grudges and unmet expectations can cause couples to treat each other in unfair ways. The negative energy each feels coming from the other can cause them to distance themselves as well. Things may continue for a while without either spouse giving voice to what's really going on in the relationship. But eventually they begin to stop being curious about the condition of each other's hearts or what's going on in one another's lives. Simply put, they disconnect by putting off conversation about issues until tomorrow. But tomorrow never comes.

Getting Naked: Creating Emotional Safety

There are two proactive aspects of a honeymoon that can help us understand how to communicate effectively throughout marriage. The first concept is getting naked.

Let's be honest, one of the most anticipated moments following the wedding is getting naked and consummating the marriage. However, what is often overlooked and yet is the glue that leads to great sexual intimacy is emotional nakedness, which is what I'm referring to in this chapter. Getting emotionally naked is one of the most freedom-giving and intimacy-building acts of marriage. But exposing our deepest feelings, dreams, and desires is also unbelievably vulnerable and can be quite scary.

Before we discuss the practical strategies for proactive communication, I want to restate the first part of the definition presented earlier: *Proactive communication* is when you intentionally seek to know your future spouse. More specifically, it involves remaining intentional, each day, about understanding the underlying motivations when he or she is communicating with you.

In the first part of John 15:15, Jesus said, "I no longer call you servants, because a servant *does not know* his master's business" (emphasis added). You must not only make it a priority to understand your future spouse's business, but you must also go one step further to understand the heart behind his or her business. This leads us to the Golden Communication Rule for getting naked (i.e., creating emotional safety).

The Golden Communication Rule

Every time the ministry situation came up in the months following our honeymoon, I did what any good husband was supposed to do—I listened to Christi. Yet as I stared at the proverbial nail in her forehead, I wanted so badly to help her realize her own unwillingness to be dutiful to the ministry I wanted her to be a part of. In doing so, I wasn't paying attention to the nail in my own forehead. I was *listening* to my wife, but I wasn't *hearing* her.

That unresolved argument the last night of our honeymoon led to countless disagreements in the first few months of our marriage. Yet it yielded one of the greatest lessons on communication that has since dramatically changed the depth of our relationship. In fact, I learned that the most romantic gesture I can offer Christi is simply asking about her day, how she's feeling, and what's going on in her heart and mind.

Good communication follows the Golden Rule: Treat others as you want to be treated (see Matthew 7:12). But it goes a step further. Replace the word *treat* with the word *understand*: *Understand others as you want to be understood.* Or put another way, "In order to be understood, you first must understand."

The problem for many of us is that we are unwilling to be vulnerable. And yet to communicate proactively as husband and wife requires it. In fact, in order to know your future spouse and seek the underlying motivation behind what is being communicated to you, you must be willing to commit to four decisions. These four decisions create the emotional safety required to engage in proactive communication.

1. *Build intimacy.* The decision to become more intimate with each other seems like a no-brainer. However, consider our previous definition: *Intimacy* is "the *willingness to endure* the negative feelings you get when you get close to another individual" (emphasis added). Getting close to someone inevitably creates negative feelings. Yet we live in a culture that says we have a right not to endure

anything negative when it comes to romantic relationships. If you never disagree with your fiancé(e), it's probably because one of you is compromising way too much in the relationship. The decision to build intimacy means you initiate and discuss issues with your future spouse before or as they arise, even if it's difficult.

You may have heard it said that "conflict builds intimacy." That's because when conflict is resolved in a healthy way, each person walks away feeling understood.

2. *Give up blame.* To know your future spouse means you must be willing to give up blame when you're accused. Let's try something. Have you ever done something stupid in your life? Write down what you did. When you originally set out, was it your intention to do that stupid act? Of course not. Yet you did it.

Early in our dating relationship, I took Christi camping with my family along a river. We camped and fished for an entire weekend with no showers or access to running water or electricity. I didn't realize how much she hated it until a few months later. My intention was to have a great weekend together so my family could get to know my girlfriend. Needless to say, trying to accomplish this worthy goal by sleeping along a riverbank with mosquitoes and no amenities wasn't the brightest idea.

When your future spouse makes an accusation against you, there might be some truth to it. Take time to pray and ask God what the truth is instead of immediately jumping to your own defense. Not meeting him or her with defensiveness will defuse his or her negative feelings. You can validate your fiancé(e)'s feelings, even if your perspective is different.

In our posthoneymoon ministry debacle, I was blaming Christi for her unwillingness to remain faithful to the duty of this particular ministry. Yet, in doing so, I was unable to see or understand her underlying motivation for not wanting to join me. Because I blamed her.

3. *Stop negative comparisons.* I mentioned earlier the negative comparisons I made when I felt that Christi wasn't living up to what *I* had envisioned for her. Whenever you compare your future spouse to others, you betray him or her.

4. *Change the only person you can.* When it comes to proactive communication, you'll get nowhere trying to teach your future spouse how to communicate. The best decision you can make is to change the only person you can—you.

To know your future spouse means understanding the underlying motivation behind his or her communication and actions. I'll never forget the plea of the young woman in marital distress who was sitting in my counseling office with her husband. Only a few years into the marriage, she exclaimed through her tears, "All I ever wanted is for somebody to love me."

Too often, as it was with this young woman, our attempts to get others to love us are filled with avoidance, blame, negative comparisons ("Why can't you be more like so and so?"), and trying to fix the other person. The ways married couples often try to build intimacy and feel loved may be sincere in motivation but sincerely wrong in approach.

The Golden Communication Rule—"In order to be understood you must first understand"—covers the first part of the definition of proactive communication (to know your future spouse). The second part of the definition involves the actual skills required for being known. Jesus said in John 15:15, "But I have called you friends, for all that I have heard from my Father I have *made known* to you" (ESV, emphasis added). This is where you communicate with each other in a manner that seeks to honor your fiancé(e)'s heart (empathy) as you reveal your desires (expressing your feelings). This manner of communicating (respect) builds deeper trust in the relationship. (Many of the principles discussed in this section are communication strategies used in cognitive interpersonal therapy, developed by Dr. David Burns. For a more in-depth understanding of how to communicate using this approach, I highly recommend Dr. Burns's book *Feeling Good Together: The Secret to Making Troubled Relationships Work*.)

To communicate proactively in marriage, you'll need to develop three essential skills.

1. *Empathy.* To communicate with empathy is to feel bad *with* somebody. To communicate with sympathy is to feel bad *for* somebody. Notice the difference. This is where knowing your future spouse is put into practice, because doing empathy is more than having empathy. You feel bad *with* your fiancé(e) by acknowledging what he or she feels and why. James instructs us, "Everyone should be quick to listen, slow to speak and slow to become angry" (James 1:19).

I'll never forget one particular couple who came to me. She was complaining about her husband's consistent absence from family functions, and her perception was that he enjoyed being at work more than being at home. Her accusation and his response went something like this:

> *Wife*: "You'd rather be at work than with us. You're always missing our most important family moments."
>
> *Husband*: "I'm trying my best. To live in the home you want and to get to the next level in the company, I have to work late some nights. I don't know how I can win here."

His response was a defensive one. It was also competitive. He saw himself in a win-lose situation. Remember, when you're being accused, even if you don't agree with it, you can always validate your spouse's experience or perspective. Validation can always calm the other person down. The more you ignore his or her feelings, the stronger those feelings get.

Here's an empathetic response to the previous scenario:

> *Wife*: "You'd rather be at work than with us. You're always missing our most important family moments."

Husband: "I know you're frustrated (acknowledge the feeling) that I'm working more often lately, because you'd like me to be here to share family moments together with you (and why she feels that way)."

An empathetic response opens the conversation to discuss the feeling behind the action and the underlying motivation behind what your fiancé(e) desires.

2. *Expressing your feelings.* When your fiancé(e) feels understood, you can then begin to express your own emotions using "I feel" statements. This has to be done sensitively and with discernment; otherwise, it could be very easy to make your fiancé(e) feel attacked. Nonverbal communication, such as tone of voice and body language, makes up more than 90 percent of communication.

Examples of "I feel" statements include

"I feel hurt when you misjudge my intentions."

"I feel pressured when balancing your needs with my parents' requests."

"I feel rejected when you're on your phone during our times together."

Being known means you share what's going on in your life. Be vulnerable. Volunteer information about your deepest thoughts, beliefs, feelings, dreams, hopes, and desires. Sharing creates closeness.

3. *Respect.* Communicating with respect means treating your future spouse with kindness and gentleness even when you may be irritated or angry. Respect is refusing to be mean and nasty even if your fiancé(e) is being mean and nasty.

Christi and I now catch each other being disrespectful and call each other out on it even in the middle of an argument. It's been fun because we can now laugh about it when we consider what we just said. For instance, Christi recently accused me of always giving in to our son when he wants something. Though I admit there is some truth to it, I gently reminded her about the time I didn't give him the electrical cord plugged into the wall to suck on. It was a humorous way for us to reconsider the word *always* in her accusation.

Black-and-white communication, using words like *always* and *never* or "I win and you lose," isn't good because it denotes a character flaw in your fiancé(e), not a time-and-place happenstance. Communicating in a respectful way means saying, "I feel _____ *when* . . ." For example:

> "I feel angry when you choose to hang out with your friends over me because I worry you don't enjoy me anymore."
>
> "I feel hurt when you arrive home thirty minutes late from work because I'm afraid you don't appreciate the work I've done to make a nice dinner for you."

Jesus warned, "Judge not, that you be not judged" (Matthew 7:1, ESV). To respect your future spouse means giving him or her the benefit of the doubt in each circumstance by not making judgmental character statements.

Items for Our Everyday Honeymoon Suitcase

Now that you've learned the key strategies of getting emotionally naked by knowing your future spouse and being known, we'll move to the second proactive aspect of experiencing an everyday honeymoon: enjoying the bliss.

I recently went through our honeymoon pictures and found shots of my wife and me kissing each other and flashing our wedding bands around for others to see. We were like two kids in a candy store having a taste of our first chocolate bars. In fact, try this out for a date night sometime. Walk around town shouting, "Woo-hoo! Look at this (as you flash your wedding bands openly for all to see)! We're married! This is awesome!"

How can you enjoy the everyday bliss you'll experience during the honeymoon period? It starts with reverence. Let's return to the honeymoon suitcase. What you pack in your suitcase every day will lead to a place where you will communicate well as a couple and feel safe with each other. The items you pack in your honeymoon suitcase—like the gear for kayaking and playing tennis—will build your marriage and set you up for everyday bliss.

In our wedding vows, Christi said, "You are my teammate." I looked at her and declared, "I will fight for you and not with you." Since our wedding day we have held an "us against the world" attitude in our marriage. We look out at the world and build prorelationship thoughts that foster emotional safety in our marriage and set the stage for everyday bliss. Because in my eyes, no woman in the world can measure up to Christi.

There's a married couple at our church who enjoys everyday bliss better than any other couple I know. On Facebook, you can find pictures of their anniversary trip and the days-long birthday party she threw for her husband. All of her pictures on social media are tagged with the caption "My Mr. Wonderful." No other man in the world can measure up to him in her eyes. That's prorelationship thinking, and it prepares the everyday suitcase for the honeymoon items to be packed in it.

Write down the following three behaviors to pack each day in your honeymoon suitcase. Hang them on your refrigerator and, most important, practice them as you prepare for married life together.

1. *Ask questions.* Asking questions of your future spouse is an art that needs to be practiced. Start simple by just making it a daily routine to ask, "Honey, how was your day?" One question will lead to another question. Try to find out something new about your fiancé(e) every day. What is it that drives him or her? What does he or she love to do? What can you start doing together to make memories? Instead of going fishing on your own, how about taking her with you? Ask him to help you cook one day a week. Whatever it is, ask at least one question every day to inquire about your fiancé(e)'s heart and where he or she is emotionally, spiritually, relationally, and so on.

2. *Give thanks.* The second item you can pack in your everyday honeymoon suitcase is gratitude. I'm not just talking here about an attitude of gratitude or about feeling grateful. What I'm talking about is *practicing* gratitude by keeping gratitude journals or a gratitude jar, or maybe even developing gratitude rituals where you verbalize something you're grateful for in your future spouse. If you practice gratitude now, while you're engaged, it'll be second nature by the time you're married!

A few weeks ago, I was late getting home from work. I thought for sure I was going to be in trouble because Christi usually makes dinner while I take care of our two children. I rushed home, ran through the door, and began apologizing repetitively before Christi could react.

Then, in her own gentle way, and much to my surprise, she looked at me and said, "Josh, you don't need to apologize. I'm just very grateful for your work ethic. Thank you for working so hard for our family."

Say what!?

I'll be honest. I wanted to get naked right then and there. When Christi expressed gratitude to me, it made me want to get home early. Why? Because it creates emotional safety. I can be vulnerable at home.

3. *Embrace moments of joy.* I believe one of the most tragic issues today is how our fast-paced culture is robbing us of experiencing joy. We miss joy when we wait for something extraordinary to happen. But real joy is different.

One research study recently looked at spouses who lost another spouse to death. Without exception, every participant mentioned something about a particular moment. Here are a couple of examples:

"If I could just walk back downstairs every morning and see my husband sitting, reading the newspaper, and drinking a cup of coffee . . ."

"My wife used to send me crazy text messages throughout the day. I would do anything to get one of those text messages again."[7]

I have a joyful moment every time I walk into my son's room in the still of the night, and he is lying there sleeping. There's nothing like standing over a sleeping child and praying for him or her.

Don't miss these moments of joy now or after you're married. Be proactive about communicating these moments each day with your future spouse.

Early on in our marriage, Christi didn't want to be a domesticated housewife. In fact, she was pretty adamant about it. Our premarital counselors worked with us on this issue and one night playfully brought up the idea that sex begins in the kitchen. My immediate response was a bit sarcastic, "Well, I have to get her there first."

Now she loves to cook, and one of my most joyful moments is watching her. It's become therapy for her. She plans meals and comes alive thinking up recipes and preparing meals for our family. I love that. I embrace those moments and share them with her.

Today, maybe your joyful moment was holding your fiancé(e)'s hand while walking in the mall. Perhaps it was simply watching him or her interact with somebody. Whatever the moment, verbalize it each day.

For your everyday honeymoon suitcase, ask at least one question of your spouse, verbalize one thing you're grateful for each day about him or her, and proactively communicate the joyful moments you never want to forget.

Tomorrow Never Comes

We have 1,440 minutes each day, but how many of these minutes become *moments*? As Christi always reminds me, we only have today to communicate who we are and how we feel. And there should be no safer person for your fiancé(e) to share it with than you.

Choose to repurpose your minutes into moments by practicing proactive, life-giving communication as you seek to know your future spouse and be known.

JOSHUA STRAUB is the president and cofounder of the Connextion Group, a company designed to build relational connections between generations. Josh speaks and writes on the two key ingredients necessary for building healthy families: intentional parenting and a loving marriage. In addition to being a family-and-relationship coach, Josh is also the coauthor of *God Attachment* and *The Quick-Reference Guide to Counseling Teenagers*. He serves on the teaching team at Woodland Hills Family Church. He wakes up each day striving to love others better, starting with his wife, Christi, and their two children, Landon and Kennedy.

Ready to Talk

1. The author of this chapter writes about the moment when he knew "our honeymoon was over." What happened next? Which of the following lessons do you see in his experience? How could they help when you feel *your* honeymoon is over?

    • Honeymoons don't last forever, so don't panic.

    • Poor communication is often the root of marital conflicts.

    • Generally speaking, you should be fighting *for* your spouse, not *with* him or her.

    • The end of the honeymoon can lead to deeper love and understanding.

    • Other _____

2. The author talks about three essential skills needed to communicate proactively: empathy, expressing your feelings, and respect. What skill is easiest for each of you right now? Which one is most difficult? Which skill do you see is strongest within your relationship? Talk about some ways you can both build on your strengths and grow where needed.

3. What are some things you plan to pack in your literal honeymoon suitcase? After reading this chapter, what communication tips will you pack in your symbolic everyday honeymoon suitcase?

Ready to Try

Sometimes it's easier to communicate when you're together, involved in a not-too-demanding task and not quite face-to-face. Cooking is a good example. Get a recipe from an in-law-to-be, Pinterest, or your favorite celebrity chef or food show. Then work together in the kitchen creating something new. It's a fun way to connect, and it can spark conversations about dinner traditions, favorite meals, and so on. Talk about your family dining experiences. Did you have dinner together often? Did family members fend for themselves? What did you like or dislike about those habits? What mealtime traditions would you like to have once you're wed?

PART 2

MANAGING CONFLICT IN HEALTHY WAYS

CHAPTER 8

WE ARE SO DIFFERENT!

John Trent, PhD

"How did we get here?"

Angelina (whom everyone called Angel) kept asking herself that question. Out of all her friends, Angel felt that she and her husband, Bryan, would sail through marriage. After all, both of their parents loved and cared for them and had modeled healthy marriages. Both came from families of genuine faith. Angel had seen so many of her friends, who grew up in tough, uncaring backgrounds, struggle later in their marriages. But she and Bryan had seen up close and personal what a strong marriage and family looked like.

Not only that, but they'd chosen to be as prepared as they could for marriage. They had listened to countless podcasts and read loads of Christian books on marriage and relationships after they got engaged. They carved out time to do their own Bible study on marriage as well. They even attended an eight-week premarital preparation course at their church—a good course that seemed to hit all the bases they'd need to have a great marriage.

Most of all, Bryan and Angel were sold-out, real-deal believers in Jesus. Not just visitors at church every other holiday. They were committed to loving Jesus personally, and both of them wanted their marriage to reflect His love. For example, the Sunday after they got back from their honeymoon, they started attending a great church near their home and serving in the children's ministry. They even joined a Life Group, a small group of couples all about their age, that met every other week. Each meeting focused on a positive way of doing life together, and the group provided a community of positive people who encouraged and cheered Bryan and Angel on in their marriage.

With all they had going for them, how could Angel be thinking about ending their relationship and running away? Equally terrible, she knew she wasn't the only one feeling that way! Angel could see that same hurt, uncertainty, and questioning every time she looked in Bryan's eyes. Even more, she saw and felt it in the way he was starting to pull away from her both emotionally and physically.

The fact was that something had changed between them. Throughout the time they dated and during their first several months of marriage, Angel had been so impressed with Bryan's drive, ambition, and energy. He was a strong, decisive leader but also respectful of others. He seemed so secure and ready to take the lead in their relationship—to move them toward a positive future.

Now, while he still looked like the Bryan she had married, it was as if someone else had taken his place relationally! The person she was living with wasn't respectful; he was a steamroller! He was loud, rash, and impulsive. He ignored her feelings, and it seemed as if he went out of his way to cut her out of decisions, large and small. In short, there was a right way, and it was his way. And if she didn't like it, there was the highway—or at least that's how Angel felt.

Where had all those positive strengths gone that had once drawn her to him?

In her heart of hearts, Angel knew that a change had taken place in the way Bryan looked at her as well. In their courtship and early in their marriage, everything just seemed so *easy*. They had just "fit." If Bryan was quick to make decisions, Angel complemented him by being methodical and making sure they sat down and worked on a plan.

Bryan had always appreciated Angel's laid-back personality and her natural ability to sense when others were hurting. If someone needed help, she was quick to jump in and serve, or she'd show up at their place with help or encouragement. He'd seen these qualities as Angel's strengths, the very reason he'd fallen in love with her. But now, after just a year of marriage—less time then they'd dated and had been engaged—those same traits had turned into teeth-grinding negatives for Bryan!

Instead of Angel being methodical, Bryan thought she was slow and asked way too many questions. She seemed fearful and unwilling to make decisions. She wasn't just sensitive; she was hypersensitive and too emotional over nothing. And while she was serving others, it seemed to Bryan that even that trait had gone from something positive to a negative. It was almost as if helping others was an excuse to get away from him, swallowing any time or goals they had together.

For both Bryan and Angel, it was as though a terrible switch had been made that was robbing them of their happiness and joy. *The very things that had drawn the two of them together were now pushing them apart.* Even to the point of questioning whether their marriage could last!

How could that have happened?

The key reason why this happened with Angel and Bryan, and why it does with *most* couples, is what this chapter is all about. Particularly early in a marriage, there is, in fact, a "switch" that impacts almost every couple to some degree. And it's linked with understanding how our unique personality differences can indeed lead us to feelings of incompatibility.

As you prepare to head into the adventure of marriage, here's the truth that can enrich or even save your relationship later on. Your own unique, God-given strengths—and the differences your future spouse brings with his or her unique set of strengths—can actually be grounds for a great marriage!

Value Your Differences for a Great Marriage!

The stress from facing differences in a marriage can be unnerving and hurtful. But it doesn't have to ruin your relationship! You can move from resenting differences to valuing them—and your spouse—particularly when *you* choose to actively and purposefully seek to understand your own unique, God-given personality strengths and those of your fiancé(e) as well.

Proverbs 3:13 tells us, "Blessed is the man [or woman] who finds wisdom [and] gains understanding." As you better understand your own and your future spouse's strengths, you'll . . .

- learn why becoming a student of his or her strengths gives you an incredible edge in solving problems and making better and wiser decisions as a couple than you ever could have made individually;

- see how a key to identifying and dealing with your own weakness, in relationships at home and at work, is learning what happens when your strengths are pushed to an extreme; and

- discover a way, together, to continue "seeing" your future spouse's strengths, which will increase caring, closeness, and positive feelings in your marriage during each new season of life.

It Starts with Understanding Your Unique, God-Given Strengths

Really "seeing" your own unique, God-given strengths, and those of your future spouse, begins by understanding that we are all "fearfully and wonderfully made" (Psalm 139:14). We are unique creations of God, crafted with strengths and abilities to reflect His love and life. For example, this idea of each of us expressing unique personality traits can be seen in Proverbs 22:6: "Train up a child . . . *in keeping with his [or her] individual gift or bent*" (AMP, emphasis added). In other words, each child has a specific "bent" or way he or she is shaped to do life—a unique set of personality strengths, gifts, and abilities (including spiritual gifts, if the child is a believer). This "bent"—our strengths—acts like a relational DNA map of how we approach life.

These personal God-given strengths are so often the very qualities that attracted you to your fiancé(e) in the first place. For example, my wife, Cindy, and I had so many differences, one of the only things we had in common was that we were both married on the same day! On a serious note, we had lots of positive things in common when we dated and married. We both shared a love for the Lord. We had a mutual desire to have a strong Christian marriage and family. But what really drew us together were our differences. And they were indeed many.

For example, Cindy is left-handed; I'm right-handed. Cindy is a saver (thankfully); I'm more of a spender (unfortunately). She's a morning person; I'm a night person. She wants to work, finish tasks, and then play. I want to play . . . and then play. My wife wants the toilet paper to go off the top of the roll. *I just want it there!*

All these differences (as well as the male-female ones, of course) deeply attracted us to each other. It was as though we were two halves of an apple coming together to make one delicious Washington State apple. But after only six months of marriage, it was more like applesauce!

Like Angel and Bryan earlier in the chapter, my wife and I had different ways we were "bent" in approaching almost every area of life. We had a different bent or approach in the way we made decisions—one fast and one slow. We were different in how we faced (or didn't want to face) problems. We were very different in the way we dealt with new people and new information. We also had different levels of trust or needs to "validate" facts or people. And we were very different in how much lead time we needed to move in a new direction. In almost everything from finances to the way we drove a car to how we did the laundry, we approached life in very different ways. And that caused stress and strain early in our marriage as we tried to understand how to blend two individual bents into one home and marriage.

Yet for Cindy and me, and for Angel and Bryan (and maybe for you and your future spouse as well), the key to turning those differences from frustration points into incredible benefits came when we chose to actively, purposefully, and positively "see" and value each other's strengths.

To help you develop this ability, I'd like you to take a short survey I first created when I was in graduate school. It's the same instrument that my lifelong friend Gary Smalley and I adapted to use in a book we wrote on blending personality strengths, titled *The Two Sides of Love*. This instrument is called the LOGB Personal Strengths Survey. You'll find a copy of this assessment in appendix B (along with instructions) for you to take. Or feel free to go to *www.strongfamilies.com* and take an online version of this same tool by clicking on a button on the website that says LOGB.

Stop! Take a few minutes to complete your personality profile before continuing. Once you've completed the profile, share your graph with each other. Then we'll look briefly at what it means if you scored high in the L, O, G, or B boxes. (Keep in mind that it's not uncommon to score high or even "tie" in more than one category.)

A "Living" Picture of Your Strengths

While most personality tools use words to describe people, I've often seen people resist the labels they're given or not understand the words that categorize them. So I decided to use a different approach to help people step toward the description of who they are. Since most people love and are very familiar with the way certain animals act, I developed the following personality-assessment tool using those animals.

As you read through the four animal descriptions (Lion, Otter, Golden Retriever, and Beaver), underline the characteristics that sound most like you. Then total your score in each category and identify the highest-scoring category to determine your dominant personality type.

If you scored high or tied on more than one scale (for example, the Lion and the Otter tied as your highest scores), carefully read *both* descriptions that apply to you. Remember that we're a blend of all four of these basic personality types, with a few of us being purebreds. And know, too, that while this instrument can give you a valid picture of who you are today, that picture can change over time as you grow, mature, and go through different life experiences.

1. *The Lion.* Those who scored highest on the Lion scale have personality strengths that motivate them to naturally take charge and be assertive. They love taking the lead and generally know which way they want to go.

That natural ability and confidence to move toward a goal or objective is a great strength for Lions. They're naturally competitive and often self-starters. They don't mind challenges. At work, they often end up as the boss or in a position that lets them jump in and be actively involved in directing activity around them. Lions want to do things "now!" and hate to waste time when they could be getting something else done. This means they generally want to make decisions *quickly*, with or without all the facts. Or they want to solve a problem "now"—even if it's eleven o'clock at night!

Lions are fast-paced, competitive, and goal driven. That often means they look at questions from others (particularly from Beavers, who *love* to ask clarifying questions) as slowing them down, not aiding or helping them. And in everyday conversation, they most often don't want to hear every detail of someone's day—just the high points.

These are all strengths, but as you'll see with Lions, Otters, Golden Retrievers, and Beavers, each person's core personality strengths, *if pushed to an extreme*, can become their biggest weaknesses in relationships (at home or at work).

Lions, particularly under pressure, can be so decisive that they struggle with slowing down to listen to or seek input from others before making a decision. They're often so driven to push forward and get something done, they can communicate by their actions or nonverbal communication that a task is more important than people, or others' feelings. Again, under pressure, if they feel their time is being wasted or a decision is being blocked, they can be impatient, argumentative, or even pushy.

Lions are great people and great spouses. They can accomplish much for the Lord and their families and raise great kids. So if almighty God has given you a Lion to do life with, look forward to accomplishing great things together.

When a Lion gains the wisdom to *slow down* and seek to include others—proactively asking for their input and valuing their questions and insights—he or she will become a great leader as well. A wise Lion will take the time to really "see" the strengths of the people God has placed in his or her life.

2. *The Otter.* Otters are fun loving, enthusiastic, playful, and encouraging. They love people and *love* to talk. That's one reason why they know hundreds of people *but don't know anyone's name*! Otters—purebred Otters, in particular—don't focus on details, like names. But they're so naturally friendly and engaging, they can form friendship bonds quickly with others and often end up being the center of attention.

They're creative and full of energy, enthusiasm, and life. For example, Otters love *starting* things. Sometimes that means they don't finish everything they start, but not finishing something doesn't bother them the way it does other personalities (like Beavers). Otters have a great time getting things launched.

Overall, Otters are optimistic and can see the potential in ideas they take to heart. But often they don't see the risks associated with those ideas—which means they don't always take time to read instructions (or a prospectus before investing!). Otters lead with their hearts and are excitable. They often use lots of words, energy, and gestures when communicating.

Take all those great characteristics and push them to an extreme, and Otters can come across as unorganized or too fun loving. Others may believe they're not serious enough when it comes to important discussions or challenges, or that they're insensitive about not meeting deadlines that affect others.

Otters love people, but again, if their strengths are pushed to an extreme, then under pressure an Otter can become a people pleaser in a way that can put real strain on a marriage or important relationships. Otters under pressure may say yes to everyone in order to be liked but not realize the impact their people pleasing may have on their loved ones, particularly when there's no time or energy left for their spouse or family after working so hard to please others.

All in all, Otters are great to have on a team or in a marriage or family, with all their creativity, optimism, energy, and life. But wise Otters know how crucial it is to value people around them who are great at following through, being sensitive, and setting a clear path (like Lions, Beavers, or Golden Retrievers).

3. *The Golden Retriever.* Golden Retrievers are considerate, good-natured, and strong team players. They're naturally kindhearted and love helping, serving, and looking for ways to come alongside others, particularly if they're around people who are hurting. For example, at work, the Lion often organizes the Christmas party (but doesn't actually go), while the Otter loves the idea of a party and tries to talk to everyone there. But the Golden Retriever will sit with *one* person at the party— either someone the Golden Retriever already knows or someone he or she wants to get to know even better or deeper. Golden Retrievers may also sit with someone who is hurting or struggling and seek to encourage and help that person.

Purebred Golden Retrievers in grade school will actually send themselves to time-out if they do something wrong (as opposed to Lion kids who send their *parents* to time-out).

Retrievers, like each of the other core personalities, are tremendous people to be married to. But if their strengths are pushed to an extreme, they, too, face issues. For example, Retrievers often tend to avoid problems (or downplay issues) at all costs, saying things like "Let's talk about that tomorrow" or "Let's deal with that later."

Again, circling lots of words in the G box means you have a great many positive strengths! Golden Retrievers rock! For example, they're world-class at seeking peace and harmony with others and in wanting to see closeness and caring in a home, marriage, or workplace. But there are times when problems need to be faced and dealt with *today*—not six months from now. Which is why Golden Retrievers need others around them, like a spouse, who have the strength of a Lion or the creativity of an Otter or the detail orientation of a Beaver.

4. *The Beaver.* Guess what's on the class ring at MIT (the Massachusetts Institute of Technology)? Or at Caltech? Both of these colleges are arguably two of the finest engineering schools in the world. And both of them have on their class rings . . . *a Beaver!* That's because Beaver personalities are God's little architects and engineers. They're organized, precise, and detailed. They catch the spelling mistakes that everyone else misses. And if they're purebred Beavers, they actually *like* to balance the checkbook! They sleep better knowing exactly, not approximately, how much money they have in the bank. In short, they're great on follow-through and completing detailed tasks.

Remember the Christmas party from earlier? The Lions organized the party, the Otters came to the party wanting to talk to everyone there, and the sensitive Golden Retrievers sat with one person who needed encouragement. But the Beavers were the only ones who remembered to bring the food! That's because "Bring food" was on their list. Beavers *love* to check things off lists!

Like every other core personality type we've looked at, when a Beaver's strengths are pushed to an extreme, Beavers can take other people apart by being critical. Perhaps not verbally or in a loud way, like a Lion who "roars" at others. But if you offend a Beaver (or a Golden Retriever, for that matter), that person can hold on to a grudge for a long time, clearly remembering the offense—and what you were wearing when you offended him or her! That's opposed to Lions and Otters who tend to get over things and move on more quickly in many cases.

One more thing. While Beavers can be critical, most often they're really good at taking themselves apart, which means they can be extremely hard on themselves, particularly if they feel they've fallen short of a goal, made a mistake, or done something wrong. Thoughts race through their minds, such as *Why did I say that?* or *What did she mean by that?* or *If only I had . . .*

It's the Beavers' attention to detail and desire to do things in a quality and correct way that makes them so incredibly beneficial in a marriage, in the workplace, and in other relationships. They can spot problems early on, even when an idea is being shared initially—which is one reason it's a good idea to invite a Beaver into a conversation. They can help others limit risk and identify challenges that can block or keep something from being successful. Beavers are also great at wanting issues to be dealt with when they're small, instead of waiting for small problems to turn into crises. For example, they don't like driving for long distances with the warning light on in the car without getting the car checked or fixed! Beavers finish tasks and close loops and plan today for a positive future—strengths that Lions and Otters often lack and need so much.

What Turned Things Around for Angel and Bryan

Remember Angel and Bryan? What turned things around for them— and what can turn things around for you when it comes to blending your differences as a couple—were three simple suggestions. These suggestions helped Bryan and Angel see their own strengths, and their spouse's strengths, more clearly. They also helped Bryan and Angel move from viewing each other as an opponent to the ally they once were.

1. *Become a student of your future spouse's strengths.* From what you've read in this chapter, it's probably not surprising that when Angel took the LOGB assessment, she discovered that she is a Golden Retriever who is also high on the Beaver scale. Bryan, on the other hand, is literally tied at the very top of both the Lion and Otter scales. This means that when it came to decisions, Angel, as a Golden Retriever, preferred to go slowly and carefully, talking through all the options before they made a

decision. She relaxed when she knew they'd covered all their bases and understood the best they could the impact a decision would have on their relationship, their finances, or even their future.

Bryan, on the other hand, wasn't only strong (a Lion); he was spontaneous (an Otter). So when decisions came up, his goal was to rush in and "get 'er done!" Time was wasting! Instead of gathering all the facts or slowing down to talk to Angel, he'd jump in and make a decision, often without even bothering to include Angel. Then he'd be shocked when she didn't appreciate and thank him for his quick decision-making skills or the direction he'd taken without her!

The more they both learned about their individual bents and their spouse's, the more they understood how differently each of them saw life—how differently they approached everything from making decisions to facing problems to picking which restaurant to go to.

And what came with understanding (which helped their relationship tremendously) was seeing *why* they did things the way they did. Meaning, Bryan wasn't trying to hurt Angel's feelings by making fast decisions. It just came naturally. And Angel wasn't peppering Bryan with questions to frustrate him. She was looking for information to make the best possible decision and help him.

It's amazing how seeking understanding in a marriage, instead of just reacting to personality differences, can strengthen the relationship and lessen frustration and conflict. And it does something else as well.

2. Be willing to ask yourself, "Are my strengths being pushed to an extreme?" Once Angel and Bryan became students of their spouse's strengths, they were able to focus on solving issues instead of just attacking each other. And they were able to do something else that's incredibly important: They became willing to take a hard look at their own lives and how they were using their own strengths with their spouse and others.

Wise couples will start looking at their individual strengths, asking if and how those strengths are being pushed out of balance or to an extreme. Just asking the simple question, "Are my strengths being pushed to an extreme?" can be an incredible help in a marriage. For

Bryan, when he chose to ask that question, it opened up an opportunity for reflection and growth that helped him not only in his marriage but at work as well. Bryan realized that not only was he being too forceful and spontaneous with decisions at home, but his strengths pushed to an extreme were negatively impacting his relationships at work. He was great at taking charge, but he became a great leader by slowing down to value and include others in decision making at home and at work.

Upon reflection, Angel had to admit that some of her strengths were being pushed to an extreme as well. She was indeed rushing off to help and serve others but not just to be helpful. She was in fact looking for something she felt "successful" at as an escape from things not going well in her marriage.

Proverbs 12:15 tells us, "The way of a fool is right in his own eyes, but a wise man listens to advice" (ESV). And Proverbs 1:5 says that "a wise man will hear and increase learning, and a man of understanding will attain wise counsel" (NKJV). By seeking wisdom and understanding, and *dropping* their pride, Bryan and Angel were able to see life from each other's perspective instead of just their own, and that lead to one final step that changed their relationship.

3. *Set aside time to blend your differences.* Blending differences in a marriage can transform how a couple makes decisions and faces problems. Bryan, who was always good at taking the lead, suggested that he and Angel do something to keep them moving toward each other, not apart. As busy as they both were working full-time, Bryan suggested to Angel that they take just one hour every Tuesday night to focus on their marriage.

Specifically, they'd head over to the local food court at the mall near their apartment. Then they'd sit down, hold hands, and do two things. First, each of them would share *one* word from the LOGB assessment that reflected a strength they appreciated about the other person. That way they'd begin their talk by affirming and choosing to value a strength they saw in their loved one. Second, they'd talk together, using each of their God-given strengths and abilities to work together to solve *one* problem or deal with *one* issue that had come up during the week.

As a Golden Retriever, Angel loved the idea of carving out time to bless and affirm each other. And she loved having a plan for dealing with problems in an honoring way. By sitting at the food court, Bryan couldn't get too loud or dramatic when they talked, which helped him (and Angel) stay positive. And Angel loved holding hands and working together to become closer and make life better for them—and eventually for their children. (For eight years, every Tuesday night Bryan and Angel showed up at the food court to affirm each other's strengths and talk.)

What this couple discovered very quickly was that *together* they had the whole zoo sitting at their table with them! Bryan brought the Lion and Otter, and Angel brought the Golden Retriever and Beaver. Not only could they make better decisions with the strengths God gave them, but they could make *great* decisions! And by learning to focus together on beating back a problem or an issue, they gained insight and wisdom that they never could have come up with alone. They actually *did* need each other!

It was almost as though God had *placed* them together—differences and all. Which, they realized, was exactly what He'd done! And that's when they finally moved away from judging each other's differences to seeing and valuing each other's strengths.

In 1 Corinthians 12, the apostle Paul shared how in the body of Christ, we're not all "eyes" or "ears" or "feet" or "hands." We each bring a unique set of gifts, strengths, and abilities to the table—like different but important parts of the body—that are *needed* if we're to have a fully functioning body. In verse 18, we see God's purpose in putting different people and gifts together: "[He] has placed the members, each one of them, in the body, just as He desired" (NASB). That word *placed* is a jeweler's term. God "places" each of us in the body with the careful skill and consideration that a jeweler does in setting a stone in a ring!

Bryan and Angel came to believe that God had placed them together—like the stone in her wedding ring—with all their differences, "just as He desired." Together, like that stone, they reflected His light in so many different ways, with each of them complementing the other. By joining together, they brought more light and love into their relationships, and more of God's love, than they ever could have separately!

Only the Wise Seek Counsel and Understanding

So here's my challenge to you. Seek wisdom and understanding as you're faced with the personality differences God has "placed" in your relationship by doing the following:

- Take time to become a student of your future spouse's strengths, which can help you gain understanding and avoid frustration.

- Be wise and godly by dropping your pride and being willing to ask the question, "Are my strengths being pushed out of balance or to an extreme?"

- Carve out precious time to sit down together as a couple (at home or at a food court near you!) to affirm and bless each other's strengths and then share and blend together the strengths God gave you when He placed you together.

For more information on LOGB, go to *www.StrongFamilies.com*. And for more tools and encouragement to build up, affirm, and "bless" your future spouse, visit *www.TheBlessing.com*, a cobranded site with Dr. John Trent and Focus on the Family that's part of the Blessing Challenge for Couples.

JOHN TRENT, PhD, has spent more than thirty years working with preengaged and premarital couples. For the past twenty-five years, Dr. Trent and his wife, Cindy, have taught a premarital course at Scottsdale Bible Church in Scottsdale, Arizona. He has also authored numerous publications and coauthored *The Blessing* and *Breaking the Cycle of Divorce*. In 2014, Moody Global Ministries in Chicago, Illinois, hired Dr.

Trent to be the voice of marriage and family as the Gary D. Chapman Chair of Marriage and Family Ministry at Moody Theological Seminary. He is also the president and founder of the nonprofit organization StrongFamilies.com and continues to write, travel, and speak on behalf of the organization.

Ready to Talk

1. If you and your future spouse were to meet on an online dating site that compared your personalities based on a list of questions, do you think you'd be declared a match? Why or why not? How important would that be to you? Why?

2. Below are various pairings of LOGB marriages. Based on the descriptions given in the chapter, discuss what you believe to be both the positive aspects of these pairs as well as the potential struggles.

   • Mr. Beaver and Mrs. Lion

   • Mr. Otter and Mrs. Otter

   • Mr. Lion and Mrs. Golden Retriever

   • Mr. Beaver and Mrs. Otter

   • Mr. Golden Retriever and Mrs. Golden Retriever

3. Based on this chapter, which of the following might you and your future mate need to watch out for? Why? How will you remind yourselves to do that?

   • Clashes between your personalities

   • Worrying too much about having different personalities

   • Expecting that opposites will always attract

   • Thinking that similar personalities will hold you together

   • Other _____

Ready to Try

At wedding receptions, best men and maids of honor often give toasts, describing aspects of the bride's and groom's personalities as they offer this tribute to them. Since you probably won't get a chance to do this at your own wedding, come up with your own toasts to each other, specifically trying to include details based on each other's LOGB assessment. Take a few minutes to think through your toasts; then deliver them. If any surprises or questions arise as a result of your descriptions, be sure to talk them over.

CHAPTER 9

WHAT DO YOU EXPECT?

Bill and Pam Farrel

WHETHER YOU REALIZED it or not, you've been building your expectations of marriage for a long time. The home you grew up in profoundly shaped how you think, what you like, and what you think is "normal" in relationships. Some of what you value is based on your reaction to your family.

You may have disagreed with some of the ways of interacting and making decisions that you observed in your family. You may have decided that you would "never be like that" or have deliberately replaced the way your family did things with new skills. These behaviors were likely developed with strong emotions, so they are very important to you. Whether you're aware of it or not, you anticipate that your spouse will value your approach, and you expect your preferences to be integrated into your life together.

Then there are your dreams about being married. Some of you have spent significant time thinking about what your future family will be like. You may have fantasized about what your wedding will be like, down to the smallest details. You may have imagined how good it will be to wake up next to someone who loves and adores you. You may have dreamed about romantic escapades and sexual freedom. The point is, we all imagine what marriage will be like before we get married. Some of what you came up with is realistic, while some of it is just fantasy.

This is your marriage, and it's intensely personal to you. It's nearly impossible for you to be objective about your relationship with your future spouse. As a result, you have expectations because your dreams span every area of your life, including the following:

- How you will be loved
- How you will make, save, or spend money
- How much attention you will get from your spouse
- How often you will engage in sex
- How romantic your spouse will be toward you
- How housework, cooking, and financial management will be dealt with
- How much time you will spend with your parents
- How many kids you hope for—and how you will raise them

If you're honest, in your mind you likely have a preconceived picture of the perfect husband or the perfect wife and the perfect marriage. When real life fails to match these portraits, negative emotions might be unveiled. You might have longed to marry Mr. Right or Miss Right; you just didn't realize that his or her first name was *Always*!

Your expectations of marriage aren't necessarily a bad thing, because they drew you into a relationship with your fiancé(e). They cultivate hope and build anticipation in your heart. One of the challenges of marriage, however, involves adapting our expectations to the day-to-day realities of a real relationship.

What Do You Expect?

Have you had the fun of taking the registry "gun" at the store and tagging all the wonderful items you hope to be given for your wedding? Did you sign up for a set of his-and-hers towels? Did you dream of cooking together as you picked out cookware? Did you envision romantic interludes as you chose the decor for your bedroom? The process of choosing gifts often reveals many of the expectations you carry in your heart about your future life together.

We all have expectations. Most of them are unwritten and unspoken, so we assume the one we love meets them . . . until he or she doesn't! It's like running headlong through a meadow toward each other, with romantic music playing and arms extended toward that loving embrace we long for. Then *bam*! We crash into an invisible wall—and it hurts!

Some of the early expectations that Bill and I (Pam) had of marriage were quite humorous:

> *Pam*: I'm marrying an architect student who loves math (not like me!), so eventually we'll be rich.
>
> *Bill*: I'm marrying a woman who loves ministry (like me), so we might be poor.
>
> *Pam*: His mom didn't cook, so my husband will cook for me!
>
> *Bill*: My mom didn't cook, so my wife will cook for me!
>
> *Pam*: He will adapt and stay up late with me (and give me massages).
>
> *Bill*: She will adapt and get up early with me (and make me a hot breakfast).
>
> *Pam*: If I say my view louder with more tears, I'll get my way.
>
> *Bill*: If I say it calmer, with stubborn silence, I'll get my way.

Pam: Wonder Bread, spaghetti, ramen noodles, macaroni and
cheese from a box, and soup from a can are kitchen staples.

Bill: Salad; grilled, lean meat; and fresh fruit are kitchen staples.

Pam: Green jello with pineapple and mini-marshmallows equals
Christmas love.

Bill: Green jello with pineapple and mini-marshmallows equals
Christmas torture.

We laugh about our different expectations now, but early on we
experienced some significant emotional turmoil over them. To avoid
banging your heads against these invisible walls of expectation, it's helpful to identify common expectations the majority of us deal with. It's
also helpful to learn how to manage differences in expectations.

Following is a chart of potential expectations you may have for
your relationship. For each, mark how strongly you expect it to happen
in your marriage. There are a few blank lines at the bottom so you
can add items that are personally important to you. Then compare
both lists, putting special focus on the expectations you have that are
significantly different. See if you can agree on what is "realistic" in
these various areas.

His List of Potential Expectations

Description	5 Gotta Have It	4 Would Make My Day	3 Negotiable	2 Could Get Used to It	1 Can't Live with It
You'll never do things for yourself that you know will upset me.		X			
We'll always be on time.		X			
You'll want to make love whenever I am in the mood.	X				
You'll want to spend your free time the same way I like to spend mine.				X	

Description	5 Gotta Have It	4 Would Make My Day	3 Negotiable	2 Could Get Used to It	1 Can't Live with It
We'll agree on most of our decisions.		X			
You'll remember important dates like our anniversary, birthdays, etc.				X	
You won't gain weight.				X	
You won't lose weight.					X
You'll make more money than I do.					X
You'll spend money the way I like to spend it.			X		
We'll have a clean and neat house.		X			
We'll eat healthy food.			X		
We'll exercise regularly.				X	
We'll exercise together.					X
You'll dress the way I like.				X	
We'll be affectionate.			X		
You'll clean up after yourself.			X		
You won't hug anyone else of the opposite sex.			X		
You won't be distracted by TV, video games, social media, or other entertainment when I'm home.			X		
You'll take care of me financially.					X
You'll avoid alcohol.			X		
You'll avoid drug use.	X				
You won't socialize without me.					X
You'll talk with me throughout the day.			X		
You won't be friends with people I don't like.				X	

Description	5 Gotta Have It	4 Would Make My Day	3 Negotiable	2 Could Get Used to It	1 Can't Live with It
You'll never lie to me.	X				
You'll be as committed to Jesus as I am.			X		
You'll be happy when I'm happy.				X	
You'll be miserable when I'm miserable.				X	
You'll be my best friend.	X				
You'll miss me a lot when we're apart.				X	
We'll spend holidays with my family.			X		

Her List of Potential Expectations

Description	5 Gotta Have It	4 Would Make My Day	3 Negotiable	2 Could Get Used to It	1 Can't Live with It
You'll never do things for yourself that you know will upset me.					
We'll always be on time.					
You'll want to make love whenever I am in the mood.					

Description	5 Gotta Have It	4 Would Make My Day	3 Negotiable	2 Could Get Used to It	1 Can't Live with It
You'll want to spend your free time the same way I like to spend mine.					
We'll agree on most of our decisions.					
You'll remember important dates like our anniversary, birthdays, etc.					
You won't gain weight.					
You won't lose weight.					
You'll make more money than I do.					
You'll spend money the way I like to spend it.					
We'll have a clean and neat house.					
We'll eat healthy food.					
We'll exercise regularly.					
We'll exercise together.					
You'll dress the way I like.					
We'll be affectionate.					
You'll clean up after yourself.					
You won't hug anyone else of the opposite sex.					
You won't be distracted by TV, video games, social media, or other entertainment when I'm home.					
You'll take care of me financially.					
You'll avoid alcohol.					
You'll avoid drug use.					
You won't socialize without me.					

Description	5 Gotta Have It	4 Would Make My Day	3 Negotiable	2 Could Get Used to It	1 Can't Live with It
You'll talk with me throughout the day.					
You won't be friends with people I don't like.					
You'll never lie to me.					
You'll be as committed to Jesus as I am.					
You'll be happy when I'm happy.					
You'll be miserable when I'm miserable.					
You'll be my best friend.					
You'll miss me a lot when we're apart.					
We'll spend holidays with my family.					

And the list goes on and on.

The goal of comparing your expectations is to grow into a "we" mind-set from a "me" mind-set. Before you get married, you only have to consult with yourself. You're free to focus on your own needs and desires. When you say "I do," you begin an entirely new journey.

When we were doing research for our book *The 10 Best Decisions a Couple Can Make*, we interviewed couples who had been married for more than twenty years to discover their secrets for lifelong love. One of the repeated comments included a commitment to an "us" approach to life. Their thoughts could be summed up as a math equation: We > Me. When "me" overrode "we," turmoil and strife characterized their relationships. When "we" trumped the "me," a buffer of unity was created that provided acceptance, cooperation, and romance.

One of the first automobiles Pam and I (Bill) owned desperately needed new shock absorbers. Every little bump was magnified as our heads hit the car ceiling above us. All it took was a new set of shocks to smooth out our ride. This is the way it is with our expectations in marriage. They work well in our single life, but they need to be changed when we switch to married life. Couples often get into a battle of wills to see whose expectations will win out. Marriage, however, isn't a competition in which the goal is to win. Marriage is a partnership in which you focus on mutual goals.

Progress is much easier to attain if you choose a common set of values upon which to base your expectations. This is why a commitment to Jesus makes it easier to succeed as a couple. He can be the shock absorber that smoothes out the ride as you build expectations based on agreed-upon godly principles. With a set of God-principled values, your expectations will move from self-centered to God-centered, which will make you more other-centered in your marriage. Before you know it, "we" will become greater than "me."

In describing a comprehensive relationship with God, Mark 12:30 reveals the four areas in which a love relationship operates: "Love the Lord your God with all your heart and with all your soul and with all your mind and with all your strength." As you learn to adjust your expectations in these four critical areas to the way God created us, you'll shift to a "we" over "me" mind-set and find marriage to be one of the greatest journeys on earth.

All Your Heart

Philippians 1:7 states, "It is right for me to feel this way about all of you, since I have you in my heart." This passage reveals one of the most important principles of relationships: When you carry each other affectionately in your hearts, you give each other the benefit of the doubt and readily serve one another. When your hearts get disconnected, you tend to evaluate each other based on your behaviors, which results in disappointment, because no one can behave well enough for long enough to meet anyone else's expectations.

This, of course, is easier to say than to do because the heart is sensitive, and we tend to protect our hearts from perceived pain. Although we all desire to be connected in a loving, committed relationship, we're afraid to trust at a level that would make it possible. There is, however, a code that will open your hearts to each other and foster trust. Just as your computer comes prepackaged with codes that run the software, God inscribed a code on the heart that unlocks love between a man and a woman.

The code needs to be discovered, because God created men with a different core need than women. This is why husbands and wives are given different directives in Ephesians 5:33: "Nevertheless, each individual among you also is to love his own wife even as himself, and the wife must see to it that she respects her husband" (NASB). There are, therefore, usernames and passwords that can give you access to the heart of the one you love.

Men, to gain access to your wife's heart, enter the following:

Username: Husband
Password: security

Women, to gain access to your husband's heart, enter the following:

Username: Wife
Password: success

Pam and I (Bill) have to admit that we were almost totally unaware of the marriage code[1] when we first got married. Pam was so easy to be around when we were dating that I thought she would be the easiest person to live with that I had ever met. She was full of energy, laughed every day, and had a simple dedication to helping others grow and learn more about Jesus. I would never have guessed that insecurity could totally interrupt her day and challenge my confidence in our relationship.

Bill was so calm and flexible with changes in life and so dedicated to Jesus that I (Pam) figured it would be simple to live with him. I honestly believed he would adjust to any emotional swings in my life, would roll with any challenges that presented themselves, and would remain steady during any stressors we faced. I never would have guessed that his need to succeed could make him stubborn and distant.

The Heart of a Woman

For the majority of women, security is their most vibrant and common need. I (Pam) agree! The need to feel secure is the need women feel most often, and it determines the quality of everything in our lives. Security is often difficult for men to understand because it's all consuming in our lives, and it can change faces quickly. Our greatest desire as women is to connect with our husbands emotionally, socially, recreationally, spiritually, and financially. Security in a woman's life includes the following:

- Feeling physically safe
- Having enough money to meet the needs of her family
- Being valued by the people she loves most
- Having opportunities to express herself and her convictions
- Having opportunities to be productive
- Having a place to call home
- Having time to take care of herself
- Being pampered every once in a while

- Knowing that her husband cares about the things that are important to her
- Enjoying the freedom to be who she is today

Without a doubt, the last statement—enjoying the freedom to be who she is today—is at the heart of what it means to be secure. As women, our lives are constantly changing. Typically this begins with the "gift" of menstruation. This lovely part of our lives guarantees that our emotions, our bodies, and our outlook on life are in constant motion. Some days we feel great about ourselves and are ready to face any challenge. On other days we feel bloated and ugly and worthless. Still other days find us sad, anxious, and overreactive. And these days come and go every month! (Yes, we're talking about PMS. You know you might have PMS if you throw chocolate chips into your omelet or you trade in *Glamour* magazine for *Guns and Ammo*!)

In our hearts, we women long to have our husbands accept and love us through good and bad days. The marriage code goes active when a man learns to enter *security* as the password for his wife. He does this when he makes it his ambition to meet his wife's security need first in all things. Any time she gets the message from him, "You are safe with me, and it's all right to be who you are right now," her heart is drawn toward him, and she relaxes in the relationship.

I (Bill) became aware of this security need on our honeymoon, when we were introduced to the guilt-free thrills of physical intimacy between a husband and wife. We went to dinner and then enjoyed what we call "red-hot monogamy." Pam was excited and "wound up" and wanted to talk. It was the last night of our honeymoon, so she wanted to make it last as long as possible. Into the wee hours of the night, I heard about every boyfriend she had ever had in her entire life! She told me she wanted to share every detail of her life. She wanted me to know *everything*. As a young, idealistic husband, I concurred and thought it would actually be possible to listen to Pam with the same level of attention with which she was sharing herself.

I held my own for the first hour, but exhaustion took over, and in the middle of a sentence, I started to doze off as my new wife was baring her soul. I awakened to a "heartquake" that registered 3.5 on our bed.

Pam was convulsively sobbing, murmuring, "I thought you loved me. How could you fall asleep on me? Am I really that boring?"

I sat up in bed, looked her in the eyes, and said, "I really do love you. I'm so sorry for falling asleep. Go ahead and finish."

"Okay," she said with a glint in her eye. "I want to tell you about the country-western songs I listened to growing up." Then she started singing!

I'd been had. Here I was trying to address Pam's stated concern, and I totally missed the real issue. The concern that was truly on her heart was this: "Bill, am I more important to you than your sleep? Are you willing to be tired to show me that I have first place in your heart?"

I've since learned that all interactions with Pam go better if I meet her need for security first.

The Heart of a Man

The belief that one can succeed is the need most men feel, and it determines the quality of everything in our lives. A man's approach to success is about spending his time, money, and energy on the areas of life he knows he's good at. Men are highly motivated to focus on these areas. At the same time, we are intensely *disinterested* in the areas of life we don't think we're good at. Success in a man's life, therefore, includes the following:

- Discovering what he does well and what he doesn't do well
- Spending time doing what he does well because it's an emotional need
- Evaluating his life based on what he does well

- Making a fierce commitment to doing what he does well

- Hoping for relationships that work

- Avoiding areas of life that don't work

- Feeling pressure when he has to work on areas of life in which he lacks confidence

- Desiring to make relationships as simple as possible to ensure success

- Becoming confused when things aren't working the way he thinks they should

The most comprehensive statement that describes a man's need for success is that he will make a "fierce commitment to doing what he does well."

The password that will give a wife access to her husband's heart is *success*. She does this when she makes it her ambition to create an environment where her husband can succeed with her. Any time he gets the message from her, "I love the way you live, and I love the way you love me," his heart is drawn toward her, and he gains confidence in the relationship. A man will conclude the relationship is working when he sees the following proof:

- Spending time with his wife lowers the stress level in his life.

- He recognizes when they are making decisions and sticking to them.

- There is laughter when he spends time with his wife.

- He has time to work on his commitments.

- His wife continues to flirt with him.

- His efforts to build the relationship are greeted with compliments.

I (Pam) remember when I first became aware of what is often called the male ego. We were at a gathering of friends where we were dancing romantically. Bill dipped me in a final crescendo, except he dropped me on the ground and started backing away. I got up and asked him what happened. He whispered, "I just ripped my pants."

Well, I thought it was funny, so I turned him around and shouted out to everyone else in the room, "Look, Bill just ripped his pants!" I laughed. Everyone else in the room laughed. Bill, however, did something very different from laughing. He grew angry and silent.

I learned that night that it isn't a very good idea to point out the flaws in my man. It's much better to help him look and feel successful.

When our core needs are met as men and women, an almost magical dynamic occurs in our relationships. We give each other grace, forgive easily, trust each other's perspective, and find value in our differences.

All Your Soul

The soul is a combination of factors that make you the unique individuals you are. It includes your physical, emotional, and motivational makeup. The starting point for loving with all your soul is your DNA, or the way God wired you as a male and a female. Estrogen and testosterone have a profound impact on how we process information and interact with the people we love. Gender goes back to the beginning of humanity: "In the image of God he created him; male and female he created them" (Genesis 1:27). It was in God's plan to make us different from each other from the moment He imagined us. You can make these God-given differences work in your relationship if you build an appreciation for the uniqueness you bring to your love. Pam and I (Bill) like to describe the basic differences in the following way.[2]

Men Are like Waffles

Men process life in boxes. If you look at the top of a waffle, you see a collection of boxes separated by walls that make convenient holding places. That's typically how a man processes life. His thinking is divided up into boxes that have room for one issue and one issue only. The first issue of life goes in the first box, the second goes in the second box, and so on. The typical man then spends time in one box at a time and one box only. When a man is at work, he is at work. When he is in the garage tinkering around, he is in the garage tinkering. When he is watching TV, he is simply watching TV. That's why he looks like he's in a trance and can ignore everything else going on around him. Social scientists call this *compartmentalizing*—that is, putting life and responsibilities into different compartments.

A man will strategically organize his life in boxes and then spend most of his time in the boxes *he can succeed in*. This is such a strong motivation that he will seek out the boxes that "work" and will ignore boxes that confuse him or make him feel like a failure. The bottom line is this: *Men feel best about themselves when they are solving problems.* They, therefore, spend most of their time doing what they're best at, while they attempt to ignore the things they are deficient at.

Women Are like Spaghetti

In contrast to the waffle-like approach of men, women process life more like a plate of spaghetti. If you look at a plate of spaghetti, you notice that there are individual noodles that all touch one another. If you attempted to follow one noodle around the plate, you would intersect a lot of other noodles, and you might even switch to another noodle seamlessly. That's how women face life. Every thought and issue is connected to every other thought and issue in some way. Life is much more of a process for women than it is for men.

This is why a woman is typically better at multitasking than a man. She can talk on the phone, prepare a meal, make a shopping list, work on planning for tomorrow's business meeting, give instructions to her children as they're going out to play, and close the door with her foot without skipping a beat. Since all her thoughts, emotions, and convictions are connected, she's able to process more information and keep track of more activities.

As a result, most women are in pursuit of connecting life together. They solve problems but from a much different perspective than men. Women consistently sense the need to talk things through. In conversation, they can link together the logical, emotional, relational, and spiritual aspects of an issue. The links come to women naturally so that conversations are effortless for them.

A husband is better able to meet his wife's need to make connections if he turns off that fix-it mechanism in his brain, packs up his bags, and learns to go on listening journeys with his wife. Since a woman builds trust by connecting her life to the lives of those she loves, a husband will find her easier to live with and easier to love if he listens to her with curiosity.

A wife is more likely to enhance her husband's interest if she "CliffsNotes" conversations and stays in the one box he is hoping to problem-solve in. When men bring up a subject to talk about, women immediately recognize all the issues that relate to that subject. It's as if a woman can see every box that is touching the box a man has opened. If she ventures into all those other boxes, he gets overwhelmed. When he has one box open, there is only one problem to solve. If he has two boxes open, there are two issues to solve. With three boxes open, there are three problems to solve, and so on. Every man has a limit to how many issues or boxes can be open at once. But if a wife will stay focused on one topic and resist the urge to open up all the surrounding boxes, she will buy her man the emotional time he needs to work his way down through the layers of the box, and eventually he will share his precious emotions with her.

All Your Mind

The way you and your fiancé(e) think about each other will affect the way you feel about each other. Think about the characteristics you love in the person you're getting ready to marry. You may be fascinated with these traits and have come to rely on them to bring joy and stability. It may be hard to imagine that these traits could ever become a source of deep frustration, but this is exactly what happens to most married couples. The traits you love most about your spouse-to-be have a darker side to them that can irritate you. Since these are powerful traits, the irritation can be just as deep as the joy you're experiencing now.

For example:

- The strong convictions your future spouse has about doing the right thing give you confidence that you can trust her. But they may become an irritation when she turns them on you and your behavior.

- The concern he demonstrates for your emotions and your well-being can become threatening when you see him showing the same concern for others.

- The strong masculinity of your groom that makes you feel safe and secure may also make you feel lonely and isolated when he doesn't talk with you the way you wish he would.

Whatever you appreciate most about your future spouse will likely be the point of highest irritation in your marriage unless you train your mind to stay focused on the positive.

I (Pam) was attracted to Bill because he's a great listener, but this means he tunes in to people and never checks his watch. (This makes him run late; thus the irritation!) I (Bill) was attracted to Pam because she is spontaneous and up for an adventure. However, her "spontaneity" leaks into all areas of our life together, including the checkbook. (So her tendency to seize a great opportunity can become my irritation!)

It can be so easy to focus on the irritations and forget why we first fell in love! We have to choose to focus on the reason we fell in love with our partner. This is part of what the Bible means when it says that "we take captive every thought to make it obedient to Christ" (2 Corinthians 10:5). If you dwell on the irritations, your love for each other will erode, and your hearts will drift apart. If, however, you're willing to zero in on the qualities you find attractive in your future spouse, you'll build a love that will grow year after year.

Learning to dwell on the best in your future spouse begins with a simple three-step process:

1. When I'm irritated, I will ask, "What is the opposite of this irritation? What did I fall in love with?"
2. I will either tell myself, "You love that!" or I will choose to verbalize a compliment instead of expressing criticism.
3. I will stay focused on the positive side, not the negative side, of that trait until I "feel" in love with my partner again.

All Your Strength

Another word for strength in the Bible is *power*. The power and strength of your love for each other will be drained if you aren't aware of the differences in how men and women manage conflict.

Men tend to bury issues and escape to their favorite recharger boxes. Women tend to bring up issues and want to talk things out. Women can easily take a man's silence or withdrawal as apathy or manipulation. In reality, he may be "emotionally flooded," as if he is drowning in a sea of turbulent emotions. If you continue to verbalize issues and problems when you notice he has shut off, it can feel like nagging to the man who loves you. At the same time, men can easily interpret a woman's attempts to bring up issues as controlling and manipulative behavior, against which he has no options. If this negative cycle continues, a couple will drift apart, like boxers sent to the corners of a fighter's ring.

It doesn't need to be this way. Conflict exists because of the powerful emotions in your relationship. For instance, studies show that when a marriage is in crisis, men actually feel it at a deeper emotional level than women, even though they may not verbalize it. At the same time, God gave women a deep-seated desire to make things better for the people they love. When God made the plants, trees, sun, moon, and so forth, the Bible says it was "good" (Genesis 1:21). After woman was created, God saw that it was "*very* good!" (verse 31, emphasis added). A woman's tenacious desire to make things better may feel like nagging to a man, when in reality, it's a powerful resource for improving a couple's life and love.

The power of your emotional reactions can be directed by mutual decisions. As we mentioned earlier, we interviewed couples who had been married more than twenty years for our book *The 10 Best Decisions a Couple Can Make*. The purpose of our research was to discover the creative ways these couples handled opposing expectations and conflict in their marriages. Our favorite idea came from two firstborns (who naturally both thought they were right). Their home was decorated with numerous bowls of bite-size candy bars. We had to ask, "What's up with the candy bars?"

It seems that as newlyweds, they tended to get worked up and argue when their expectations collided. Instead of continuing to say things they would later regret, they decided to stop and eat a candy bar. The time it took to eat one of their chocolate snacks was just the right amount of time to calm their emotions. Over the years, if they sensed emotions rising, either could ask, "Want a candy bar?"

Every decision you make about how you communicate, how you manage expectations, and how you approach conflict will increase the power of your love and draw you closer together as a couple.

BILL FARREL has been influencing lives for over twenty-five years as a senior pastor, youth pastor, radio talk show host, community leader, and sought-after conference speaker. He and his wife, **PAM**, have written more than thirty books, including *Men Are like Waffles—Women Are like Spaghetti* and *Red-Hot Monogamy*. Bill and Pam are cofounders and codirectors of Love-Wise, an organization to help people connect love and wisdom and bring practical insights to their personal relationships. Bill and Pam have been married more than thirty years and have raised three young men who love Jesus.

Ready to Talk

1. What expectations about marriage might the following people have had from their growing-up years? Why?

   • Cain and Abel

   • Bart and Lisa from *The Simpsons*

   • The children of Brad Pitt and Angelina Jolie

   • The children on *Modern Family*

   • The children of Billy and Ruth Graham

   • Your spouse-to-be

2. If you haven't already done it, complete the his-and-hers charts of "potential expectations" in this chapter and compare your results. Was it hard to be honest about your expectations of marriage? Did you tone them down to appear more realistic? Do you still harbor higher hopes in some areas? What might it take for you to feel safe enough to admit what you're feeling and work together on a "we" mind-set?

3. How have your expectations about marriage changed as a result of reading this chapter? Which of the following comes closest to your answer?

   • "I see now that I was expecting too much."

   • "I'm thinking of breaking off the engagement."

   • "I feel better prepared."

   • "I think we have more discussing to do."

- "I'm glad to know there are ways to deal with potential disappointment."
- Other _____

Ready to Try

Pack a lunch and take a hike together! If you live in an area without good walking trails, try driving to a local park. Over lunch, talk about your hopes, dreams, and expectations for a family. Do you both want children? If not, is that a deal breaker? If you both want children, when would you prefer to start a family? Right away? In a few years? Just for fun, do you have any favorite girl or boy names? Expectations about a future family are some of the most significant hopes and dreams a newly married couple has. Although we cannot predict the future, and things can change as marriage progresses, it's good to be thinking through these things now.

CHAPTER 10

FIGHT OUR WAY TO A BETTER MARRIAGE

Dr. Greg Smalley and Erin Smalley

It is sometimes essential for a husband and a wife to quarrel—they get to know each other better.

—GOETHE, CIRCA LATE 1700S

YOUR MARRIAGE NEEDS CONFLICT.

Now before you call us crazy and toss the book aside, give us an opportunity to prove one of the greatest truths that we've learned after twenty-three years of marriage and thousands of hours working with couples: Healthy conflict can be the doorway to the deepest levels of intimacy and connection in your relationship.

We know this sounds counterintuitive. Conflict and intimacy together seem paradoxical or even absurd. Maybe you grew up in a home where your parents fought all the time and never really got along. Perhaps they avoided conflict altogether and existed like two ships silently passing in the night or as "roommates." Many parents divorce claiming "irreconcilable differences" because they can't successfully navigate their differences—to make their differences work *for* them instead of *against* them. Some of you watched your parents go behind closed doors to argue, and you don't have the foggiest idea how they worked through their problems. But none of this matters now.

No matter how your parents handled (or didn't handle) conflict, you can create a new legacy for *your* family. You and your future spouse have the opportunity to use conflict—those times when you're hurt, annoyed, frustrated, wounded, confused, angry, and discouraged with each other—to actually grow closer together. This isn't fancy double-talk or a sales pitch. We believe that next to your relationship with the Lord, this is one of the most important aspects of preparing for a satisfying, lifelong marriage.

It's imperative that you learn how to face your differences as a couple and work through disagreements and hurt feelings. But this will require a different mind-set. Refuse to subscribe to the prevailing wisdom in our culture that says a lack of conflict is a sign of a healthy marriage. That's insane! It's not possible to take a man and a woman whom God created so wonderfully different and expect that they'll never disagree. That's ridiculous. You *will* argue, quarrel, wrangle, bicker, and clash from time to time. As author Max Lucado put it, "Conflict is inevitable, but combat is optional."[1]

In other words, you will disagree (accept this fact), but what is optional is how you manage those moments when you don't see eye to eye or you hurt each other. You can choose to manage your conflict in either healthy or unhealthy ways. Allow this truth to penetrate deep within your mind and heart: Conflict is good; combat is bad.

Facing your differences and problems is a healthy aspect of a strong marriage. We believe that's why Jesus strongly encouraged us in Matthew 5:23–24 to deal with relationship problems so that our hearts can be right:

> If you are offering your gift at the altar and there remember
> that your brother has something against you, leave your gift
> there in front of the altar. First go and be reconciled to your
> brother; then come and offer your gift.

On the other hand, yelling, withdrawing, belittling, criticizing, avoiding, and escalating (combat) will ultimately ruin your marriage. As a matter of fact, some of the best marriage researchers on the planet can predict with a high degree of certainty whether a marriage will succeed or fail simply based on how a couple deals with conflict. If they argue without ever resolving their issues or consistently avoid conflict altogether, their marriage is at risk for divorce.[2] The apostle Paul recognized this same truth when he wrote, "If you keep on biting and devouring each other, watch out or you will be destroyed by each other" (Galatians 5:15). It's not how many arguments you have with your future spouse; it's how you manage them that makes all the difference.

Proverbs 18:19 tells us, "An offended friend is harder to win back than a fortified city. Arguments separate friends like a gate locked with bars" (NLT). The bottom line is, your marriage will not last if you're unable or unwilling to work through your issues.

By the way, we're not saying that you should "like" conflict or intentionally create it. This is why the apostle Paul wrote, "Shall we go on sinning so that grace may increase?" (Romans 6:1). Obviously we shouldn't go looking for a fight or intentionally push each other's buttons. You're never going to like conflict in your relationship. We all hate to feel disconnected, hurt, frustrated, and shut down with each other. The only one who ever wins if you stay in disharmony is the Evil One. He wants to "steal and kill and destroy" your marriage (John 10:10).

So hear us correctly. We're not suggesting that you should strive to enjoy conflict. Instead, use those moments of disagreement to strengthen your marriage. We really like how marriage expert Dr. John Gottman puts it:

> If there is one lesson I have learned from my years of research it is that *a lasting marriage results from a couple's ability to resolve the conflicts that are inevitable in any relationship*. Many couples tend to equate a low level of conflict with happiness and

believe the claim "we never fight" is a sign of marital health. But I believe we grow in our relationships by reconciling our differences. That's how we become more loving people and truly experience the fruits of marriage.[3]

Otherwise, poorly managed conflict is always buried alive, and it often festers until it becomes a much bigger problem. In the end, buried issues end up exploding like a massive volcano, leaving your spouse in its destructive wake.

So don't put your upcoming marriage at risk; instead, learn how to successfully manage those times when you experience conflict. Make a decision today that you will keep short accounts with each other. Keeping short accounts isn't about keeping score, sweeping your problems under the rug so that they mount up, or arguing in unhealthy ways. Instead, it means that you work through conflict as quickly as possible and in healthy ways—the opposite of combat. The goal is never to avoid your problems and keep peace at any price.

As one author wrote, "Peace . . . is not just the absence of war. It's the opposite of war."[4] Make your goal to quickly repair your relationship. We really like how author Sabrina Beasley McDonald describes it:

> Keep short accounts and extend forgiveness regularly. Nothing will ruin a desire to be with your spouse faster than resentment and bitterness. In return, it also ruins your spouse's desire to be with you. Fights are going to happen in marriage; there's no way around it. But you can choose to handle these conflicts in the right way and build up your marriage instead of tearing it down.[5]

Now let's turn our attention to the difference between unhealthy conflict and healthy conflict.

Why Do We Fight?

We hope you're hearing us say that conflict in a marriage is inevitable, and it can actually be a really *good* thing for your marriage if you manage it in healthy ways. But unfortunately, the old adage "Easier said than done" aptly applies when talking about conflict. In other words, it's one thing to say that conflict can benefit our marriages—in theory that makes sense. However, it's quite another thing to go from a disagreement to connection. Make no mistake; it's hard to put into practice healthy conflict principles. We were reminded of this reality not too long ago when we were doing a marriage seminar in Tokyo, Japan.

Before the start of the seminar, Erin, our seventeen-year-old daughter, Murphy, and I (Greg) took a few days to sightsee around Tokyo. As the travel planner, I bought a great book on what to do in Tokyo. One of the most popular tourist destinations turned out to be a beautiful park called Meiji Shrine. It's located in a dense forest that covers about 175 acres. There are several ponds, old bridges, and paths that zigzag throughout the park. In preparation for our day trip, I thoroughly researched how to walk there from our hotel, which paths to take in the park for the best sightseeing spots, and a variety of other important information. I had this all worked out and planned perfectly.

However, it took us a long time to walk to the park because I got us lost a few times, so by the time we arrived at the entrance gate, we were pretty exhausted. Once we got into the park, the path immediately forked. I had planned on us taking the long way through so we could see this one particular bridge overlooking a gorgeous pond. But when we arrived at the fork, Erin and Murphy wanted to take the shortest route because they were already worn out from all the walking we'd done just to get to the park.

So instead of following me as I turned down the path I had mapped out, Erin and Murphy started walking the other way.

"You're going the wrong way," I cautioned.

"We're tired," they said in unison, "and this looks like the shortest route."

"But this way is the more picturesque way, and I want to take a family picture by the bridge and pond."

"But we're exhausted," Erin responded.

"Fine," I snapped, "let's go *your* way." And I started walking in their direction—the opposite way.

I think Erin and Murphy were stunned by my reaction. I really don't think they realized how much I wanted to go the other way. So once they realized how important the "scenic" route was, they started walking in that direction—my planned-out route. However, I was already huffing and puffing down the shorter path, not even looking back because I was frustrated with both of them.

I remember evenutally looking back at my wife and daughter thinking they'd turn around and follow me. I'm sure they thought the same thing about me: *Surely he won't leave us and storm off mad.*

Sadly, my wife and daughter greatly underestimated my stubbornness! Once I realized that they weren't going to follow me, I really got upset and wanted to teach them a lesson. Since I had carefully studied the map, I knew that the two paths would eventually merge back together farther into the park. So I figured that I could angrily march my way for a while, and then we'd meet up and the girls could apologize. Remember, I still thought I was the one who'd been wronged!

My revised plan seemed perfect, until the girls didn't show up at the spot where the trails merged back together. I waited and waited until I realized something awful: *My wife and daughter are lost . . . in a foreign country . . . without any money or clue where they are.* I quickly surmised that I was in big trouble!

So before I explain how this conflict could possibly have a happy ending that resulted in a deeper level of connection and intimacy with my wife, I want to explain an extremely important point about conflict. As in our story, when you argue, it's never really about whatever the issue or topic is that you're fighting about (such as money, household chores, children, sex, work, leisure time, in-laws, which walking path to take, etc.). These topics appear to be what's driving the conflict, but it's an illusion.

What is really happening during an argument is that your "button" gets pushed. I'm sure you've heard the expression, "He just pushed my button" or "She is totally pushing my buttons." When you argue, picture that big Easy button from Staples (the office-product retailer) getting pushed. We all have "easy buttons" (or "hot buttons" as they're sometimes called) throughout our bodies. One author describes them this way:

> Everyone has "hot buttons." They're your tender spots, the places where you're most sensitive, the points where you get irritated, or hurt, or angry, and have to respond. . . .
>
> Hot buttons are . . . triggered by specific events or circumstances. . . . When triggered they typically take over and direct your behavior. They also carry a strong emotional charge when they're activated, so that behavior is going to be emotional and extreme. There's nothing rational or considered about a response that comes from a hot button. It's pure emotion. . . .
>
> You'll know you were acting under the influence of a hot button when you regret what you did or said the moment you cool off. The words just popped out; you turned away and slammed the door behind you. You didn't think about it until afterwards. At the time, it was simply what you had to do. *That* was a hot button.[6]

Buttons represent sensitive emotions that are easily triggered. We're not talking about simple feelings like anger, annoyance, worry, sadness, jealousy, boredom, or tiredness. Instead, buttons are intense feelings that are often beyond our awareness. For example, a button is a deep, sensitive emotion that can cause you to feel . . .

Unloved	Inadequate
Disrespected	Worthless
Rejected	Not good enough
Failed	Invalidated
Controlled	Unimportant
Abandoned	Misunderstood

Therefore, beyond the fact that we have a sin nature and our default setting as humans is selfishness, a more accurate way to explain what happens when we get hurt or frustrated or argue is that our "emotional buttons" get pushed. Remember, it's not the day-to-day squabbles over money, chores, in-laws, or directions that drive conflict. The real issue is our sensitive emotions that get triggered and all stirred up. This is what's so misleading about most arguments. We get so focused on the topic (e.g., money) that we miss the underlying root cause of conflict: the button that got pushed (e.g., feeling controlled).

Once a button is pushed, our hearts close instantly. This is one of the most important parts of understanding conflict. Think of those little roly-poly bugs. You know the ones we're talking about? Those little grayish armadillo-like bugs that roll up into a small ball when they're touched. Our hearts act just like those roly-poly bugs. When we feel emotionally "flicked," our hearts shut down and roll up into a tight ball. Just as you can't force open a roly-poly bug without killing it, once your fiancé(e)'s heart closes, you can't pry it open either. Over time, if a couple continues to practice unhealthy conflict, a closed heart will eventually harden. This is how unresolved or unhealthy conflict can kill a marriage.

The conflict goes from being an internal storm to a full-blown hurricane after our buttons have been pushed and our hearts close. We instantly go into reaction mode. This is never good! When we're all stirred up internally (buttons pushed) and our hearts are shut down, we're capable of saying or doing any number of things (reactions). Every reaction will be either a "fight" or a "flight."

Fighters directly engage the other person in order to persuade him or her in some way. They don't back down or remain silent; they go toe to toe or pursue their spouse around the house. They might get angry, use calm logic, criticize, get sarcastic, yell, throw a tantrum, debate their position, make belittling comments, defend themselves, invalidate their spouse's feelings, try to fix the problem, find a solution, complain, and so on. It's as if the Fighter ends up thinking, *Since we aren't going to connect relationally, I might as well win the argument.* Fighters jump right into conflict and advocate for their own opinion, viewpoint, or perspective. Thus, Fighters spend the majority of their time in persuasion mode, defending their point of view. The problem with this reaction style is that it always sends the same message: *I'm not safe for any meaningful interaction with you.*

On the other hand, Flighters emotionally disconnect. We "flight" when we avoid conflict or withdraw from difficult conversations. The key trait of a Flighter is a reluctance to get into a disagreement (avoidance) or to stay with an important conversation (withdrawal). Flighters don't want to rock the boat, so they fly below the radar or stay out of the fray.

Withdrawal can be as obvious as walking out of the room or as subtle as staying put but logging off emotionally. A Flighter may withdraw by becoming silent or may quickly agree to a solution just to end the discussion with no intention of ever returning to the conversation. It's not as if they don't talk or interact; instead, they avoid sensitive issues, work hard to minimize conflict, and believe there is little to gain from getting upset. Their motto is "Relax! Problems have a way of working themselves out." In avoidance mode, Flighters may use the phrase *agree to disagree* time and time again—which means they avoid conversations they think will end in conflict. A person who chooses to "flight" and disengage always sends the same message: *I'm disconnecting from any meaningful interaction with you.*

To recap, unhealthy conflict happens when your buttons get pushed, your heart closes, and you go into reaction mode (fight or flight). Do you see why this doesn't help a marriage thrive, and why this can kill a marriage? Nothing good will ever come from this unhealthy cycle because it's the exact opposite of love. Whereas love is patient, kind, content, humble, polite, selfless, calm, grateful, and so on, closed-heartedness generates these negative reactions that drive you both apart.

Sadly, when your heart is closed, God's love is no longer flowing between you and your future spouse. And this is exactly where Satan wants you—loveless, disconnected, and isolated. This is why we're warned in 1 Peter 5:8, "Be self-controlled and alert. Your enemy the devil prowls around like a roaring lion looking for someone to devour." Satan wants to devour you and your marriage. And all he needs is a small foothold that instantly appears when you argue. Ephesians 4:26–27 says, "In your anger do not sin: Do not let the sun go down while you are still angry, and *do not give the devil a foothold*" (emphasis added). So instead of staying in reaction mode when you experience conflict with your spouse-to-be, how can you use the disagreement to drive you to the deepest levels of intimacy and connection? We promise it's possible!

Managing Conflict in Healthy Ways

To break out of an unhealthy cycle of conflict, you must first understand a commonly held myth about working through an argument. In our culture, the most common advice for a married couple who is in the middle of a conflict goes something like this: You need to sit down and calmly talk through the issue. It isn't that Erin and I (Greg) don't agree with the advice. Ultimately, we do need to resolve our conflicts, and that takes communication. The problem we have with the advice is the *when*. At what point should a couple begin to talk through the problem?

To answer this question, think about the last time you were hurt or frustrated with your fiancé(e)—a time when your buttons were pushed, your heart was closed, and you were in reaction mode (fight or flight). Now, when you were in that state, when was the last time you were genuinely able to have a good, productive, Christlike conversation with your fiancé(e)? By the way, most people answer with a resounding "Never!"

Honestly, most people don't end up having a healthy discussion, because it's almost physically impossible. They're too stirred up emotionally, their hearts are closed, and they're reacting. When you're in this state of mind, reflect on what's going on physiologically in your body—your heart races, your blood pressure rises, and rational thoughts are no longer possible. This is why Erin and I think the worst advice we could give a couple in conflict is to encourage them to first work out the problem together. When your buttons have been pushed, when your heart is closed, and you're in reaction mode, the unhealthiest first step is to attempt to work out the problem relationally—between you two.

Instead, the best first step is found in Matthew 7:3–5:

Why do you look at the speck of sawdust in your brother's eye and pay no attention to the plank in your own eye? How can you say to your brother, "Let me take the speck out of your eye," when all the time there is a plank in your own eye? You hypocrite, first take the plank out of your own eye, and then you will see clearly to remove the speck from your brother's eye.

This is amazing advice from Jesus Himself, and it's the perfect first step to breaking out of unhealthy conflict. Here, Christ is saying that before you focus on your fiancé(e) and his or her speck, you need to *first* get the log out of your own eye. In other words, before you try to have a conversation together and talk through the conflict, first deal with you. Therefore, we say that the best thing you can do after your buttons have been pushed is to get *your* heart back open so that instead of reacting, you can *respond* to your fiancé(e). Responding is the opposite of reacting. Responding is Christlike because the focus is on loving, caring, listening, understanding, validating, and empathizing. This is why King Solomon wrote, "A wise man's heart guides his mouth" (Proverbs 16:23). In other words, an open heart will guide a healthy conversation. So how do you get your heart to open up again? Let's go back to Tokyo and to the Meiji Shrine.

I (Greg) ended up searching for Erin and Murphy for about thirty minutes, to no avail. The longer I looked, the more my worry and frustration mounted.

Finally, I found my wife and daughter as they exited the temple shrine. By the way, the shrine tour was the whole reason we had walked there in the first place—and they did it without me.

I was fuming!

"Where were you guys?" I shouted.

"Once you left us," Erin sarcastically answered, "we just kept on walking. We assumed that you would eventually show up and apologize."

"Apologize!" I reacted, "*Me*? You're the ones who left me. We were supposed to do the tour together. Besides, I'm the only one who knows how to get home!"

At this point Erin and I will spare you the rest of the conversation. We're quite certain you can imagine how our conflict quickly spiraled downward. However, we hope you see how pointless it is to attempt to work out a conflict as a couple *before* your hearts are open.

As we walked back toward our hotel in complete silence, we eventually followed Christ's directive in Matthew 7, and we each stopped focusing on what the other person did or didn't do—we focused on the log in our own eyes.

Over the years, we have found three simple steps that help us get our hearts open.

1. *Call a time-out.* Instead of continuing to argue and debate the situation, hit the pause button. In other words, get away from each other for a brief amount of time in order to de-escalate your stirred-up emotions. This is exactly what King Solomon wrote about: "A fool gives full vent to his anger, but a wise man keeps himself under control" (Proverbs 29:11). Instead of continuing to react (fight or flight), you want to keep yourself under control and calm down.

Some of the things that can help defuse your pushed buttons include taking some deep breaths of air, exercising, taking a walk, cleaning the house, listening to music, praying, journaling your feelings, and so on. The key is to create some space from each other and do something that will calm you down. As you create some space, make sure to let the other person know that you're taking a time-out to get your heart back open and that you'll be back later to finish the discussion. This is not withdrawing. Withdrawal is an extremely deadly flight reaction. Calling a time-out insinuates that you just need a short break before you continue the conversation. Research suggests that you might need about twenty minutes to calm down when your buttons have been pushed. Erin and I have made it a rule that the person who calls the time-out should also be the one to initiate getting back together to talk about the conflict—but only when both hearts are open.

2. *Identify your emotions.* This next step is an important shift in what you're thinking about. When we're hurt and frustrated, our thoughts are racing with what the other person did or didn't do. This is called "stewing." We can't stop stewing about how much we were wronged or mistreated. If we continue to think about "them" and replay the conflict over and over in our minds, we'll stay stirred up. Remember Matthew 7:3: "Why do you look at the speck of sawdust in your brother's eye and pay no attention to the plank in your own eye?" If you're going to get your heart open, you have to shift from thinking about your fiancé(e) to focusing on yourself. The way to make this important shift is to do what King David suggested: "In your anger do not sin; when you are on your beds, search your hearts and be silent" (Psalm 4:4).

While you're in your time-out, start focusing on your emotions—the voice of your heart. Ask yourself, "What button just got pushed?" You want to name the button (identify the emotion). This will continue to calm you down and open your heart. You might be thinking, *Whatever, Dr. Smalley!* However, there is actual research from UCLA that shows by simply naming what you're feeling, your brain activity will shift from the amygdala—your fight-or-flight center—to a much more rational part of the brain—the prefrontal cortex.[7] This simple act not only begins to impact the state of your closed heart, but it impacts what is going on in your body physiologically. The goal is to defuse your buttons, and identifying what you're feeling allows this to happen!

After the Meiji Shrine incident, as I (Greg) walked in silence behind my wife and daughter toward the hotel (in my self-imposed time-out), I started trying to put a name to what I was feeling, identifying the buttons that had been pushed. I quickly realized that I felt disrespected and unappreciated. It wasn't that Erin or Murphy were trying to disrespect me or not appreciate me, but this was how I interpreted their behavior. I had put a lot of time into researching the attractions at the park. It was very stressful to be the one in charge of planning our trip. To me, it felt like they weren't respecting or appreciating how much work I'd put into figuring out all of the details.

Erin and I always tell people to treat their feelings as information. Emotions are neither right nor wrong, good nor bad; they're just really helpful pieces of information. When a warning light goes off on your car's dashboard, it's a good idea to figure out what it means. In the same way, God created your emotions to function just like your car's warning lights. When you're feeling something or a button has been pushed, it's a source of great information. The amazing part is how simply putting a name to your emotions can calm you down.

Armed with some great information about your emotions, now you're ready for the final step.

3. *Discover the truth.* One of the biggest mistakes people make with their emotions is to either ignore them or act upon them. Remember, emotions represent nothing more than information. But we should never mindlessly act on any information without evaluating it first. The best way to evaluate your emotions or feelings (the buttons) is to take that information to the Lord. You're searching for His truth about you and your fiancé(e). As humans, we aren't the source of truth. The Scriptures make it extremely clear that Christ is truth: "Jesus [said], 'I am the way and the truth and the life'" (John 14:6).

If you try to determine the validity of your emotions and thoughts about your future spouse, you're at risk of believing lies. Remember, we have an adversary. Satan is the "father of lies" (John 8:44), and he wants you to believe lies about your fiancé(e). He wanted me to see Erin as a disrespectful and unappreciative wife. But I don't want his lies; I want the truth. This is why the apostle Paul wrote, "Set your minds on things above, not on earthly things" (Colossians 3:2). I don't want to trust my own interpretations and perceptions of what my wife does; I want God's perspective, because ultimately, He is the source of truth.

When my heart is closed, my view becomes distorted. I lack God's insight, wisdom, and truth. The apostle Paul put it this way: "They are darkened in their understanding and separated from the life of God because of the ignorance that is in them due to the hardening of their hearts" (Ephesians 4:18). This final step is all about abandoning your own conclusions about your fiancé(e) and pursuing God's truth. The great news is that God is faithful. He only wants what's best for you and your fiancé(e), and He is committed to restoring unity. He wants us to follow the apostle Paul's plea: "I appeal to you, brothers, in the name of our Lord Jesus Christ, that all of you agree with one another, so that there may be no divisions among you and that you may be perfectly united in mind and thought" (1 Corinthians 1:10). God will give you a peace about your emotions that "surpasses all understanding" (Philippians 4:7, ESV) and will help you see the truth about your fiancé(e).

As I walked and prayed that day in Japan, God gave me such clarity about my wife and daughter. I quickly realized the truth: They were tired; they weren't trying to disrespect me. After realizing what was actually true and working to reopen our hearts, we were then ready to talk and restore our relationships. Do you see why it's so important to first get your heart open before you attempt to talk through a conflict with your fiancé(e)? To us, this is why King Solomon's advice—"A wise man's heart guides his mouth"—is so appropriate. We'll never have a loving, Christlike conversation until our hearts are open.

As the three of us walked toward the hotel, I gently asked if we could talk about what happened—"A gentle answer turns away wrath, but a harsh word stirs up anger" (Proverbs 15:1). I knew my heart was fairly open and that I had a pretty clear sense of God's truth. So I asked Erin and Murphy to help me understand what happened at the fork in the path—what it felt like when I walked off upset.

Erin talked about how she felt "misunderstood" and "misjudged." These were the buttons that got pushed for her. In the first place, she didn't understand how important going the long way was to me. She thought that I was judging her for something that she didn't even know about and that I didn't take time to understand how much her feet were hurting. Once she realized that I really wanted to go the scenic route, she had then wanted to please me. But when I walked off upset, it confused her and left her feeling misunderstood and judged.

Since my heart was now open, I was able to validate the feelings she expressed. If my heart had still been closed, I would again have begun to defend my actions. If this happens to you, start over with step one—a time-out. The important thing to realize is that it's worth it! Until your heart is open, the conversation will never go anywhere helpful or satisfying, because ultimately a closed heart will just do further damage to the one you love most!

Murphy felt controlled and abandoned when I walked away. She has such amazing strength and is independent just like Erin. I love this about my wife and daughter. But when I tried to get Murphy to go the longer way, she felt like I was trying to control her. And then when I stormed off, she felt that I abandoned her. Wow! I had no idea that Murphy would ever feel abandoned by me.

Once I listened, understood, validated, and empathized with Erin and Murphy, their hearts quickly softened toward me. Then they asked why I had left in the first place. It felt great to have them validate and appreciate the difficult job of being tour guide. The three of us stood hugging in the middle of the sidewalk in downtown Tokyo. I'm sure we received some strange looks and interesting comments: *Those crazy Americans!*

The Real Value of Conflict

Certainly the Smalley family didn't handle the beginning of the Tokyo argument very well. Some might even suggest that it was rather unhealthy. And yet when it has to do with conflict, what ultimately matters most is not how you begin but how you end. This is something that Erin and I (Greg) have learned over and over in our marriage: When conflict is managed in a healthy way, people feel safe to open their hearts and reveal who they really are. They feel open to display their uniqueness and opinions and share their concerns, hurts, fears, and frustrations. This is true intimacy. This is why conflict is a doorway to intimacy and why your marriage needs conflict.

Sadly, many couples don't see the value of conflict because of past negative experiences. Maybe they didn't see healthy conflict modeled growing up, or perhaps they haven't handled disagreements successfully over the course of their marriage. Thus, most couples fail to notice the potential benefits just waiting to be discovered.

Healthy conflict . . .

- brings problems into the light.
- provides an opportunity to break old, ineffective patterns.
- helps you better appreciate the differences between you and your future spouse.
- gives you a chance to care for and empathize with your fiancé(e).
- fosters humility, and "God gives His grace to the humble" (see James 4:6).
- gives you great insight into your own issues. [This especially applies to the ones you will bring with you into marriage. We all have them, and they repeatedly show up in our views, our reactions, and our perspectives of our life partners and situations.][8]

Isn't this a great list of what conflict can do if we learn to walk through it in a healthy way? It can "bestow on [us] a crown of beauty instead of ashes," as the prophet Isaiah put it (Isaiah 61:3). This is exactly why healthy conflict can be a doorway into intimacy and connection. The moment you get into an argument with your future spouse, there is an open door to discover something new about him or her, your relationship, and yourself. Instead of reverting to old patterns of reactions when our buttons get pushed, why can't our mind-set be, *I'm thankful for this disagreement because we have an opportunity to deepen our understanding and intimacy?*

We want to leave you with this observation about conflict from my (Greg's) father, Dr. Gary Smalley:

> Conflict is inevitable in relationships. It rears its head in even the healthiest, most deeply intimate of marriages. It is how you handle conflict that will determine how it affects your relationship, for better or for worse. Again, the most important aspect is not how much you love each other or how committed you are to your relationship or the strength of your faith; *optimum relationships depend on how adeptly you handle conflict.* Every instance of conflict represents two divergent paths: you can use it to either grow together or grow apart[9]. . . . Open the door. Walk through—and you learn more about the delights of marriage than you ever dreamed possible.[10]

Erin and I love that thought—we can use conflict to either grow closer together or further apart. And we hope you now see that tapping into the power of healthy conflict is a matter of opening the door, not closing it. Sometimes you may want to slam the conflict door shut or at least lock it when your future spouse has an issue with you. However, look at the growth opportunities you'd be missing out on.

You have a choice to make. You can use unproductive patterns of dealing with conflict or walk through the doorway of healthy conflict into the deepest levels of intimacy and connection to the place the apostle Paul envisioned for marriage:

> Let all bitterness and wrath and anger and clamor and slander
> be put away from you, along with all malice. Be kind to one
> another, tenderhearted, forgiving one another, as God in Christ
> forgave you.
>
> EPHESIANS 4:31–32, ESV

The choice is yours!

Ready to Talk

1. What's your definition of *fight*? By that definition, have you and your future mate had your first fight yet? If you'd read this chapter first, how might that fight have gone differently? If you haven't had a fight yet, what ideas from this chapter could you use to make sure your first major conflict is a constructive experience?

2. How do you typically handle conflict with your fiancé(e)? When your buttons get pushed within your relationship, are you more of a "fighter" or a "flighter"? What are some of the ways that you typically react (e.g., defend yourself, withdraw, stuff your feelings, emotionally log off, debate, become angry or saracastic, criticize, give the silent treatment)?

3. What conflict-triggering "buttons" do you have? From the following list, what are some of the more sensitive emotions that get triggered when you get into an argument or when you feel hurt, frustrated, upset, or fearful?

Unloved	Worthless
Disrespected	Judged
Rejected	Invisible
Failed	Invalidated
Controlled	Unimportant
Abandoned	Misunderstood
Inadequate	Powerless

Talk about where some of these buttons came from. It might be a specific experience growing up or just an emotion you've become sensitive to. Be careful not to joke about or minimize your fiancé(e)'s buttons.

Ready to Try

Together, watch a TV sitcom or drama featuring a couple who argues, bickers, or trades insults. (If you don't want to view a whole episode, look for YouTube clips.) Then talk about the episode. Does the fighting seem funny, painful, or sad? How do you feel when you see or hear a couple fighting? Do you have memories of parents yelling or giving each other the silent treatment? Do you avoid conflict as a result? Or do you think it's normal—or even to be encouraged? In what ways do you want your fighting to be like or unlike what you've observed at home or in entertainment?

CHAPTER 11

TEAMMATES: ENDING THE CHORE WARS BEFORE THEY START

Susan and Dale Mathis

DOESN'T IT FEEL GREAT to do something special for another person, just to bless him or her? There's something so gratifying about helping an elderly woman with her groceries or a small child tie his shoe, or sending a get-well card to someone who is sick, or taking a plate of cookies to a busy mom. It warms our hearts even as it blesses the other person. And it often means more than we realize. Each act of service is a tiny way for us to be like Jesus, and it's a beautiful thing.   LOVE LANGUAGE

According to God's plan, you are here on this earth to love and serve, so that's why you find joy in doing things for others. If that's the case, then your future role as a husband or wife should primarily be to love and serve your mate.

When it comes to roles and responsibilities in marriage, the reality is that there will be times when one of you will need to do a lot of extras. It'll feel as though you're pulling 90 percent of the load, and your spouse isn't doing his or her fair share. But that's what having a servant's heart is all about. Dale and I (Susan) learned about this firsthand not long after we married. I was busy launching a new magazine, and Dale stepped up in amazing ways to serve me during that time.

I was working fifty to sixty hours a week, and it was a stressful and exhausting time. It was difficult for me to juggle the household responsibilities and the extra work, but Dale selflessly picked up so much of the slack—shopping, cleaning, cooking—nearly doing it all! He didn't complain or make me feel guilty; he just served. And because I knew he hated shopping and cooking but did it anyway, I felt cherished even during such a stressful time when I felt bad about not doing my part.

Shortly after that, Dale was dealing with some serious health issues, and I had the opportunity to serve him. In fact, after much discussion and prayer, I left the work I loved to be home with him, support him, go to his doctors' appointments with him, and be there for him.

In the course of daily life, married couples can become distracted and forget about the joy and rewards of doing acts of service for each other. All too often, they begin to view the duties, everyday tasks, stress-producing errands, minute-by-minute decisions, and even their roles as husband and wife as irritations rather than opportunities to serve. When this happens, they simply miss the precious blessing found in serving one another.

Ephesians 6:7 says, "Serve wholeheartedly, as if you were serving the Lord, not [people]." Wow! If only we applied this to our everyday responsibilities and roles, what a difference it would make in our marriages.

As you begin your life together, what do you think it will look like to intentionally and regularly serve each other—with a whole heart? Whether it's cooking, cleaning, working in the yard, caring for the kids, running errands, or showing love for each other, if the responsibilities and decisions that need to be completed each and every day are done with a servant's heart, the benefits you reap will be worth the effort! Conflict will be alleviated, you'll be more productive, and your hearts and home will be much more peaceful. That's pretty amazing!

Ephesians encourages us to have a servant's heart, to put our needs behind other people's needs, and to have an unselfish determination to serve others. Jesus Himself spent His life serving others, and the Bible is filled with stories of how He served people by healing the sick, feeding the multitudes, and even washing His disciples' feet. Then He gave His life for us all—the ultimate sacrifice. He set a very high standard for us to emulate, but whenever two people choose to selflessly serve each other, there is peace, contentment, satisfaction, and love like nothing else.

Preparing for the adventure of marriage by cultivating a heart to serve can make your daily life a joy. And choosing to have a servant's attitude toward all the responsibilities, duties, chores, and roles of married life will help you find balance as a couple and give you a healthy way of sharing the workload to accomplish the everyday stuff of family life.

Let's take a look at roles, responsibilities, and decision making in marriage from the perspective of serving each other. We think you'll see how it can make a positive difference in navigating the challenges of everyday life.

Roles

Children who grew up in a home with both parents inevitably witnessed the roles their parents modeled as husband and wife—for good or bad. They also saw how responsibilities and decision making worked and watched the way their parents served in the home—or not. The culture, our peers, our churches, our education, and the media also taught us about roles in marriage.

As you prepare for marriage, now is the time to analyze and assess what you experienced in your family of origin and decide what you want to take into your marriage and what you want to intentionally leave behind. What you learned growing up, either consciously or unconsciously, can often influence your thinking now. And some of what you learned about marital roles may conflict with other views and leave you with confusing messages. But if you start out your marriage basing your roles upon a foundation of selfless service, the power games and control issues that couples so often face should be infrequent and may even melt away in love.

Karen and Matt grew up in traditional homes where the male and female roles were clearly delineated, so they unconsciously fell into doing the same things their parents did. Karen cared for the kids and the inside of the home, while Matt took care of the outside and brought home the bacon. But their marriage was littered with frustration, power games, manipulation, control, stubbornness, and dissension—until they discovered God's thoughts on the matter.

One day Karen had enough. Matt's increasing demands and self-centered actions became unbearable. She had a heart to serve, but there was only one servant in the house, and that was one too few. Something needed to change.

She stomped her foot and shook her head. "I slave every day cooking and cleaning and keeping this house immaculate. The least you could do is help me once in a while!"

"I work hard all day, and I'm tired when I come home," Matt said. "Besides, that's woman's work!"

"Are you serious? I work hard all day too, and yet you come home and sit in front of the computer or TV all night long. When do I get a break?"

"Would you stop all this drama?"

Karen looked at him, appalled, and then stormed out of the house. She was done.

Clearly Matt was lacking a servant's heart, and the roles Karen and Matt had fallen into when they first married weren't working. Karen was tired, and Matt was inconsiderate. Below the surface was a bigger issue: the stereotypical beliefs about the roles they expected each other to fulfill.

From the very beginning of your marriage, and even before, all kinds of decisions, duties, and responsibilities will need to be fulfilled. Just planning your wedding entails making lots of decisions. Who will be responsible to do what? How will you complete it all in time? For many couples, this becomes the first big challenge in marriage: fulfilling their roles and responsibilities together. When you're married, working out the responsibilities of life becomes a daily—and sometimes hourly—opportunity to serve each other well or rub one another the wrong way. Preparing for the adventure of daily life—before you get in the middle of it—is a wise way to go!

How will you divide up all the tasks that need to be done, including the chores, finances, work, duties, and decisions? How will you get everything done with the limited time you have? Who will run which errands or do which chores? It can become complicated, stressful, and frustrating if you let it fall to chance.

And what about the roles you will be expected to fulfill every day? You'll soon take on your roles as wife and husband, and someday you may have the roles of mother and father. But you'll also maintain the roles of adult child, friend, employee, citizen, church member, and so on. Each of these roles comes with certain expectations and obligations, and with them responsibilities, duties, and stresses. So how will you intentionally prepare to navigate the roles of husband and wife?

The roles that Karen and Matt stumbled into became an unhealthy pattern of relating to each other that eventually threatened to destroy their relationship. Matt thought that a man's role was to keep things in control, to lead, to pay the bills, and to demand submission. Karen fell into her role by default, until she could stand it no longer. Finally they both realized that their marriage was dysfunctional at best, so they decided to get some counseling. Once they understood God's better plan for their life together as husband and wife, they were able to make some life-changing adjustments. They found that serving each other selflessly was a wonderfully liberating way to live together!

Keep in mind that however you view your roles, it's important to share your feelings with each other and agree on what will work for both of you—you're on the same team. The process you use to arrive at a win-win decision is more important than the actual decision. God created the man to be the provider and protector of his wife and family. As a servant-leader, he is called to gently and patiently guide his family in much the same way Jesus guided and led His followers.

God created the woman to be a completer and helpmate for her husband and family. As a life-giving servant, she can bring nurturing and balance into family life in a beautiful way that only a woman can.

Selfishness and self-centeredness are contrary to the Ephesians 6 command. Serving and sacrifice are at the center of it. With these qualities as a firm foundation for marriage, the man's role as a servant-leader and the woman's role as a servant-helper become amazingly gratifying and wonderfully bonding.

Moreover, it takes two people serving each other to make a healthy marriage. While dating, we often hide our natural, self-centered tendencies and put on our best appearance. Though we're all imperfect people struggling to do our best, each of us can be a little selfish at times. We can all get moody or lazy, stubborn or inconsiderate. But what you want to discern before your wedding day is whether your future mate really does have a servant's heart, or whether he or she has a pattern of selfish behavior that will become detrimental to your marriage.

Is your future mate humble and flexible? Does he or she have a cooperative attitude and a serving mentality? If so, you're blessed. On the other hand, does your future mate have control issues, resist submitting to authority, or have a view of roles or accepting responsibility that worries you? Then you should consider the consequences of living with that challenge long term and deal with it now. You may need to speak with a mentor, counselor, or pastor. Share your concerns honestly. Now is the time to deal with any potential challenges.

Responsibilities

Marriage can be quite an adventure—like two people canoeing down a mountain stream in a single canoe. The lead oarsman and the co-oarsman are on the same level, and they work together for a common goal as they stay in sync with each other. They row toward the same destination, but the lead oarsman, who sits in the back, usually steers the canoe, keeps the pace steady, protects them from potential dangers, and works with his partner to reach their destination. They must stay balanced, or the canoe may stray off course. They must stay in sync and connected as a team, or they may tip. They must communicate and adjust to one another, or they'll have trouble.

So it is with marriage. According to God's Word, the man is the leader, but he is to lead like Christ—a servant-leader. He is not to be controlling, dominating, or overpowering but to lead the team, like a lead oarsman does, by sacrificially serving his wife, deferring to her, and having the same goals. And the woman should serve, defer, and be in sync with her husband as well.

As husband and wife, each of you will have some special and unique responsibilities that only one of you can fulfill. Though your roles may be different, keep in mind that you are equal in God's eyes. Both of your roles should work together to make your marriage the great adventure it's meant to be.

Let's Talk to the Guys

As the husband and the leader of your home, you will have the awesome, God-given responsibility of loving your wife in the same way "Christ loved the church and gave himself up for her" (Ephesians 5:25). You should be willing to sacrifice your life for her, if need be, just as Jesus did for us. But what does that look like in practical terms?

Your fiancée needs to know that your commitment to her is forever. She needs assurance that you will be faithful, loyal, and devoted to her forever. It's your privilege and responsibility to love her so deeply that she will continually be assured of your commitment to her through the thick-and-thin seasons of married life.

As you embrace your role, you'll also need to set aside your own needs and desires. Since a husband's responsibility is to serve his wife as Christ would, that means her needs will often come before your needs.

Another aspect of being a servant-leader is being patient and understanding as you journey together through the ups and downs of married life. The apostle Peter offered this advice:

Live with your wives in an understanding way, showing honor
to the woman as the weaker vessel, since they are heirs with you
of the grace of life, so that your prayers may not be hindered.

1 PETER 3:7, ESV

One of a woman's greatest needs is to connect with her husband, to be cared for, supported, accepted, and understood. As a husband, you'll have a great opportunity to meet your wife's needs in a special and unique way. You can also show your servant-leadership by protecting her physically and emotionally, and this in turn will fulfill her desire to be cherished and cared for. As you serve her in this way, you'll help her feel safe and valued, accepted and loved. Listen to her. Talk with her. Spend time with her. Serve her with your mind, heart, and body, whether by helping her with the kids or the housework, or by giving her time with her friends when she needs it.

This is all part of God's amazing design for marriage, which reflects Christ and His church. As you serve each other in love, you'll be creating a healthy relationship and a life full of joy and peace.

And Now the Ladies

As a wife, you'll also have the awesome responsibility of serving your husband in a special way. You can help him to be all he can be, and you can serve him in so many large and small ways. You, too, will find yourself sacrificing at times as you serve your husband. But what does that look like in practical terms?

As a helper and completer, and depending on your lifestyle and schedules, the greater share of homemaking responsibilities may fall to you at certain times. However, you and your husband will need to determine what works best for both of you. Marriage is a journey, and you and your future spouse will experience different seasons of life over the years. It's important to be flexible and willing to serve, as you are able, during each season.

Just as a wife needs to be assured of her husband's faithfulness (a husband needs that kind of assurance as well), a husband also needs to be respected, appreciated, and affirmed (Ephesians 5:33). When he works hard to provide, or when he protects you, notice the things he does, big or little, and acknowledge them. Whether it's checking to make sure the doors are locked at night, opening your car door for you, or maintaining your vehicles, show him you appreciate him and verbally affirm him regularly. Though your husband will never be perfect—and neither will you—do your best to applaud the good things he does.

Another important way to serve your husband when you're married is to respect him. You can show respect by your words, the tone of your voice, and your body language. Love and respect seem to breed love and respect, so that's a winning plan to implement in your marriage early on.

Many of these things might seem trivial, but they aren't. They are ways to become the wife God has called you to be. Love and marriage are blessings. Loving the man God has placed in your life is a privilege. As you do these things, I can imagine God saying, "Well done, good and faithful servant! You have been faithful with a few things; I will put you in charge of many things" (Matthew 25:21).

Daily Life

So how will you get all those boring, mundane daily duties done, accomplish the never-ending chores, and keep your marital peace and harmony? It's all about doing what you do best and having a loving attitude of serving each other. It also requires a teammate mentality. Once you're married, you and your spouse will be on the same team. Therefore, you'll either win together or lose together. There's no such thing as a win-lose scenario in a marriage. You can't win while your spouse loses. That's an illusion.

When you make decisions about roles and responsibilities in your marriage, make sure you first remind each other that you're on the same team, and the only acceptable solution is doing something you both feel great about. In other words, make sure you approach decisions with a servant's mind-set and a teammate mentality. As the apostle Paul wrote, "I appeal to you . . . in the name of our Lord Jesus Christ, that all of you agree with one another so that there may be no divisions among you and that you may be perfectly united in mind and thought" (1 Corinthians 1:10).

Let's face it, all married couples get weary doing the mundane tasks of life—the endless cooking, cleaning, grocery shopping, laundry, taking out the trash, and so much more. It can be overwhelming at times. Then kids come along and add lots of extra chores, duties, and responsibilities.

From the very beginning of their marriage, Angie and Chad decided to play to their strengths and "divide and conquer" when it came to their roles, responsibilities, chores, duties, and other everyday tasks. Their plan has been very successful, even years later. Throughout the week, they make a list of what needs to be done and divvy up the list over breakfast. Then on a Saturday morning, they plan their chores and tick them off—whether it's cleaning, shopping, or running errands.

Over the years they've been willing to be flexible. When children came, Chad pitched in to provide extra help around the house and with the kids, and when he had a major job promotion that required travel and longer office hours, Angie understood and did many of Chad's regular chores. They both hold their list of jobs loosely, and their to-do list is a team project, so they get it done with love and grace. In fact, they use these ten great tips from 1 Corinthians 13:4–7 as their guide:

1. *Be patient.* Chores are simply a part of life, so be content doing them and avoid grumbling about what needs to be done.

2. *Be kind.* Serve each other by doing a chore without your partner knowing it or by making dinner when he or she has had a tough day.

3. *Don't envy.* Envy and power struggles are unproductive and unloving. Don't be tied to traditional roles and duties, and be careful not to envy your spouse's talents. If you're a good mechanic and he's a good cook, go with your strengths! Be willing to use your skills and abilities for the good of the team.

4. *Don't be boastful or proud.* Tackle daily duties and chores with a humble and sacrificial attitude, and prioritize what's most important—with both of you in mind.

5. *Don't dishonor each other.* Be careful to appreciate the work each of you do, and avoid nit-picking when your spouse doesn't do something the way you would do it.

6. *Don't be self-seeking.* Don't expect your spouse to do most of the work. Do your fair share and pull your own weight.

7. *Don't be easily angered.* When you need to take up the slack and do more than usual for a time, like when one of you is sick or extra busy at work, maintain a heart to serve instead of getting angry or annoyed.

8. *Don't keep a record of grievances or wrongs.* Don't keep score when you feel you're pulling more of the load in your marriage. Be a team, choose duties fairly, and work together to compromise peacefully.

9. *Don't delight in evil but rejoice in the truth.* You can always procrastinate or ignore what needs to be done, but if you manage your time well and deal with things honestly and in a timely manner, both of you will succeed.

10. *Always protect, always trust, always hope, always persevere.* Just do it! Lovingly serve each other day in and day out.

The mundane tasks of married life can be transformed when you view them as opportunities to serve and love each other.

Exercise: Who Will Do What?

How will you decide who does what in your marriage? Divvy up the following chores and responsibilities according to your individual strengths. Remember, there will be times when you'll have to adjust your duties as life changes. But the following list is a good starting point.[1]

- Cooking and preparing meals
- Cleaning up after meals
- Cleaning bathrooms
- Doing the laundry
- Taking out the trash
- Shopping for groceries
- Decorating
- Taking care of household repairs
- Servicing the car

- Doing the yard work
- Planning trips
- Planning nights out
- Buying and giving gifts
- Planning and shopping for holidays
- Corresponding with family and friends
- Caring for aging parents
- Caring for pets

Decision Making

Married couples are faced with hundreds of decisions to make every day, whether small or large. From deciding to make the bed to choosing when to go to bed, their days are filled with choices and decisions. Before you became engaged, you may have gone through a season of singleness when you learned to be independent and make decisions on your own. You did things the way you wanted, how you wanted, when you wanted. Your decisions were yours and yours alone, and not making a decision became a decision made by default.

Now, your days of independent decision making are about to change. Even if you and your fiancé(e) have been making decisions together during your engagement, married life will take this to a whole new level. When you marry, you and your spouse will need to learn how to become interdependent. Your roles, responsibilities, and decisions as a couple will become intertwined, much like a rope, and you'll need to figure out how to navigate these overlapping areas and find balance in your life together. The way you approach the decisions and responsibilities of married life will make all the difference in the world. So be sure to approach each decision as a team.

For Leon and Chandra, it was another busy day. With three children, two jobs, a home to maintain, sports, activities, and school, family life was more than full—it was too full. They had too much on their plates, and their family schedule was getting out of hand.

The kids were involved in several extracurricular activities, Chandra was involved in three demanding church groups, and Leon played sports and served on the church elder board. Their family time was nonexistent, and their couple time was suffering too. They had some hard decisions to make, but most important, they needed to make a decision to say no to so much busyness. As a couple they worked together, reevaluated their commitments, and made some big changes. In the process, they found balance again.

As you make decisions, assume responsibilities, and fulfill your roles in marriage, it will help if you figure out how to do this in an *interdependent* way. For some couples, that's not easy. The key is learning to work together as a team and finding balance as a couple. But that can go against the grain if you have an independent nature.

How will you and your spouse make decisions, delegate responsibilities, and assume differing roles once you're married? You'll need to figure out what will work best for your relationship and how you can best serve each other. Since every couple is unique, intentionally preparing now for the responsibilities to come and discussing them will make life easier later on.

Scripture instructs each of us to "use whatever gift [you have] received to serve others, faithfully administering God's grace in its various forms" (1 Peter 4:10). That can sure help you figure out how to delegate marital responsibilities. Ask yourselves, "Who is most gifted in accomplishing certain tasks?" If you or your future spouse has the gift of time or the skill to cook, there's your answer.

Scripture also says,

> Have nothing to do with foolish, ignorant controversies; you know they breed quarrels. And the Lord's servant must not be quarrelsome but kind to everyone, able to teach, patiently enduring evil, correcting his opponents with gentleness.
> 2 TIMOTHY 2:23–25, ESV

Wow! If you can avoid arguing over how to fold clothes or do dishes or drive, what a difference it will make in getting daily chores done with peace and kindness.

Finally the Bible tells us that "if anyone serves, he [or she] should do it with the strength God provides" (1 Peter 4:11). The truth is, you can't do this on your own. The daily roles, responsibilities, decisions, chores, duties, and obligations of marriage will wear you down if you don't rely on God's strength day in and day out. He will strengthen you, empower you, and encourage you as you choose to serve each other unselfishly.

As you use your gifts, avoid arguments, and rely on God's strength, your daily life together can be productive and peaceful. And as you share the workload as a team and find balance so that no one person ends up doing it all, the everyday challenges of married life will be accomplished more easily.

A Better Way

As a couple, you'll have to make some pretty big decisions throughout the course of your married life. How will you work together to make those bigger decisions—like moving or having a baby or changing jobs,

ALL 3 SOON

churches, or houses? Each decision should be given as much time, attention, and discussion as each of you needs so that you can come to a mutual decision as a couple. Take your time to make wise decisions, and always approach decision making as a team.

The truth is that making wise decisions can get tricky sometimes. Are all decisions made on a fifty-fifty basis in marriage? What happens if there's a stalemate? Who makes the final decision when there's a disagreement as to what the decision might be?

Relational decisions can also get rather sticky. How will you spend your time? When will you have couple time, alone time, or time with friends? And what about church, tithing, moral standards, and giving?

It's important to try to come to a mutual agreement, no matter how big or small a decision might be. As much as possible, look for a win-win for both of you. To do this, you'll need to use the communication and conflict-resolution skills presented in this book, cooperate with each other, and compromise when you need to.

Philippians 2:3–4 offers some really good advice: "Do nothing out of selfish ambition or vain conceit, but in humility consider others better than yourselves. Each of you should look not only to your own interests, but also to the interests of others."

Pray together about the decisions you need to make, employ God's Word, and make sure your decisions align with your priorities as a couple. Keep each other's needs, goals, values, and dreams in mind, but make decisions that will work for both of you. One of you can't hang out with his or her friends every night while the other sits home alone. Likewise, one of you can't rack up credit-card bills and ignore the budget.

When you make the wrong decision about something, whether together or separately (and you will!), admit your mistake, forgive each other, learn from it, and avoid blaming one another. Consider getting some outside counsel so you can learn what you can do better the next time around.

Above all, as you begin your life together, keep this in mind: In everything—your roles, responsibilities, duties and chores, and decisions—work together as a team and serve each other selflessly. In doing so, you'll build a marriage that's filled with love, productivity, peace, and promise!

SUSAN and DALE MATHIS are the authors of *Countdown for Couples: Preparing for the Adventure of Marriage* as well as *The ReMarriage Adventure: Preparing for a Lifetime of Love and Happiness*. Dale has two master's degrees in counseling and has worked in counseling and human resources for more than thirty years. Susan is the founding editor of *Thriving Family* magazine and the former editor and editorial director of twelve unique publications. Susan now serves as a speaker, freelance editor, and writer. For more than a decade, Susan and Dale have worked with couples in premarital counseling and have been mentors and facilitators for a megachurch premarital ministry. Their purpose is to encourage and equip couples with vital and helpful information that will make for a healthy marriage.

Ready to Talk

1. What does the following relationship truth mean to you? "In a marriage, you and your spouse are on the same team; thus, when you are making decisions, you either will win together or you will lose together—there is no other option." Talk about when you played a team sport or participated in a team activity. Was there ever a time that you did really well but your team still lost? What was that like? How will you both function as a team when making decisions as a couple?

2. During your engagement so far, how have you tended to divide up the following chores or activities? How did that happen? Will the same approach to assigning tasks work when you are married? Why or why not?

- Planning a date night
- Initiating premarital counseling
- Planning where you will live after the wedding
- Paying for meals and movies
- Praying before eating
- Planning the wedding
- Planning the honeymoon

3. Look at the story of Mary, Martha, and Jesus in Luke 10:38–42. What were their attitudes toward getting things done? What did Jesus seem to be saying about the relative importance of chores? What do you think He would tell a couple in which one spouse felt like Martha and one acted like Mary? What is the difference between *serving* your future spouse and *sacrificing* for your future spouse? How will you incorporate serving and sacrificing into how you make decisions as a couple?

Ready to Try

If possible, take a tour of the place where you'll live once you're married. (If not, take a tour of a friend's or relative's home.) Pause in each room or area to consider the chores that may be performed there.

- Meal preparation
- Clearing the table after meals
- Loading and unloading the dishwasher
- Laundry
- Clothing repairs
- Balancing the checkbook
- Preparing the taxes
- Decorating the house (painting, wallpapering, picture hanging)

- Cleaning the house (scrubbing toilets, vacuuming, dusting)
- Changing the sheets
- Trash removal
- Car maintenance (oil changes, license plate renewal)
- Minor home repairs (a broken screen door, a rusty hinge, a loose stair tread)
- Yard work
- House maintenance tasks (cleaning gutters, painting, repairs)
- Cleaning the garage
- Writing letters or e-mails to update the extended family
- Keeping track of birthdays
- Buying gifts for extended family members
- Maintaining the social calendar and planning social events

Who completed these tasks in your families of origin? Who will do them in the family you're forming? Which responsibilities could be shared? Who wants to be the King of Vacuuming or the Queen of Car Washing? Don't try to set these roles in stone, but take a first step toward negotiating a balanced arrangement that takes preferences, skills, gifts, feelings, and fairness into account.

CHAPTER 12

OUR MONEY RELATIONSHIP

Scott and Bethany Palmer

TAKE THE PLUNGE. Tie the knot. Get hitched. Jump the broom.

Ever wonder, *Why all the scary phrases?*

Your wedding day will be one of the most cherished days of your life, but the fact is that change can be scary. Never fear, you've got each other now! No matter the location, whatever the style, your wedding day will be an extraordinary picture of love shared with your family and friends. The aisle, the vows, the hope, the music, the kiss! Pucker up and leave your fears behind!

And yet we've found something most engaged couples are seriously afraid of: talking about money. The majority of couples find money discussions scary and uncomfortable, so they typically avoid talking about dollars and cents before they tie the knot.

We certainly did. Just like most couples, we didn't talk about money before we got married. There were so many other fun subjects to explore or discuss, plus all of those details to attend to—and money never seemed to be one of them.

When we were engaged, we were like every other couple in that respect. One of us thought everything would just work out naturally (Bethany). While the other one was truly very nervous about money before the wedding (Scott) but didn't really want to talk about it.

Knowing what we know now, we had nothing to fear. Nor do you, because "God gave us a spirit not of fear but of power and love and self-control" (2 Timothy 1:7, ESV).

The truth is that conflicts over money can poison our relationships and ruin our marriages, but that doesn't have to be the case for you and your forever mate. You've got this! You don't need to fear talking about money (or tripping and falling in front of all your family and friends). You can tromp arm in arm right through any money fears and find freedom right from the start in an area that is tearing marriages apart every day.

Ten Money Relationship Questions

- How do you like to celebrate birthdays?

- What is the biggest gift you've ever purchased for someone?

- What kinds of vacations do you like?

- How often should we have date nights?

- How many times each week should we dine out?

- Is the appearance of our home important to you?

- How did your parents talk about money?

- How did your parents argue about money?

- What stresses you out when it comes to money?

- How often should we go on vacations?

Why Are Couples Fighting About Money?

It seems every couple fights about money. Did you know that 70 percent of all divorces cite money as the number one cause for calling it quits?[1] One of the reasons is the dailyness of it. Money impacts practically every decision we make every day: Do we want home-brewed coffee or a fancy latte at the drive-through? A smartphone or the same old dumb one? Generic groceries or name-brand? To have lunch out or to brown-bag? Money affects even how many hours we spend working each day!

Those daily choices you and your honey make where money is involved form your *Money Relationship*. If you didn't realize you even had a Money Relationship, you're in good company. The majority of couples don't realize their daily money choices affect their relationships.

When we talk to couples about money, we find it helps to make the distinction between money and finances. Your *Money Relationship* refers to your day-to-day spending decisions, while your *financial plan* refers to those long-term, big-picture matters like debt, budgets, retirement, insurance, investments, taxes, and estate planning. Money and finance are related but very different.

Understanding this distinction helps clarify and compartmentalize these discussions into two categories, which helps to decrease that feeling of being overwhelmed and fearful about money discussions. This distinction is a precursor to stamping out money fear and adding strength and freedom to your relationship.

We applaud your quest to avoid those alarming divorce statistics with money as the culprit, and we want to help you turn your money fears into money freedom with these two steps: (1) Identify your fears, and (2) share your perspectives.

You can tackle a topic that needlessly frightens most couples with God's Spirit of power, love, and self-discipline and make money discussions a strong tool to divorce-proof your precious marriage.

Step 1: Identify Your Fears

We all know people who love to go to scary movies. The spooky music, the creaking door, the abandoned building, the shape-filled shadows, the scary noise in the distance, and the figure in the dark who wasn't there before. The suspense and uncertainty of what may happen next chills and thrills scary-movie fans.

But uncertainty about money and finances isn't so thrilling! And yet there's a way you can flip on the lights, look those fears straight in the eye, and conquer your fears and uncertainty about money as an unshakable team.

Let's start by identifying the fears. As we said, most couples fear talking about money. In fact, research shows that more than half of couples have negative feelings about discussing finances with their fiancé(e).[2] Your particular, individual fears may be very different from your fiancé(e)'s, because everyone has a different perspective about money. God made every one of us unique and different, even when it comes to our views of money. We each have a special way of looking at money that is God-given and hardwired into us right from the start—just like the color of our eyes or how tall we are.

Ten Financial Planning Questions

- Do you track your savings and spending?

- Would you describe yourself as conservative or aggressive in your investing?

- What mistakes have you made with money?

- How do you feel about debt?

- Do you think joint or separate checking accounts are best in marriage?

- Do you give to charitable organizations?

- Do you want to rent or own a home?

- Will we be a dual-income family, or will one of us stay home with our children?

- Do you think paying bills should be done separately or together?

- Should we have a financial adviser?

Maybe you've never considered what your personal perspective on money is, but you can probably relate to one or more of the following opinions:

- I love using coupons. Who wouldn't want to save extra?
- Coupons are a hassle. Who hauls those around just to save pennies?
- I'm always looking for an opportunity to give someone a gift—big or small. *B E L*
- Giving gifts is overkill and unnecessary. *M E*
- Life is short. Your money should provide lots of adventure.
- Life is short. Keep your money secure.
- Vacations are the perfect time to see something new. *M E*
- Returning to our annual vacation spot ensures a great time.
- Talking about money kills the romance and adventure in our relationship.
- Not talking about money makes me nervous about the future. *B E L*

Did a few of those opinions resonate with you? Did a couple of them sound a little like your fiancé(e)'s perspective on money?

Our individual perspective on money is so much a part of who we are that it's easy to think others think about money the exact same way we do. When driving down a highway, have you ever noticed that you think everyone going slower than you is nuts, and everyone going faster than you is crazy? You think the right speed is the speed you're going. Your perspective on money is the same way. You're probably convinced that your future spouse thinks about money like you do. We've found that's not usually the case, and that can be scary.

It's easy to fear the future when you see that your future spouse doesn't have the some perspective about money as you. That fear may stir up thoughts like these:

- What will happen if, for the rest of our lives, we can only go out to eat where they offer coupons?
- What will happen if he thinks I'm going to work forever and not stay home and raise our children?
- Now that I'm getting married, will every conversation be about taxes and money?
- How can we build up savings if he always likes to be the guy who picks up the tab for everyone?
- Is she going to ask me about every purchase I make? Every time? Forever?
- She knows that credit-card purchases have to be paid back at some point, right?
- Is her sense of adventure and love of risk going to make us rich or break us financially?
- Will I have to give up all exciting or risky ventures once we're Mr. and Mrs.?
- If we make every moment count, will we have any money left to count?

You can feel the fear in these statements. And they're all valid concerns. But when you identify and discuss them, you fast-track your relationship from money fear to money freedom.

Your goal in step 1 is to identify the fearful aspects of your relationship related to money. Fear comes from the unknown.

Remember when you wondered if you'd ever find that perfect someone? Then when you finally met him or her, all of the uncertainty from the unknowns faded away. The more you learned about each other and your relationship, your fears began to shrink. The fact that you're reading this book together demonstrates that you're ready to learn, craft a game plan, and secure some tools to empower you to squash those fears and have the absolute best marriage possible!

Identifying your individual perspective on money is such a powerful solution for eliminating money fear. We created a scientific, easy, and *free* way for every couple to determine theirs. As financial advisors, after witnessing the alarming rate of divorce among our clients, we spent time researching how to stop this frightening trend. We identified the 5 Money Personalities to make it possible for all couples to better understand one another and communicate positively about money.

We then worked with a statistical scientist to develop an assessment we placed online for free. This Money Personality Assessment calculates both your Primary and Secondary Money Personalities. The assessment is painless and takes about ten minutes apiece. We hear over and over from couples—dating, engaged, and married—what a game changer this information was for their relationship.

So stop! Do not pass go. Take the Money Personality Assessment right now at TheMoneyCouple.com. Flip a coin to see who goes first, take the assessment, and then let your fiancé(e) take a turn. (If one of you asks to keep the coin you flipped, you may already have an insight into one of the Money Personalities in your relationship.)

After one woman took the assessment, she told us, "The clouds parted. The angels sang. I got it! I understood myself better after that ten minutes than I had my entire life."

Good luck on the assessment! This is one of those awesome assessments where there are no incorrect answers. You'll do great! . . .

Welcome back and congratulations! You should be proud of

yourselves for taking the time to get to know yourselves and each other better than most couples who have been together for decades. Your investment in your relationship is priceless.

Now that you know your Primary and Secondary Money Personalities, let's tackle potential fears related to your unique money perspective.

The following chart shows a sampling of the fears of each Money Personality. Take some time to look at the genuine fears associated with your Primary and Secondary Money Personalities. (If you haven't taken the assessment yet—though we hope you have—you can still read through to see which fears you connect with.)

Saver fears:	My spouse will spend too much money. My spouse will pay full price on purchases. My spouse won't respect my savings. I will be viewed as cheap all the time. My spouse won't stick to the budget. We will go into debt.
Spender fears:	My spending will be under a microscope. I won't have the freedom to spend. I will be viewed as materialistic. I won't be able to give gifts when I want. I won't have enough money to spend.
Risk Taker fears:	I won't get to be adventurous anymore. My spouse will slow me down. I'll get trapped in a rut. Marriage will limit my flexibility to pursue new business opportunities.
Security Seeker fears:	We won't have a long-term plan. How will I take care of everything and everyone? I will be seen as a worrier. We won't have plans for retirement.
Flyer fears:	I'll have to get involved in the finances. My spouse will want to talk about money all the time. My spouse will care more about money than relationships and people's feelings. I will have to follow a plan all the time.

We all know that fear is a vital response to physical and emotional danger. If we didn't feel it, we couldn't protect ourselves from legitimate threats.

Now that you've faced your fears with courage, read back through the list with your fiancé(e)'s Money Personalities in mind.

Neither of you needs to feel silly or embarrassed for feeling fearful about money or viewing money the unique way you do. Few of us can explain our fears of snakes, heights, or even public speaking, but those fears still feel very real.

Step 2: Share Your Perspectives

Now that you've spent some time thinking through your own money fears and learning your honey's money fears, it's time to bring those fears out into the light as you share them. Listening to each other's money fears helps propel your relationship from fear toward money freedom.

Observe some standard "good communication" guidelines as you share with each other: Connect visually, remember that timing is everything, listen well, be positive, stay on topic, and speak to one another with love. Start the sharing with these two questions:

1. With your Primary Money Personality in mind, what is one money fear you have? (Limit: ten minutes.)
2. With your Secondary Money Personality in mind, what is one money fear you have? (Limit: ten minutes.)

Well done, fear facers!

Mark Burnett, vocal Christian and creator of *The Voice*, *Survivor*, and *The Bible* miniseries reminds us, "Facing your fears robs them of their power." We agree and pray you rob your fears of their power and not let money fights rob your relationship of peace.

If you're struggling to understand your future spouse's Money Personalities, we want to suggest a simple—and maybe even fun—exercise. Take a day, or half a day, and try to live out your future spouse's Primary

Money Personality. Pick an upcoming day when you'll be together, and prepare to be amazed. As the day progresses, one of you has the spotlight and should talk aloud about the money decisions you are making.

Here's an example of a Spender and a Saver who recently told us about trying this exercise:

Tom, a Primary Spender, told his fiancée, "I wake up and go to the closet to get dressed for the day. I look around the closet and think, *When I look at my clothes, I see a bunch of stuff I'm tired of wearing. I like to feel good about how I look, so I could really use some new shirts.* Then I think about what we're doing today and wonder if we'll be near a store where I could grab one or two."

Heidi admitted her heart started to race. Heidi is Tom's sweetheart and a Saver. Her heart pounded quite vigorously at the thought that her soon-to-be-spouse was already thinking about spending money, and he hadn't even left his bedroom.

Tom said he saw the fear in Heidi's eyes from this new revelation, so he suggested they go grab brunch to talk about it.

Heidi's blood pressure crept up again. She thought, *He wants to go spend money to talk about spending money? Brunch always costs so much, when toast and a glass of milk at my place would be fine.* But she smiled and grabbed her purse.

As Tom and Heidi moved through their day, Tom, the Spender, kept talking about what he was thinking and why he was thinking it. Heidi, the Saver, listened and did everything she could to learn about her beloved's perspective.

The next day it was Heidi's turn. She told Tom, "For starters, I woke up to my cold apartment . . . that you make fun of. But the cold reminds me that I'm doing a good job lowering my heating bill this year. And that feels good to me."

Now it was Tom's turn to keep his lips zipped and discover the inner workings of his future spouse's Money Personality.

As they went through the morning, they made more decisions involving money: Should they grab coffee on the way to church? How much should they put in the collection plate? The youth group was having a bake sale to raise money for a missions trip. Should they buy brownies or not?

The Saver needs to talk her honey through her thought process on every one of those choices. By lunchtime Tom said he was amazed at how heavily money decisions weighed on his sweetie, the Saver.

Let us be clear, we're not telling you to go out and spend money you don't have or to give your spouse free rein to destroy your finances just for an exercise.

If you'd rather make hypothetical decisions, that's fine. Try some questions like "If we went into your favorite store right now, what would you do first?" or "If you got a small bonus at work, what would you want to do with it?" The point of this exercise is to build understanding and respect for your future spouse's Money Personalities, and you can do that without spending a cent.

So now that you've started a great discussion about money fears, you can leap with strength into money freedom. A next step is discussing both of your Money Personality needs.

Each Money Personality feels liberated when his or her needs are being met. Now is a great time to think about and talk through your money needs. Most couples are terrible at telling each other what they need, especially when it comes to money. A husband assumes that his wife knows he has a hunting weekend planned for the same weekend every year, or a wife assumes her husband knows she needs a new outfit for a big presentation at work. The spouse *might* know, but clear communication removes any doubt.

Being honest about your needs shows your future spouse that you trust him or her, you value the insight he or she has to offer, and you believe the two of you can work together to solve problems.

Use the following chart to see how you can help your mate-to-be experience money freedom in your relationship.

Saver wants:	My spouse to acknowledge the cost and be open to a good deal. Discussion of any debt and plans to reduce or eliminate it. A commitment, however small, to start saving. Careful use and management of any credit cards.
Spender wants:	My spouse to allow for spending liberties. To know details don't bog down every purchase. A gift account to buy special surprises for my new mate. Flexibility within the budget.
Risk Taker wants:	My spouse to listen and respond to new opportunities. To share excitement without all the details initially. Possibility of liquid funds to invest an agreed-upon amount—big or small—in "the next big thing," on occasion. Freedom to be ready to consider and discuss anything.
Security Seeker wants:	My spouse to be supportive of a future plan. My spouse to be willing to pay for higher quality. Time to analyze spending decisions. Wise use of money with guaranteed future returns.
Flyer wants:	My spouse to recognize the value of relationships over money. Not to be put in charge of the planning or details. My contentment not to be mistaken for not caring. Easy, automatic ways to save or grow finances.

Freedom is life-giving. Did you feel a little elation when you read your Money Personalities' freedom needs? Freedom!

Now go back through the list and find your future spouse's Money Personalities and note the ways you may offer him or her freedom.

Take some time and discuss the freedoms your Money Personalities need to thrive. Start with these questions:

1. With your Primary Money Personality in mind, what gives you a sense of money freedom? (Limit: ten minutes)

2. With your Secondary Money Personality in mind, what gives you a sense of money freedom? (Limit: ten minutes)

Well done! That wasn't so scary, was it? You carved out the time and made the effort to take a huge step forward that most couples skip. Now that you've identified your money fears and shared your Money Personalities, you can move from money fear to money freedom in your relationship. You'll avoid fights and misunderstandings and be able to see eye to eye on day-to-day spending. This understanding, appreciation, and acceptance of your future spouse and the way he or she approaches money will strengthen your relationship and, we pray, help make it divorce-proof.

Opposite Dynamic

We're sure you discovered during your discussion times that there is a lot to discuss regarding money and finances that you wouldn't normally think about. You may also have found two competing viewpoints, an Opposite Dynamic, in your relationship. Quickly identify whether you have an Opposite Dynamic in your relationship. See if your Money Personalities are on the opposite side of the spectrum.

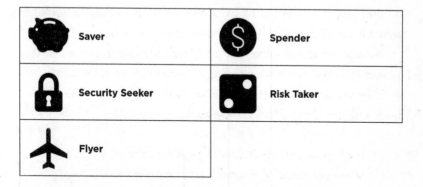

🐷 Saver	💲 Spender
🔒 Security Seeker	🎲 Risk Taker
✈️ Flyer	

Don't worry. A vast majority of couples we talk to have an Opposite Dynamic in their relationships. At first that dynamic may cause conflict and misunderstanding, but take heart, it can ultimately create a wonderful, healthy balance in your home.

Take, for example, Joe and Ann. For the most part, they have a strong relationship. However, the little differences between them are starting to add up and cause tension in their marriage, because every decision they make involves their competing Money Personalities.

Ann wants to go skiing over the holiday. Joe wants to stay home and watch it snow. Ann wants to try out a new restaurant. Joe wants to stick with the value menu at their neighborhood burger joint. Joe is thinking about turning his hobby into a small business. Ann is scared they'll lose their hard-earned savings.

The Opposite Dynamic in their relationship means that Ann and Joe see the world through very different lenses. And the differences are starting to wear them down.

Some couples have multiple opposite traits; others have only one. The number of differences isn't critical. What matters is your awareness of these potential areas of disagreement and misunderstanding. Knowing where and how you see things differently can help you make money decisions with care and kindness.

Once Joe and Ann uncovered the Opposite Dynamic in their marriage, choosing a restaurant stopped turning into a fight and became a chance for them to break some bad habits. Instead of going out to eat because they didn't feel like cooking, they mutually agreed to splurge on a couple of great meals a month rather than eating at a convenient place twice a week. So Ann's Spender Money Personality got to indulge a bit, while Joe's Saver Money Personality could feel good about the reduction in their eating expenses. Eliminating the regular quick bites at a restaurant helped them discover that they liked making simple meals together at home.

Recognizing an Opposite Dynamic in your relationship isn't a free pass to no more conflict, but it is a way to recognize that those conflicts don't have to get personal or painful. You can address problems as partners, not as adversaries, because you know that your honey is coming at the problem from the legitimate perspective that just happens to be different from yours. When you know that, you can work through problems with respect and a true desire to find middle ground.

A strong Money Relationship won't just happen overnight. (To dig deeper and master all the communication tips and tricks for avoiding money fears and fights, you might want to pick up our book *The 5 Money Personalities: Speaking the Same Love and Money Language*.)

Celebrate the fact that you care enough about your life together to learn now how to change your money fears into money freedom and help divorce-proof your marriage. The more you communicate and clarify now, the fewer surprises and less tension you'll encounter in the future.

A Special Note About Debt

Many couples today start their marriages with some amount of debt. Debt can be a huge source of tension and fear. There are five main types of debt: student loans, credit cards, car loans, personal loans (including loans from friends), and home loans. Hiding debt and starting out with financial secrets is never the way to go.

Talking openly about your debt is an opportunity to communicate, understand one another, and come together as a team. If one or both of you have debt, once you're married, that debt becomes both of yours. Take some time and discuss this challenge.

1. Write down the amount of debt.
2. Talk through these questions:

   • How do you feel about debt?
   • How do you feel your particular Money Personalities helped or hindered your debt situation?

- What steps can you take going forward?
- How can we help each other in this area?
- What scares you about debt?
- When will you feel freedom from worrying about debt?
- Is there an amount of debt you are comfortable with?

3. Make a month-by-month plan to pay it off.
4. Make sure that you both agree about how you will approach any future debt.

Communicate openly and honestly. Evaluate your level of comfort with debt so you both understand what you're getting into and how you can move from fear to freedom in regard to debt.

SCOTT and BETHANY PALMER, the Money Couple, have dedicated their lives to helping others strengthen their relationships by knowing the 5 Money Personalities. With forty-three years of combined financial-planning experience, they launched The Money Couple. They are regulars on national TV and radio and speak internationally about love and money. Scott and Bethany enjoy an active lifestyle with their two sons, Cole and Cade.

Ready to Talk

1. If your spouse-to-be could travel back in time and see you in the following situations, how might it help him or her understand your current views on money?

- The way you were dressed in third grade
- What happened when one of your parents lost a job or got an inheritance
- Christmas morning, age twelve

- The time you first realized that some people had a lot less or a lot more than you did
- Other _____

   Since time travel hasn't been invented, what do you need to explain to your future mate about your financial past? Why?

2. How would you rank the following, from the least scary to the most terrifying? Why does your spouse-to-be need to know your answers?

   - Managing the bills
   - Losing a job and not being able to find another
   - Having to figure out a budget
   - Having to live on a budget
   - Going bankrupt
   - Being married to someone who spends too much
   - Being married to someone who won't let you spend enough
   - Serving money instead of God

3. What are your primary and secondary Money Personalities? According to the chapter, what steps might help you work together on your finances?

Ready to Try

If you haven't registered for wedding gifts yet, set aside time to go to a few stores where you can register for home supplies (such as kitchenware, towels, dishes, and decorative items). Before you start tagging items, talk about what you're most excited to look for. Pots and pans? Power tools? Offer honest opinions about what you like and what you think things should cost. Avoid dismissing each other's choices and opinions about what's extravagant and what isn't—you're building a home together! This is a good time to discover your future spouse's likes, dislikes, and feelings about possessions. When you're done, consider whether the experience felt fun or stressful. Do you work well as a team? Are you more eager than ever to start your life as Mr. and Mrs.? If so, great! If your quest was more tense than tranquil, talk about that openly. How might things have gone more smoothly?

CHAPTER 13

STORM SHELTER: DEALING WITH STRESS AND CRISES

Dr. Greg Smalley and Erin Smalley

I (ERIN) CAN REMEMBER the day as if it were yesterday. My husband, Greg, walked into the room after being on the phone and announced, "Hey! We've been invited to China to do a marriage seminar! What do you think?"

My anxiety level shot through the ceiling as a million questions and concerns arose immediately.

"Who would keep the kids? We've never left them to go so far away!"

"It's a foreign country, and a lot of things are different there. What if they don't like what we teach?"

"What if our plane crashes?"

It just continued to spiral downward from there. Some fears were rational, and others were completely irrational. I knew that in my head, but it was hard to move my heart beyond them.

I had never dreaded anything more than the weeks leading up to boarding the airplane to China. I cried, I read books (Mark Batterson's *In a Pit with a Lion on a Snowy Day*), I turned my fears over to God (again and again and again), and I had others praying for me. I was petrified to go to this foreign place where I didn't know the language, the culture, the people, or the customs.

When we arrived in Kunming, China, I quickly realized that this place was as different as I had feared. It smelled strange, the sounds were confusing, the language was mysterious, and the food was different. And the biggest one—the driving was *crazy*! When in the "tiny" van, I mainly closed my eyes and prayed for survival! It was also very crowded in China, and there didn't seem to be a moment when our personal space wasn't being invaded.

At the end of the first week, we were scheduled to travel to Beijing. By that point the entire experience had left me worn out. I just wanted to go home. And there seemed to be a theme in our trip: Of the four couples traveling with us, we—Greg and Erin—never had an airline reservation that was correct. After being turned away at the American Airlines counter for the third time, I was certain that we should just go home, back to everything we knew—our food, our language, our culture, and our children!

I felt like the children of Israel after they made it out of Egypt:

> In the desert the whole community grumbled against Moses and Aaron. The Israelites said to them, "If only we had died by the LORD's hand in Egypt! There we sat around pots of meat and ate all the food we wanted, but you have brought us out into this desert to starve this entire assembly to death.
>
> EXODUS 16:2–3

Just like the Israelites, I had no idea why God had brought us to China.

However, with my husband's encouragement and the help of a few people who knew English, we ended up on our flight to Beijing. Thankfully,

I spent the next week in China bliss. We went to the Great Wall, shopped at the Pearl Market, and ate the most amazing food I'd ever had.

I never imagined that I could fall in love with a people I didn't even know. But my heart changed, and I did—I fell in love with China.

I never dreamed that we would get the opportunity to return to China, but we've been back *six* times to do marriage ministry. The absolute best surprise was when God allowed us to adopt our daughter, Annie, from China.

I'm so glad that I didn't "grumble" and complain my way out of China that first time when things felt so foreign and confusing. Just as He did with the children of Israel, sometimes God takes us into the wilderness before we enter the Promised Land. More than anything else you'll ever learn about marriage, it's amazing what happens when you venture together into the unknown—through the stress, challenges, and differences that life will bring.

Stress and Change During the First Year of Marriage

As you're preparing for marriage, you're embarking on a lifelong journey to a "foreign" country—much as Greg and I (Erin) did when we traveled to China for the first time. We're sure you're experiencing different emotions at this point—excitement, joy, anticipation, and yes, even fear. There are not only a lot of unknowns in marriage, but there will be a lot of changes as soon as you say "I do!" As you adjust to your new marriage, there will be both internal and external stressors that you will encounter together.

Internal stressors are the changes that occur *within* your relationship. Think about the many changes that you will most certainly face as a first-time husband and wife:

- Taking a new name
- Moving into a new residence (across town or across the country)
- Starting a new job

- Completing undergrad schooling or entering a graduate program
- Living with someone 24/7
- Adjusting to financial changes
- Leaving your family for the first time
- Doing laundry for two
- Cooking for two
- Deciding which side of the bed to sleep on
- Finding "your" church
- Deciding how to spend free time
- Dealing with new household responsibilities and chores
- Building a support system
- Managing arguments and conflict
- Experiencing an unexpected pregnancy (We had a baby girl before our second wedding anniversary!)
- Encountering mental-health issues (depression, anxiety)
- Coping with busyness
- Building a sexual relationship as husband and wife
- Managing expectations
- Learning to deal with countless differences
- Reorienting old friendships

The list could go on and on. There will be a lot of changes during the first year of your marriage. It will look different for each couple, but what we can promise is that there *will* be change. Much like we experienced going to China, sometimes the unknowns of living in this foreign land of marriage can create stress and conflict between you and your new spouse. Sometimes couples forget that even positive changes create stress.

As if the previous list of internal changes that happen within your marriage wasn't enough, you'll also experience *external* stressors that originate outside your relationship. However, these external challenges will impact your marriage just the same. Here are some of the most common external stressors that couples encounter:

- Sickness or the death of a family member
- Financial crisis (bankruptcy, debt, unexpected expenses, etc.)
- In-laws
- Spiritual warfare
- Job loss or unemployment
- Being sinned against (physical or sexual assault, burglary, scams, etc.)
- Car trouble
- Things breaking around your house
- Failed business
- Legal problems (DUI, being sued)
- Natural disasters (tornado, earthquake, hurricane, flooding)
- Extended-family conflict
- Dependent family member
- Electronic distractions (social media, constant texting, checking e-mail)

We're certain that we've left some challenges off this list that you may encounter during the first few years of your marriage. At some point, in the midst of one of these trials, you may even feel like the Israelites and wonder why God brought you together only to experience such misery: "All the Israelites grumbled against Moses and Aaron, and the whole assembly said to them, "If only we had died in Egypt! Or in this desert!" (Numbers 14:2). This is exactly how newlyweds Chris and Rachel felt right after they walked down the aisle.

Chris and Rachel met while attending college, where they became well-acquainted friends. After a year of friendship, they took the next step into a dating relationship. After about six months, Chris excitedly proposed to the love of his life, and she 100 percent agreed to be his wife. Everything was on course—he was about to graduate and had landed a youth-pastor job at their church while working on the side at Starbucks. And Rachel worked to complete her senior thesis and internship so she could graduate within the next year. Wedding plans were interwoven with late-night study sessions and many specialty coffee drinks delivered by her favorite barista. Their engagement season was as good as it gets. They had each other, a future together, and coffee. What more did they need?

They spent one last holiday with their respective families in Seattle and Colorado prior to getting married. When they returned from their holiday travels, they were thrilled to be back together. They decided to have some fun their first night back and make paper snowflakes while watching a Christmas movie. After what seemed like a picturesque reunion, Chris walked home to his apartment only a few blocks away. Blissful was what life seemed to be—for now and forever.

However, within twenty minutes, everything changed. As Rachel was getting ready for bed, she heard the doorbell ringing violently. *What in the world?*

Her roommate tentatively approached the front door, where she met Chris crying.

Rachel's heart started beating wildly as she tried to imagine what could possibly be going on. Twenty minutes earlier, as Chris kissed her good-bye, this scene never would have crossed her mind. But now she was facing a distraught, tear-stained man. To her shock, he pushed out the grief-stricken words, "My dad . . . my dad is dead."

Rachel reported,

It was the most confusing, tragic, and desperate twenty-four hours I've ever experienced. It was so difficult to see my beloved Chris be filled with questions, doubt, confusion, and deep, deep sadness. And the worst part, there was absolutely nothing I could do but be there. The next day we flew out to Colorado in total disbelief and shock.

I had met Chris's parents during my earlier visits. I loved being with his parents and knew them to be very funny, loving, and generous. As for his mom, Carol, I knew I definitely liked this lady who had a deep laugh and a deep faith, and we often shared lovely phone conversations in French.

However, the dynamic changed quickly because I was thrust into this tragedy. She was no longer the happy, soon-to-be mother-in-law with her husband by her side supporting and cheering us on. Instead, as you can imagine, she was grieving deeply, and the roles suddenly shifted. We were no longer being supported by two amazing people who were anticipating our special day and helping us plan out wedding details. We were now comforting and supporting Carol as we planned her husband's funeral. None of this seemed imaginable.

Although I wasn't quite part of the family yet, I did my best to be helpful. I chose to sleep by Carol's side and do the tasks that needed to be completed, like laundry, preparing food, and cleaning. I was doing everything I could to give Chris's family space to grieve without being in the way. However, the most difficult part of all was calling their friends and family to tell them of Robert's death. All of them should have been getting a wedding invite from me instead of a phone call with tragic news.

That November day when we buried Chris's father was bitter cold and snowy. Six months later, in May, I graduated from college, and Chris stepped down from his pastoral job. In mid-June we were married, and by the end of July, we packed up everything and moved to Colorado to live with Carol in her basement.

We spent the first year of our marriage living with Carol,

and although this was good for her, it was helpful for Chris as well. It allowed him to fully grieve his father's death.

All I can say is that marriage definitely wasn't what I had anticipated. We shared all of our dinners, movie nights, and game nights with Carol. We really felt called to care for her and not allow her to be alone. Every night we maintained the family tradition of bedtime prayer, which was filled with a strange mix of tears, sorrow, praise, and thanks.

After about a year of living life this way, my heart began to close. I was a new wife, and I had desired to care for Carol and Chris. However, my inner struggles were beginning to win. I desperately desired to have our own space and home. My desires weren't wrong, but sometimes my behaviors were. Soon Chris and I transitioned into our own home and life; however, I knew everything in the future would be colored by the absence of my father-in-law.

This definitely wasn't what Chris and I had expected during our engagement and first year of marriage. However, we all will have different crises, stresses, and trials throughout the journey of marriage. That's why they call it a journey.

Greg and I (Erin) wouldn't wish what Chris and Rachel went through on any newly married couple. And yet stress, challenges, and painful trials *are* going to be part of your relationship—sooner or later. The Scriptures make this fact clear: "Dear friends, do not be surprised at the painful trial you are suffering, as though something strange were happening to you" (1 Peter 4:12). The key isn't to hope that nothing bad will come your way until you've had time as a couple for your relationship to develop the necessary coping skills. The key is to learn how to manage the stress and challenges that are inevitable in marriage.

Sadly, when many newly married couples face outside trials, research suggests that they are "more likely to report problems within their relationship, more likely to experience declines in satisfaction over time, and quicker to dissolve their relationship entirely."[1] But this doesn't have to be your story. As Rachel so eloquently wrote, part of the adventure of marriage lies in facing external difficulties together and growing stronger through these trials. Couples who thrive in their marriages don't have fewer problems; instead, they work together and take the view that tribulations are opportunities for growth and positive change. The apostle Paul spoke about this in Romans:

> We rejoice in the hope of the glory of God. Not only so,
> but we also rejoice in our sufferings, because we know that
> suffering produces perseverance; perseverance, character; and
> character, hope. And hope does not disappoint us, because
> God has poured out his love into our hearts by the Holy Spirit
> whom he has given us.
>
> ROMANS 5:2–5

Take hope. No matter what comes your way during your first year of marriage, you have the power to ultimately write your own story. Your marriage story doesn't have to end in massive hurt and frustration as you face stress and challenges. Instead, your story can be personally fulfilling and can be a beacon of light for those who are watching your journey.

But how do you face challenges and protect your marriage? The answer begins with understanding the unhealthy ways we deal with stress.

Unhealthy Ways of Dealing with Stress and Challenges

Two years into our marriage, one of the biggest stressors that we dealt with was busyness. I (Greg) was in full-time graduate school, pursuing my doctorate in marriage and family. We had a baby girl to care for and a household to manage. Erin was working full-time as a labor-and-delivery nurse, and I needed to make extra money so we could afford to live in Southern California. I ended up getting a part-time job leading drug-and-alcohol recovery groups for a local high school. Many of these teenagers were considered high-risk students (delinquent, using drugs or alcohol). But I loved these kids. One time I shared that Erin had been harassed at the local grocery store by some punks. I'll never forget these hard-core boys, whom I wasn't supposed to connect with, passionately promise that they were going to "take care" of these other boys who had threatened Erin. I spent the rest of the meeting talking them out of war with a rival gang. Now when my friends are teasing me and I tell them to be careful because "I know people," I'm actually not kidding!

What a crazy season. Although Erin and I didn't experience a death like Chris and Rachel, we were massively busy, and it was beginning to take its toll on us as individuals and in our relationship. As I look back on that stressful, busy season, I realize that we both started to cope with the busyness by doing some very unhealthy things. When I feel stressed out, I go into the "cave." I withdraw and isolate. On the other hand, Erin does the exact opposite when she experiences stress. She gets overly social and feels the need to connect with her girlfriends and our couple friends. Whereas I didn't want to be around anyone because I was exhausted and stressed out, Erin wanted to be around people what seemed like every night. As you can imagine, this caused plenty of conflict in our marriage.

What about you? How do you handle stress? We're sure you have both healthy and unhealthy coping skills. The key, however, is to become aware of the *unhealthy* things you do to manage stress. Here are some of the more popular ways that people attempt to handle stress that don't work:

- Minimizing or normalizing it—explain away stress as temporary ("I just have a million things going on right now"), see it as an integral part of your life ("Things are always crazy around here"), or blame it on your personality ("I'm a type A person, that's all")
- Ignoring it   *Me*

BEC
- Obsessing about it— to fixate on or be completely consumed by what is causing you to be stressed
- Withdrawing from friends, family, and activities
- Living life through your brain (brain-only decisions) ME
- Taking out your stress on others (lashing out, angry outbursts, physical violence) ME
- Becoming a workaholic
- Overeating or undereating (turning to your "other" friends—Ben and Jerry, Ronald McDonald, Sara Lee, Little Debbie, or Russell Stover) to cope with stress, or not eating at all.
- Being a couch potato—zoning out for hours in front of the TV or computer, or playing video games
- Procrastinating MEP
- Engaging in "retail therapy"—buying yourself something to boost your mood when you're feeling low or really stressed out
- Filling up every minute of the day to avoid facing problems BEC
- Giving in to the demands of others
- Using legal or illegal drugs (illegal drugs such as marijuana or cocaine; legal drugs such as prescriptions or over-the-counter pain or sleep medication, caffeine, alcohol, and cigarettes)
- Escaping—distracting yourself with shopping sprees, pornography, adrenaline-junkie activities, etc.
- Shutting down—you stop functioning because your stress level has overwhelmed your physical and mental reserves.

What do you do when you're stressed out? The problem is, when you deal with stressful events in unhealthy ways, you exacerbate the negative effects of stress and create new problems in your health and relationships. Let's take a look at what happens.

The Impact of Stress and External Challenges

First, stress takes a toll on us as individuals. According to WebMD, when you are stressed, your body thinks you're in danger. "It makes hormones that speed up your heart, make you breathe faster, and give you a burst of energy. This is called the fight-or-flight stress response. Some stress is normal and even useful. . . . But if stress happens too often or lasts too long, it can have [negative] effects. It can be linked to headaches, an upset stomach, back pain, [as well as short temper, anger, depression, anxiety], and trouble sleeping. It can weaken your immune system, making it harder to fight off disease."[2]

Stress creates exhausted people who are empty inside—drained physically, emotionally, mentally, and spiritually. When we're worn out, we have nothing to give, and our marriages suffer—we end up serving relational leftovers. Best-selling authors Les and Leslie Parrott explain the devastating impact of exhaustion on our marriages:

> Busy people rarely give their best to the ones they love. They
> serve leftovers. We're not talking about the kind that come
> from your fridge. We're talking about emotional and relational
> leftovers—the ones that remain after the prime energy and
> attention have already been given to others. This is sometimes
> known as sunset fatigue. It's when we are too drained, too tired
> or too preoccupied to be fully present with the ones we love
> the most. They get what's left over.[3]

A marriage can't survive on leftovers forever. A thriving marriage requires time, attention, and energy. Our marriages need our highest priority because of what stress does to them. Listen to how author Judy Ford described the impact of stress on a marriage: "Stressed-out couples quarrel and fight more often, withdraw from each other, [and] feel disconnected, sad, frustrated, [and] angry." When stress is allowed to continue unchecked, it can lead to even bigger problems. According to

Ford, "Long-term stress can turn to depression and isolation resulting in a frozen and distant relationship."[4]

When stress happens, couples suffer relationally:

- Their interactions are hurried.
- They have increased conflict and arguments.
- They disconnect—turning away from their spouses and toward friends or another support system.
- They suffer from a decreased libido and a decreased sex life.
- They communicate less—they start keeping things to themselves or stop sharing innermost secrets.
- They spend less time together—they prefer to be with other people than to be alone with their spouses, or they're relieved when their spouses leave.
- They experience decreased fun and laughter.
- They stop talking about enjoyable things and end up "administrating" their marriage (talking only about the budget, problems, household responsibilities, etc.).
- They react more intensely or strongly to daily ups and downs of married life.
- Their stress is contagious—the tension bounces back and forth between partners. Partners become unable to relax and enjoy each other.
- They fantasize about divorce or separation.

Several problems occur when stressful events hit a new marriage. First, stressful events demand time that newlywed couples can't afford. As Chris and Rachel discovered, a grieving mother-in-law requires time and energy. This impacts a couple because maintaining their relationship takes time and energy as well. Stressful events change what the couple needs to talk about and the time available to talk about it. Thus, the more time they spend dealing with stressful events, the less time they have to spend on the marriage. Marriage researchers Lisa Neff and Benjamin Karney perfectly explain this dilemma:

> Despite our best efforts, there are only 24 hours in a day. Time that couples spend deciding how they are going to cut back to get their bills paid, or negotiating who is going to take off work to care for a sick relative, is time that is not spent on other activities, like having sex or participating in shared interests, that are more likely to promote closeness. As a consequence, couples are likely to perceive more unresolved problems within the relationship during periods when they are facing especially high demands outside of the relationship.[5]

Furthermore, stressful events reduce the ability of couples to successfully manage their issues. Stress is like a circuit-breaker box that gets overloaded. When a circuit box has more electrical connections than it's supposed to have, it becomes overloaded, the circuit trips, and the power goes off. We've all almost killed ourselves stumbling around the garage or basement in the dark trying to find the circuit-breaker box. The same thing happens in our marriages. When stress overloads a couple, they "trip" or shut down and thus have a difficult time dealing with the crisis. Lisa Neff and Benjamin Karney explain this problem:

> Stress diminishes the capacity of couples to resolve their issues effectively. In our labs, we have documented this effect by showing that the same couples who are perfectly capable of effective relationship maintenance when times are good (e.g., they tend to forgive each other, they avoid making big issues out of small ones) become significantly less able to engage in these adaptive processes after periods of stress. And the same couples do better at relationship maintenance again after their stresses alleviate.[6]

Another problem with stressful events is that they cause couples to "react" (fight or flight) more intensely to relationship challenges.

The greater the stress in our lives, the more reactive we are to the normal ups and downs of our relationships. When under increased stress, for instance, one spouse may feel perceived slights from her significant other more acutely. Or the husband may hear something more in the tone of his wife's voice when she asks him to take out the trash. Relationships exposed to high stress for a long period of time are bound to falter, no matter how well each individual's relationship skills are developed. During such times, couples are more likely to see their relationship as negative, not realizing the impact stress is having on the validity of their evaluation. Stress colors their perception of the relationship itself. Remove the stress, and a couple's positive relationship skills can once again—and usually do—take over.[7]

However, the most devastating effect of stressful events is that they make people feel unsafe. As we mentioned earlier, it's like that roly-poly bug that rolls up into a tight little ball when it feels threatened. Stressful events make people feel threatened or unsafe. And when people feel unsafe, they shut down and their hearts close. Unfortunately, over time a closed heart will begin to harden. And a hard heart is a major red flag in a marriage.

The only time Jesus ever talked about divorce, He mentioned a hardened heart: "Moses permitted you to divorce your wives because your hearts were hard. But it was not this way from the beginning" (Matthew 19:8). Notice the last phrase: "But it was not this way from the beginning." As you are getting married, our guess is that your hearts are open to each other. This is how we usually start marriage: with open hearts. However, over time, as conflict and stressful events happen, our hearts take a beating and can eventually close.

What we're really trying to guard against is allowing our hearts to harden. This is the kiss of death for a marriage. As noted in chapter 4, author Max Lucado agrees:

A hard heart ruins, not only your life, [but your marriage as well]. . . . Jesus identified the hard heart as the wrecking ball of a marriage. . . . When one or both people in a marriage [harden their hearts], they sign its death certificate.[8]

So how can you tell if a heart has closed? Here are some signs:

- No eye contact
- Folded or crossed arms
- Withdrawal
- Resentment
- Negative body language
- Attack mode
- Avoidance of touch
- Insensitivity

- Relationally disconnected
- Selfishness
- Unforgiveness
- Emotionally distant
- Faithlessness
- Hopelessness
- Anger

How would your fiancé(e) know when your heart is shut down? Remember, one of the greatest negative effects of stress is also the least talked about. Over time, poorly managed stress tends to shut down our hearts. Refuse to allow your heart to close. King Solomon, the wisest man who ever lived, gives us this encouragement: "Above all else, guard your heart, for it is the wellspring of life" (Proverbs 4:23). One of the best ways to guard against a marriage that feels unsafe and hearts that are closed is to learn how to manage stressful events in healthy ways.

Guarding Our Hearts: Healthy Ways of Dealing with Stress and Challenges

The best way to manage stressful events is to understand your responsibility as an *individual* and then as a *couple*. Let's first look at what you can do to cope with stress and challenges *as an individual*.

1. *Recognize it.* According to author Judy Ford, "Couples often become so accustomed to unchecked stress that they barely recognize [it]

and often overlook the destructive ramifications."[9] It's as if we miss the warning signs and have become immune to the signs of stress because it has become such a normal part of our everyday lives. So how do you know when you—or your fiancé(e)—are stressed? Here are some of the signs:

- Tension in your shoulders and neck
- Clenching your hands into fists
- Anxiety
- Back pain
- Constipation or diarrhea
- Depression
- Fatigue
- Headaches
- High blood pressure
- Insomnia
- Problems with relationships
- Shortness of breath
- Stiff neck
- Upset stomach
- Weight gain or loss[10]

2. *Analyze it.* Discover what's causing stress in your life—both the large, obvious stressors as well as the small daily hassles and demands. Here are some of the obvious causes:

- Getting married
- Being laid off from your job
- The death of a loved one
- An illness

- An injury
- A job promotion
- Money problems
- Moving   *BEC* (handwritten)

Following are some examples of small daily hassles and demands:

- A long commute
- Endless errands
- Family responsibilities
- Career responsibilities
- Household responsibilities (cooking, cleaning, lawn care, etc.)
- A never-ending stack of bills
- Volunteer work
- Balancing work and marriage   *ME* (handwritten)

Most of University of Texas psychologist Lisa Neff's work on stress and marriage shows that the best way to keep stress from weakening relationships is to cut out as many stressors as possible. As you both think about the obvious and subtle stressors, what might you cut out or deal with before you walk down the aisle?

3. *Do great self-care.* Once you can identify your stress and understand where it's coming from, the key is to take great care of yourself, as Jesus stressed in the greatest commandment: "'Love the Lord your God with all your heart and with all your soul and with all your strength and with all your mind'; and, 'Love your neighbor as yourself'" (Luke 10:27). We want you to focus on the very last two words—"as yourself." Stressful events will always be part of our lives. Thus, we need to keep our focus on learning to manage stress. Here are some ideas that will help you to take great care of your heart in the midst of stressful events:

- *Get your heart open.* Remember, when you experience stress, the net effect is that it closes your heart. What you're trying to guard against is your heart hardening over time. We love that the Lord wants to heal our hearts: "'Even now,' declares the LORD, 'return to me with all your heart. . . . Rend your heart and not your garments. Return to the LORD your God, for he is gracious and compassionate, slow to anger and abounding in love, and he relents from sending calamity'" (Joel 2:12–13). Do whatever it takes to get your heart back open.

- *Express your feelings.* Don't stuff or ignore your emotions. Feelings give our hearts a voice. If you don't voice your feelings, resentment will build, and the situation will likely remain the same.

- *Slow down the pace of life.* Intentionally change your pace and create margin—the space between your workload and your limits. Robert Barron wrote, "The deepest part of the soul likes to go slow, since it seeks to savor rather than to accomplish; it wants to rest in and contemplate the good rather than hurry off to another place."[11] Thus, you must ruthlessly eliminate hurry from your life!

- *Get plenty of sleep.* As adults, we need about eight to nine hours of sleep each night. ~CREW REST~

- *Rest and relax.* Try to keep at least one day a week free from obligations and make it a day of rest and relaxation to recharge your batteries. Genesis tells us that "God blessed the seventh day and made it holy, because on it he rested from all the work of creating that he had done" (2:3).

- *Get regular exercise.* Physical activity is a great way to release pent-up energy, stress, and tension. Try to engage in at least thirty minutes of exercise, three times per week. ~PA'S~ ~CHECK~

- *Keep your sense of humor.* Laughing helps your body combat stress. "A cheerful heart is good medicine, but a crushed spirit dries up the bones" (Proverbs 17:22).

- *Learn how to set boundaries and say no.* Whether at work or at home, know your limits and refuse to accept added responsibilities when you're close to reaching them.

The bottom line is that taking good care of yourself is always in the best interests of you and your fiancé(e) because you can't give what you don't have.

Now let's look at what you can do *as a couple* to manage the stresses and challenges you encounter.

1. *View your marriage as a journey.* We love to use the analogy of the explorers Lewis and Clark to describe marriage. They went on a great expedition down the Missouri River with a group called the Corps of Discovery. Why we think this is a perfect description of marriage is that you are about to embark on a great adventure as well. Since Lewis and Clark traveled by canoe, they never knew what was around the next bend of the river. Sometimes the river was easy—calm and peaceful. Other times, the river was difficult—filled with unexpected raging rapids, plunging waterfalls, and hostile situations. Although they didn't know what was awaiting them around the bend, they were in the canoe *together*. This is what marriage is like. You are about to start your own "Corps of Discovery" adventure together. The point is that you're in the amazing adventure called marriage *together*. Whatever happens, you can face it as a team.

We recently read a story that perfectly illustrates this journey perspective of marriage:

> Shortly after [the] wedding, [a] wife was diagnosed with
> a virulent form of cancer requiring a debilitating round of
> treatments. It was an awful and difficult time for both of them,
> but she survived. The cancer went into remission . . . and the
> two of them proceeded to have a long and happy marriage. "So
> you see," [the husband explained], "the key to having a strong

marriage is experiencing stress. The way we figure it, after beating cancer, we knew just how much we could depend on each other. After that, the rest was easy."[12]

We love the husband's perspective! As the rough waters approach and changes happen—and they will—always maintain a mind-set that you are unified teammates. Remember, the first year of marriage gives you plenty of opportunity to apply this, thus laying the groundwork to use this mind-set throughout the many years of your marriage journey together.

The word *unity* means "the state of being united or joined as a whole." This couldn't be a better definition as it applies to marriage, because as you and I know, when we're married, we become a "whole" or a unit—"The two will become one flesh. So they are no longer two, but one" (Mark 10:8). Therefore, when we approach changes, conflict, and stressors as individuals, more difficulties arise because we're fighting what is true—we are one or a whole.

When you are unified, you can tackle any storm that comes your way! Therefore, we encourage you to apply this wisdom in your relationship— especially during the first year.

2. *Treasure-hunt when trials come.* Much like Chris and Rachel, you cannot predict what will come your way during your marriage. The Scriptures are clear that you will have trials in life, but God will use those very struggles to strengthen your marriage. This is exactly what 1 Peter 5:10 promises: "After you have suffered a little while, the God of all grace, who has called you to his eternal glory in Christ, will himself restore, confirm, strengthen, and establish you" (ESV).

Your first year of marriage may not look the way you planned— because of either internal or external stressors. However, much like I (Erin) learned in China, persevering through fear, anxiety, conflict, and misunderstandings can lead to unexpected blessings and gifts.

Lisa Neff's work on stress and marriage showed that "couples who had good coping skills and were exposed to mild to moderate stress as newlyweds were more resilient in the face of later stressors, including parenthood, than those who had good coping skills but saw relatively little stress during the early phases of matrimony."[13] There will always be difficulties in marriage that you won't be able to control. But that's okay. Facing challenges together can bring you and your fiancé(e) closer as long as you possess the necessary tools to address the trials successfully. In the end, it's powerful to be able to look back and say, "That was brutal, but we made it through!" This is why we really like Lisa Neff and Elizabeth Broady's encouragement:

> Beginning a marriage with little-to-no stress robs the couple of the opportunity to put their relationship resources to the test, and this can leave couples at risk for marital declines when future stressors, such as the transition to parenthood, are encountered. . . . [For] spouses who . . . possess adequate initial resources for coping with . . . stress [that is, couples who begin with good communication abilities, supportive social networks, a willingness to see things from the other's perspective, etc.], increases in stress from low to moderate . . . provide . . . a training ground in which to hone their coping responses.[14]

Greg and I experienced many changes that happened quickly in the first months of our marriage. Greg had been attending Denver Seminary, so I joined him there, and we moved into our first apartment on campus. I worked at a new job in a high-stress environment, and Greg attended school full-time. I had a new address, a new name, a new city, a new climate, new friends, a new church denomination, was away from my family for the first time, and was officially sharing a bathroom with someone for the first time! It was a recipe for stress and possible conflict especially because we hadn't participated in premarital counseling. So we were given the opportunity to seek *postmarital* counseling. It was very helpful to us amid all the changes. And we can say confidently that twenty-three years later, those "rough waters" were instrumental in building the marriage relationship we have today. God promises to use our trials for good in our lives, and if we allow them to, they will strengthen our marriages as well. We really like Dr. Larry Barlow's encouragement to couples who are facing stressful events:

> When you work together through . . . all [the "rough spots" in your marriage] in a constructive way—you're communicating, you're appreciating each other, you're putting each other's needs above your own—you come out stronger and closer. You'll then have confidence to face the next issue down the road.[15]

We can't predict what is around the bend for each of you. As we started this chapter saying, you are guaranteed to experience enormous change after saying "I do." This is a normal part of adventuring into the unknown—much like traveling to a foreign country. And as we mentioned earlier, many of the stressors will be internal or within your relationship, and other stressors will be external or outside the relationship, as Chris and Rachel's story illustrated. But teammates work together for the good of the whole as they journey together.

By developing a healthy pattern of coping in your first year of marriage, you'll be much more likely to continue dealing with issues as a team over the years. It seems so simple, and yet it will have a profound impact on your relationship. So no matter what trials come your way, always remember that you're now on the same team!

Ready to Talk

1. Consider Erin's comparison of embarking on the lifelong marriage journey to traveling to a foreign country. Have the two of you traveled together before now? If so, how did you prepare for the journey? If not, are you excited to travel together, or does it make you a little nervous? How might your upcoming marriage be like going to a foreign country?

2. Share a story with each other about a stressful time in your life. How did you respond to the stress? What happened?

3. In this chapter, Greg and Erin give several ideas to care for yourself in the midst of stressful events. What can you start doing to care for yourself during the stress of planning your wedding?

- Get your heart open.
- Express your feelings.
- Slow down the pace of life.
- Get plenty of sleep.
- Rest and relax.
- Get regular exercise.
- Keep your sense of humor.
- Learn how to set boundaries.

Ready to Try

Have you planned your honeymoon yet? If so, talk about the details of the trip. (If you haven't, or if the honeymoon is a surprise, just talk about a future trip that the two of you would like to take together.) Write out your goals for the trip. Do you hope to do a lot of sightseeing? Or is relaxation high on your to-do list? Are you an "adventure" traveler (someone who likes to be on the go and see and experience as much as possible)? Or are you a laid-back traveler (someone who doesn't like a lot of structure, who takes a go-with-the-flow approach to experiencing new things)? What would your dream vacation look like? Talk about what you'd need to pack for the journey and how much preparation would be involved. Do you think you both take similar approaches to travel? If not, come up with at least three ideas for how you can merge your travel personalities in order to enjoy new adventures together.

CHAPTER 14

HOW TO HAVE A GREAT FIRST YEAR OF MARRIAGE

Tim Popadic

IN THOSE EARLY WEEKS and months of my marriage, I'll never forget thinking, *Why didn't anyone tell me it would be like this?* The fact is that marriage might be different than you think it will be, no matter how you pictured it, how much you prepared, and how many people you talked to about it ahead of time. The picture is usually different for each of us, whether for better or for worse.

My wife, Beth, and I had a beautiful wedding surrounded by our closest friends and family. It took place in a picturesque mansion in Connecticut on a beautiful June day, without a cloud in the sky. What could be more perfect?

But when we pulled up to the 1776 Townhouses, our home for the next few months, the perfection quickly fizzled. I could instantly see why they named them "1776"—our townhouse looked as if it hadn't been updated since the 1700s! As I opened the door, I could see Beth's countenance fade as she surveyed the depressing little place with wall-to-wall brown carpeting (except for several stains that left bleached-out spots), brown cabinets, and brown counters—you get the picture. And this was way before HGTV deemed brown to be an "in" color for homes. Since we had only one car, this townhouse was to be Beth's backdrop for the start of our life together. While I was at work, she was blessed to be confined to this delightful space, knowing no one but me and with no means of escape. This was just the beginning . . .

After recently graduating from college, getting married a month later, starting a new job as a youth pastor (me), moving eighteen hours away to finish up some schooling for four months, having a car blow up, having emergency surgery (Beth), coming back to the youth-pastor job, moving four more times, and living in three more apartments, Beth and I finally settled in to begin married life.

By the end of the first year, reality had set in. We'd been thrown into the fire of so many new decisions, circumstances, jobs, relationships, locations, and emotions, some serious triage needed to take place. We were left in a fog of smoke those first several months as we tried to figure out where we had been burned and which areas needed treatment first. Although I don't wish for you a situation like ours, it did draw us together in ways that only hard things do.

Many couples will say that their first year of marriage was difficult. For some reason, we think that two totally different people coming together to share life will be easy. Two people from two different families with different upbringings, ideas, thoughts, feelings, and emotions—no problem. Happily ever after, right? Well, yes and no.

Your first year of marriage is key in helping lay the groundwork for learning how to build and protect your relationship. There will be mountaintop highs, fun, adventure, joy, pleasure, laughter, thrills, and many amazing firsts. Delight in these moments! This is why you got married. There will also be obstacles, confusion, doubt, panic, and fears. It might not be as easy or simple as you think it will be. Fight for your spouse in these moments. This is also why you got married. Some rude awakenings may be mixed in with the sweet times, and some startling things may be revealed. This is where the true work begins. Roll up your sleeves, grease up your elbows, and get ready. You're in for the greatest ride of your life!

There are ten things you should know by the end of your first year:

1. Your feelings aren't reality.
2. You are not Ken, and she is not Barbie.
3. Your mother isn't the benchmark of your wife.
4. When you ask him what he's thinking and he says "Nothing," he means nothing.
5. When you ask her what she's thinking and she says "Nothing," what she really means is that she's thinking about every detail from marriage until eternity.
6. He thinks about sex the way you think about money.
7. You both are more selfish than you thought you were.
8. Contraception is 99 percent effective. (Just ask Greg and Erin!)
9. Your husband might not understand the concept of calling you in the middle of the day just to check in.
10. Marriage is amazing, but it's also work.

Some of these statements are shockingly true. There is one thing, however, that all couples face during their first year of marriage: opposition in succeeding in the marriage. Opposition happens in a couple's life for many different reasons and can come in many different forms. The target of opposition is to keep your marriage from its God-given destiny—becoming what God intended it to be.

As Greg and Erin discussed in the previous chapter, the attack and opposition can come from different sources and external circumstances, be it from finances, your job(s), the influence of culture and entertainment, friends, family, and so on. There are internal attacks, such as self-doubt, criticism, the pressure to find our own identities as individuals, and how to fit in within the marriage. Attacks can be sudden and come without warning. One thing is for sure: You cannot fight these battles alone!

Build and Protect Your Marriage

One of my favorite stories in the Bible is from the book of Nehemiah. It's such a rich book with so many life lessons woven into it. Although it isn't a story about marriage, while reading it, I can't help but be moved, convicted, and inspired about the parallels and principles it can bring to marriage.

Nehemiah tells the story about the Israelites rebuilding the walls of Jerusalem. The city of Jerusalem was the city of God, the place where the Israelites came to worship. Considered sacred, a city without walls, it lacked protection from an enemy attack.

This is how the story began:

> "Come—let's build the wall of Jerusalem and not live with this disgrace any longer," [Nehemiah said to the people.] I told them how God was supporting me and how the king was backing me up. [And the people] said, "We're with you. Let's get started." [So] they rolled up their sleeves, ready for the good work.
>
> NEHEMIAH 2:17–18, MSG

How does this account relate to the first year of marriage? The city of Jerusalem represents marriage. Just as God had a desire and a destiny for the city of Jerusalem, He has a desire and a destiny for each marriage. Nehemiah cared deeply about the city. It was where his family lived, it was sacred to his community, and it represented something much larger than himself. The walls had been placed around the city to protect the work that was going on in the city. Although Nehemiah was in charge of rebuilding the walls, he couldn't do it alone. The task would require a community of people willing to work and stand guard and use their time and talents for a specific outcome.

This community of Nehemiah's was strategic: "The common laborers held a tool in one hand and a spear in the other" (4:17, MSG). The people knew that while rebuilding the walls (using the "tool"), they had to simultaneously protect themselves and the city (using the "spear"). As you begin to build the foundation of your marriage, it's crucial to be on guard, protecting it at all times.

Building your marriage while protecting it go hand in hand. Stone by stone, brick by brick, you can build your marriage by using the twelve key behaviors you've learned in this book:

1. Leaving your parents and cleaving to your spouse.
2. Making a lifelong commitment by eliminating divorce from your vocabulary and reminding each other that you'll be together "until death do us part."
3. Honoring each other, cherishing your spouse as a priceless treasure, and regularly nourishing your spouse in ways that speak love to him or her.
4. Sharing spiritual intimacy and connecting spiritually by attending church regularly, studying the Bible, and praying together.
5. Cultivating a mutually satisfying sexual relationship.
6. Fostering positive communication—knowing your spouse and being willing to be known.
7. Valuing your unique differences.
8. Creating realistic and clear expectations.
9. Practicing healthy conflict management so you can move into the deepest levels of intimacy and connection.
10. Sharing responsibility as a team—making decisions as teammates around roles and household responsibilities in a way that feels good to both of you.

11. Pursuing financial peace and harmony by managing your finances in a way that honors God and your spouse.
12. Coping with stress and crises by guarding your heart and marriage when storms and trials hit.

These twelve behaviors are powerful, but I want to add another powerful habit that will help build and protect your marriage during the first year: *Surround yourselves with a godly community*. A community like this should foster vulnerability and accountability so that each person will feel valued and cared for while being held accountable to live according to biblical principles and values. Finding a great couple to mentor you is another means of protection. Having this third party to bounce things off of and to guide you in the right direction will be priceless for your relationship.

Identify Your Community

We learn best when we expose our weaknesses to others and allow our vulnerability to guide us into a process of growth through the power of authentic community. Community is a vital part of marriage. Surrounding yourself with a few key couples will be essential to the success of your marriage. The best way to do this is to look around in the circles you're already a part of and identify a few couples whom you respect and who share like-minded values.

Chances are that you're already doing life with these people, and just taking a few steps of intentionality can help you build a stronger relationship with them. A great way to do this is to start or join a small group together, or even set specific times to get together to talk openly and honestly with each other. In our busy lives, it's so easy to miss being intentional with relationships. Take them to the next level, beyond the surface, and engage in true community the way God designed it to be. He never intended for you to walk alone, even as a couple, but to be in community together.

Do Life Together

The book of Acts describes what genuine community looks like:

> They devoted themselves to the apostles' teaching and to the
> fellowship, to the breaking of bread and to prayer. Everyone
> was filled with awe, and many wonders and miraculous signs
> were done by the apostles. All the believers were together and
> had everything in common. Selling their possessions and goods,
> they gave to anyone as he had need. Every day they continued
> to meet together in the temple courts. They broke bread in
> their homes and ate together with glad and sincere hearts,
> praising God and enjoying the favor of all the people.
>
> ACTS 2:42–47

As you look around at your friends, if you realize that you don't have these kinds of couples in your life, maybe it's time to find some new friends. The community you surround yourself with has the power to build up or tear down your relationship with your future spouse. Choose wisely. Pray and ask God to help you choose those you will allow to invest in your lives. Also ask God whose lives He would like you to invest in. Just because you're new at this marriage thing doesn't mean you can't pour yourselves into others' lives as well. While it's important to surround yourself with people who will care about you both and keep you accountable in your Christian walk, it's also okay to find friends who aren't just like you. Shine a light for others in your community who may still be searching when it comes to faith.

Practice hospitality. Invite friends into your home as well as into your life. Share meals together. Don't worry about having the perfect place settings or whether you can serve a gourmet dinner. People just want to be included and loved, even if it's over pizza and plastic plates! Be intentional about building *real* relationships.

Don't Give Up

Another essential principle to apply during your first year of marriage is perseverance. Nehemiah described this principle in action as the Israelites rebuilt the city walls: "We kept at it, repairing and rebuilding the wall. The whole wall was soon joined together and halfway to its intended height because the people had a heart for the work" (Nehemiah 4:6, MSG).

There is no magic formula to finding the right people to be a part of your lives, but one thing is critical, they have to know and love you enough as a couple to speak truth into your lives. They have to "have a heart for the work." Feel-good friends, who care too much about what you think of them to speak truth to you, won't be a helpful resource long term. You need people who will create objectivity and movement in your relationship—people who love you just as you are but can see the potential of who you can be.

I recently heard a story of a couple who was in such a community. Tiffany and Jeremy Lee, caught up in the busyness of life, drifted apart. They found themselves disagreeing on everything and came to the conclusion that their marriage just wasn't working out. Ten years and two kids later, they were ready to call it quits. A few weeks later, Jeremy moved out.

Tiffany called one of their close couple friends and told them what Jeremy had done. On the other end of the line, the husband had to excuse himself for a moment because he became physically sick. Once he was able to compose himself, he returned to the call and said, "I'm sorry, but we're not going to allow your marriage to fall apart." He hung up the phone, prayed, and came up with a plan to help.

Are there people in your life who care that much about you and are willing to dive in for the sake of your marriage? This is the kind of community you need to find—the kind of community that will encourage you but loves you too much not to take action.

Thankfully this story had a happy ending. In the four months that Tiffany and Jeremy were separated, their close couple friends gathered many other couples around them to speak truth into their lives and help get them back on track. Two months into the separation, Tiffany and Jeremy started dating again. Two months after that, he moved back home.

Now this couple is using their story of how God used community to save their marriage to help and encourage other couples who are in the same place they were.

Simple Ways to Approach Your First Year of Marriage

As you get closer to your wedding day, it's important to remember that you want your marriage to have a strong start. Let's look at a few practical ways to build and protect your marriage during your first year.

Take a "Leave of Absence" from Other Relationships

Think of the way the military grants time off to its soldiers. A *leave of absence* is defined as "permission to be absent from duty, or the period for which such absence is granted." Interestingly, the Scriptures make this same provision for newlyweds:

> If a man has recently married, he must not be sent to war or
> have any other duty laid on him. For one year he is to be free
> to stay at home and bring happiness to the wife he has married.
> DEUTERONOMY 24:5

As a newlywed couple forms their marital relationship, the two need to be given permission to be absent from the "duty" of being someone's son, daughter, sibling, or friend. A new couple needs a period of time to formulate their new relationship without the pressure of maintaining other kinds of relationships.

Once you get married, you'll literally need a leave of absence in which others don't expect you to be proactively working on outside relationships. For a period of time, you'll need to disengage from anyone or anything that could potentially interfere with "cleaving" to your new spouse. But remember, as Ted Cunningham talked about in chapter 2, you're not severing your relationships with parents, siblings, extended family, and friends. *Leave of absence* means "permission to be absent from duty, or the period for which such absence is granted." *Severing*, on the other hand, means that you totally cut off those relationships and allow them to die in the same way you would amputate a diseased, dysfunctional limb. I'm not advocating *that*! Leaving means reprioritizing your relationships: God is number one, your spouse is number two, and others are number three. You are lessening the emphasis you formerly placed on previous core relationships.

A logical question might be, "How long should the leave of absence last?" After all, most workplaces give new parents six weeks' leave of absence. Since couples differ, no standard amount of time exists. Instead, I encourage you to think about what specific things need to take place to cement your new relationship. Once those things occur, then you could end the leave of absence.

One word of caution: Feeling a special closeness and bond as friends, boyfriend and girlfriend, and as one another's fiancé(e) is much different than cleaving as husband and wife. If you've had a long dating history or engagement, or if you've known each other many years, you'll still need extended time to become one as a married couple. Take a leave of absence.

Find a Good Church to Plug In To

This has been touched on before, but it bears repeating: As a couple, you'll need to find a place where you can connect to other believers, grow closer to Jesus and to each other, serve others, and pour out your faith in practical, tangible ways. For Christians, a church community is a great place to fill these needs. Nothing good ever comes from isolation. In isolation you grow skeptical, critical, judgmental, selfish, and weak. You weren't meant to be alone, in fact; you were designed for community. That's why, in Matthew 18:20, Jesus said that "where two or three come together in my name, there am I with them." Yes, He is always with you, even when you're alone, but He emphasized community because there is power in it. After all, Jesus is community—the Father, the Son, and the Holy Spirit. If you're working to become like Jesus, then community isn't an option. It needs to be part of your lifestyle. In community, you can fully flourish as a couple.

Multiple transitions or moves before you find the right church community that fits your needs is very normal. Be committed to finding a biblically based church that prioritizes community. A great place to start is to check out churches via their websites. Typically a church will share what is most important to them. If they seem to be family friendly, they most likely have plenty of programming for young couples and families. Once you identify a few churches that seem to be the right fit, take the next step and check them out with a visit. Be sure to explore their statement of beliefs to confirm that they line up with Scripture (since, of course, that's the most important aspect of a church).

Be consistent. Plugging in to community isn't a two-week or two-visit process. It requires time. Measure it in months, not weeks. Relationships take time to forge, and often it's the second or third interaction with another couple that finally clicks. Consistency in your pursuit will help decrease the amount of time it will take for you to get connected into the right group. Plugging in to a class or small group in your life stage is a great place to start. Be patient!

Find a Couple to Mentor You

Nehemiah highlighted another essential for your first year of marriage:

> So I stationed armed guards [mentors] at the most vulnerable places of the wall [your relationship] and assigned people by families [community] with their swords, lances, and bows. After looking things over I stood up and spoke to the nobles, officials, and everyone else: "Don't be afraid of them [the enemy]. Put your minds on the Master, great and awesome, and then fight for your brothers, your sons, your daughters, your wives, and your homes."
>
> NEHEMIAH 4:13–14, MSG

Throughout our twenty years of marriage, my wife and I have been blessed with great mentors who have come alongside us and have carefully spoken words of wisdom, affirmation, and correction into our lives. Although these couples have changed through the years as we've moved to different places and have been in different seasons of life, the profile of each couple was essentially the same. They were all at least somewhat older than we were, they loved God and put Him first, they had been through hard times and had a thriving marriage because of it, and they loved us and wanted to see our marriage succeed.

As you can imagine, their influence helped form and shape the couple we are today. God strategically placed these priceless people in our lives to encourage us and challenge us. We'll always be thankful and grateful for all they invested in us. They have been the inspiration and motivation behind our passion and drive to pour ourselves into others' marriages and lives.

Mentors are so important in our lives, and being a mentor is too. I love John Maxwell's concept of the 360-degree leader who understands the importance of having an older mentor in his or her life, the importance of peer mentors, and the importance of being a mentor in someone else's life. The visual is this: one in front (older mentor), one on each side (peer mentors), and one behind (the person you are mentoring).

I hope you've been regularly meeting with a mentor couple as you work through this book. If so, I encourage you to meet with your mentor couple once a month during the first year of your marriage. Trust me, once you start the daily process of building a marriage together, many of the things you've read and learned in these pages will make sense in a very different way. Having a mentor couple during this pivotal time will pay dividends beyond your wildest dreams. If you haven't had a mentor couple up to this point, the process of finding one doesn't have to be difficult. A great way to find one is similar to what I shared earlier about finding your community. Share a meal together, serve together, and be intentional with the people who are already in your life. Once you identify a couple, ask them if they would consider mentoring you or meeting with you and your fiancé(e) on a regular basis. It would be rare for a couple to pass up this opportunity, especially if they already have a connection with you.

Often, churches have established mentoring programs that you can plug in to. This can be another way to get started if you're new to the area or just aren't sure how to go about finding a mentor couple to walk alongside you.

Find Ways to Serve

The key to success for Nehemiah's community was that they were willing to roll up their sleeves and get to work. They valued service as critical to caring for one another and accomplishing their goals. When we serve, our attention moves from us to others. Being a servant is at the heart of marriage. Making a habit of serving others early on in your marriage is so valuable. It will draw you together as you give of yourselves. It's just another step in your pursuit of becoming more like Jesus. Serving alongside others also provides the opporunity to build friendships and meet others who are like-minded and share some of your values.

Great places to serve are in your local church or community. I don't think you'll be hard-pressed to find opportunities. As a wife, you might volunteer with the women's ministry at your church, which is a great way to build female friendships. As a husband, you might join a men's Bible study, offering to help with setup and takedown after each meeting. This is also a great way to build relationships with guys in your community.

Other possibilities include serving in the nursery at church or in a children's Sunday school class, feeding the homeless at your local soup kitchen, visiting with residents at a retirement home, or volunteering to watch a neighbor's kids so she can spend a few minutes at the store without begging kids in tow.

Some of the greatest holiday memories for my wife and me over the years have included serving the homeless at Thanksgiving, giving out gifts at Christmas to parents who can't afford them, and holding babies in orphanages in Panama. It's amazing how putting others first helps put a fresh perspective on our relationship. It makes us thankful and grateful for what we have, while feeling blessed that we can share our abundance with others.

Don't Stop Dating!

Community is very important, but so is having time alone as a couple. After the wedding, couples may find themselves thinking that now that they're married, there is no need to date. After all, their life is one big date. They eat meals together, do chores together, watch TV together—everything they do is together. Apart from their time at work, their lives are one big togetherness. Because this is true, it is easy for couples to let their marriages turn into the routine, the mundane, the regular, the comfortable, and the boring. Dating is the art of saying, "You're still special! I still want to get to know you more. What you have to say is valuable. You're still fun to be with, you're still worth spending money on, and you're still worth pursuing." Most often dating is seen as the precursor to marriage. In reality, it's a vital ingredient for a thriving marriage.

Couples have all sorts of excuses for why they stop dating after marriage:

- It's too expensive.
- It's too complicated. Who will watch the kids (once children come along)?
- It's too hard to carve out time around all of our other activities.
- It takes too much thought and planning.

And the list goes on!

Do you know that married couples who date on a regular basis significantly increase their relationship satisfaction?

Why is that? Because married couples who date . . .

- have figured out the importance of being intentional,
- understand the need to continue to invest in their relationship,
- make the other person feel valued,
- know how to have fun together,
- learn better conflict resolution, and
- model for their kids the importance of their relationship.

Dating and spending time together apart from your regular routine will help keep your marriage healthy and vibrant. Especially as kids enter the picture, it will say to them that your husband-wife relationship is important, valuable, and set apart. In addition to dating, I highly recommend making time for weekends away, special trips together, and marriage retreats. Any extended time together out from the ordinary can give you a fresh perspective and time to focus on each other.

As you continue through this first year of marriage and into the years ahead, I want to offer you some encouragement. Becoming one as a couple isn't an instantaneous occurrence that takes place after the pastor pronounces you Mr. and Mrs. Rather, it's a lifetime in the making. So drop those preconceived notions and cut yourselves some relational slack. You may think you know each other now, but you have no idea what time and circumstances will expose. What joy and hardship will reveal. How growing to be more like Jesus will change the couple you are today.

Babies are born into this world with about 300 bones (give or take a few). And they need every one of those 300 bones to make it through the birth canal. A baby's skull, alone, is comprised of forty-four different bones! These bones are pretty flexible—still essentially cartilage at this stage—so they can fit a head the size of a coconut through an opening the size of a plum. You see, it takes about eighteen years of life for a baby's bones to fuse together. By the time they reach adulthood, they will have a total of 206 bones. Amazing, isn't it? Three hundred to 206 bones—now that's a big difference! It takes the process of time, growth, and sometimes even pain to conform to the design God intended.

Marriage is like a baby. You come into this union with a total of 600 bones. You'll need every one of those 600 bones to make it through the birth canal of your first few years of life together. Your bones need to grow hard and strong to support the structure of your marriage in the years ahead. As you grow closer, learn more about each other, compromise, let God transform you, let your community speak into your relationship, and selflessly serve others, your marital bones will begin to fuse together. As with a baby growing into adulthood, there are no shortcuts to this process. Much time and effort and a lot of prayer will need to go into the process for the two of you to become 412 bones—for the two of you to become one.

weird

analogy

I'm so excited because you have the opportunity that many couples miss! You can learn to build and protect your marriage from the day you say "I do." You can be intentional about surrounding yourselves with a great community. You can pour yourselves into others' lives and marriages as you learn to serve sacrificially together. Like Nehemiah, you can take action, press through, pray and obey, work hard, refuse to give up, thwart the Enemy's schemes, follow God's lead, organize, encourage, meet opposition head-on, confront injustice, refuse discouragement, and never stop until the walls are built.

God has great plans for your marriage, and this is just the beginning!

TIM POPADIC is president of the Relationship Enrichment Collaborative. He travels around the country helping churches, communities, and organizations create Date Night programs to impact the relationships within their communities (DateNightComedyTour.com). Tim has been in full-time pastoral ministry for the past twenty years. Most recently he served as the pastor of marriage and family at Christ Fellowship Church in Palm Beach Gardens, Florida. He's worked with thousands of couples and families across the country helping enrich couples in their relationships, as well as training up hundreds of mentor couples. He is a trained marriage and family therapist (MFT) and speaks nationally at conferences and workshops on being intentional in relationships. Tim and his wife, Beth, have been married for twenty-one years and have four boys.

Ready to Talk

1. Besides your immediate family, can you think of three people who really want your marriage to succeed? How do you know they're committed to your success? How could you thank them for caring and make them part of your support system?

2. Think about your current church involvement. Does it really provide you the kind of community that will help your marriage stay strong? If so, how? If not, which of the following might get you to the next level?

   • Getting to know the pastor better
   • Joining a small group
   • Meeting people by working together on a project
   • Signing up for a class on marriage
   • Finding a different church
   • Other _____

3. When you hear the term *marriage mentor*, what do you think of? What teachers, coaches, or tutors helped you learn school subjects or athletic skills, or mentored you in other areas? How did that mentoring relationship work out? What would it take to convince you to try that kind of approach to improving your relationship?

Ready to Try

Feeling hesitant about the idea of sharing with others the "secrets" of your relationship, especially mentors who might give you advice or hold you accountable? You're not alone. Try just a small first step and see how things go. Start by asking another couple—perhaps good friends with whom you're both comfortable—to conduct a little experiment with you. Invite them to spend an afternoon or evening with you doing something that doesn't require great skill or concentration (e.g., going to an art festival or zoo, window shopping, miniature golfing, etc.). Ask the other couple to give you feedback afterward on the way you and your future spouse appeared to relate. Let them choose the aspect to comment on—the tone of voice you used, perhaps, or whether you seemed to be listening to each other. Try to avoid being on your best behavior for them. The goal is to find out what it's like to be open to someone else's observation and feedback—not to impress anyone. Finally, discuss with your spouse-to-be what you might learn from the other couple's impressions.

COUPLE CHECKUP: GETTING YOUR MARRIAGE OFF TO A SMART START

Dr. David Olson and Amy Olson

MARRIAGE CAN BE ONE OF the most gratifying and fulfilling relationships in your life, but it can also be one of the most frustrating relationships. About 50 percent of marriages end in divorce, which makes marriage one of the riskiest choices individuals voluntarily make in their lifetimes. It's so risky, in fact, that no insurance company has been willing to offer divorce insurance.

While the overall divorce rate remains about 50 percent, the divorce rate is about 40 percent for those who are getting married for the first time and 60 percent for those getting married a second time.[1] For those married before, the divorce rate is high, often because children and stepchildren add complexity and stress to those marriages.

The Value of a Good Marriage

The benefits of marriage have been well documented in numerous studies, and the benefits are even greater for those who are happily married.[2] Married people live longer, have more wealth and economic assets, and have more satisfying sexual relationships than single or cohabiting individuals. In addition, children generally fare better emotionally and academically, and they have lower rates of substance abuse and crime when they're raised in two-parent families.

Public figures have affirmed the value and importance of marriage to individuals and families. Mohnish Pabrai recalls that when Warren Buffett, who is one of the most successful billionaires in the world, was asked to give Pabrai's daughters some advice he told them that "the single most important decision they would make in their lives was who they decided to marry."[3]

David Brooks, a highly respected columnist, said, after finishing a book on well-being,

> Marital happiness is far more important than anything else in determining well-being. If you have a successful marriage, it doesn't matter how many professional setbacks you endure, you will be reasonably happy. If you have an unsuccessful marriage, it doesn't matter how many career triumphs you record, you will remain significantly unfulfilled.[4]

Love Is Not Enough for a Successful Marriage

Love is a poor predictor of marital success. Why, you ask? Because almost all individuals are "in love" when they get married, and yet 50 percent of those marriages fail. One aspect of being in love is that people tend to be idealistic and see their relationship through rose-colored glasses. So most premarital couples are wearing rose-colored glasses, and they see the world, and especially their relationships, in an overly positive way.

If love isn't a predictor of marital success, what factor is most predictive? The answer is having and using good relationship skills. In a national study of fifty thousand married couples from the ages of twenty to sixty-five, researchers found that the following five relationship skills are most accurate in predicting a happy marriage: communication, closeness, flexibility, personality compatibility, and conflict resolution.[5]

You can learn and use these five relationship skills to develop a more healthy and mutually happy marital relationship. *Communication* is important because it indicates your ability as a couple to share feelings and ideas and know your partner understands you. *Closeness* involves feeling emotionally connected to your partner. Being *flexible* represents the ability to change when necessary and being open to doing things differently. *Personality compatibility* involves being able to accept your personality differences and use those differences to better work together as a team. *Conflict resolution* is the ability to resolve ongoing issues so that you can create a more harmonious relationship.

The Couple Checkup: Marriage Maintenance Is Critical

Would you let your car go one hundred thousand miles before getting an oil change? Would you go for a dental checkup just once in twenty years? Would you get a physical exam only after you've been in pain for weeks?

The obvious answer to these questions is no, and yet married couples rarely ever have a checkup for their marriages. Couples invest a great deal of time and money on their weddings, but then they begin to take their marriages for granted. It's increasingly clear that without ongoing work on the relationship, marriage can lose its vitality. Like any other checkup, the sooner a person identifies the issues, the easier they are to solve.

A couple checkup is like a diagnostic assessment of your car. Though it takes time and money for a car tune-up, it's worth the investment because it prevents future problems. By identifying a potential problem like a leaky hose, the cost of repairs is minimal compared to repairing the car after the hose bursts while you're driving.

Prevention is very important in all health fields, including medical care, dental care, and mental health. Early cancer detection is a good example of the value of the preventive approach in reducing the mortality rates of cancer patients. Early detection, prevention, and education are also important for relationship issues. Unfortunately, most distressed married couples don't seek counseling until one or both are considering divorce. In fact, treating couples who wait too long to come for marital therapy is much like treating terminal cancer. The relationship has been so destroyed that it's difficult to rebuild the marriage.

Improving Your Chances of a Happy Marriage

The Couple Checkup is an accurate and helpful map of your relationship. It's an online assessment and program tailored to the unique stage and structure of your relationship. The checkup assesses about thirty areas that researchers have identified as key areas for healthy relationships. The questions are also designed to increase a couple's connection by encouraging self-awareness and partner awareness and dialogue in these key areas. The Couple Checkup identifies both relationship strengths and growth areas.

The Couple Checkup is based on the highly successful PREPARE/ ENRICH program, which has been used by over one hundred thousand counselors and clergy to help three to four million couples prepare for marriage and/or enrich their marriages. Couples who have taken the PREPARE/ENRICH program have reduced their chances of divorce by 30 percent.

A Comprehensive Picture of Your Relationship

The Couple Checkup explores about thirty important aspects of your marital relationship. As illustrated in the following figure, the scales are organized into a variety of important areas:

Ten core scales. The ten core scales of the Couple Checkup include the most common and important aspects of your relationship, such as communication, conflict resolution, finances, affection/sexuality, role relationship, and spiritual beliefs.

Relationship dynamics. This assessment explores positive and negative relationship patterns in your relationship.

SCOPE personality scales. Five personality traits are assessed for each of you, which helps you better understand your personality similarities and differences as a couple.

Couple map. The map explores how each of you feels about emotional closeness and your ability to handle change in your relationship. These areas are important dynamics that can help you build a more healthy relationship.

Family map. Each of you describes your families of origin in terms of closeness and flexibility. The map can help you better understand the family dynamics in your families of origin and how those dynamics compare with your partner's family.

Cultural context. The diversity in families today in terms of ethnicity, level of education, financial conditions, and family structure adds to the complexity in a marriage. This assessment offers information about these topics for you to share and discuss.

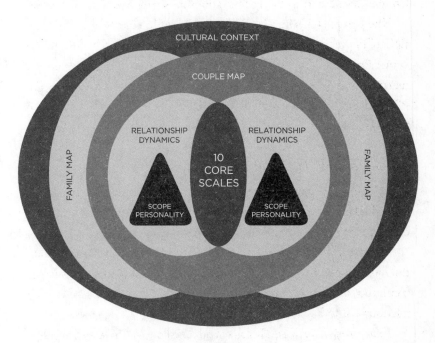

Major Goals of the Couple Checkup

Thomas Carlyle wrote that a "block of granite, which is an obstacle in the pathway of the weak, becomes a stepping-stone in the pathway of the strong." A major goal of the Couple Checkup is to turn stumbling blocks (issues) into stepping-stones (strengths). You can achieve this goal by taking the checkup and then reviewing, discussing, and processing the results with your fiancé(e) or spouse. The Couple Checkup is designed to help couples in the following ways:

1. *The checkup stimulates you to talk about your relationship.* Couples rarely talk directly with each other about their perceptions and feelings about their relationship. It's easier to talk about their work, children, daily activities, and interests, but not about their relationship. Relationship talk is hard because it leaves you vulnerable when opinions, feelings, and needs are openly shared. Answering questions about your relationship creates curiosity in how your partner answered the questions. This can stimulate you to talk about your relationship.

2. *The checkup identifies and helps build your relationship strengths.* One of the advantages of doing a Couple Checkup is that it will reveal your relationship strengths, including some you may not have been aware of or perhaps have never discussed. Couples often assume they know each other, but our studies have found they only agree with each other on the characteristics of their relationships about 33 percent of the time. This means that rather than assuming you know your partner's feelings and ideas, you should assume your guesses will often be incorrect. You can greatly benefit from taking an assessment that will reveal how each of you feels about different aspects of your relationship.

3. *The checkup identifies and encourages you to resolve relationship growth areas (issues).* An important goal of the Couple Checkup is to help couples build new strengths by resolving current issues. All intimate couples have issues and areas where their relationships could improve. Quite often, couples have difficulty resolving current issues, or they simply try to avoid discussing problematic areas in their relationships. This leaves couples feeling that their issues never seem to get resolved. In fact, one of the top issues men and women complained about from a list of survey items was "Some of our differences never seem to get resolved." For men, this statement was the third most cited issue, and it was the second most common issue for women.[6] Unless you're able to

resolve issues in your relationship, tension will build and create more problems.

4. *The checkup helps you learn effective relationship skills.* Four of the top five predictors of a happy marriage are relationship skills: communication, conflict resolution, couple closeness, and couple flexibility. You can learn skills to improve these areas in your relationship. Once learned, these skills can be used not only in your marriage but in other relationships as well.

5. *The checkup helps turn your stumbling blocks (issues) into stepping-stones (strengths).* The Couple Checkup Report and an online discussion guide are resources designed to give you power to resolve ongoing issues and create a stronger relationship. Ultimately, you need to feel equipped to resolve issues so you can turn relationship challenges into strengths. With a good base of knowledge and some relationships skills, you can tackle many difficult issues in marriage and increase relationship satisfaction.

Benefits of the Couple Checkup for Your Relationship

The seven letters in the word *checkup* can help you remember the advantages of taking the Couple Checkup with your partner:

C—*Create positive change.* You can create positive changes in your relationship by establishing new habits that promote a more satisfying relationship. The checkup will help you brainstorm new ideas to change your relationship in positive ways.

H—*Healthy for your relationship.* Checkups promote and maintain relational health. Just as a physical exam or a dental checkup identifies ways to improve your body, the Couple Checkup identifies ways to improve your relationship.

E—*Evaluate where you are now.* The best way to identify areas of improvement is to evaluate your current relationship. In fact, the first step in most medical treatment is a diagnostic assessment.

C—*Communicate more effectively.* The checkup gives you the opportunity to share and discuss the specific results that reveal how each of you sees the many aspects of your relationship.

K—*Kick-start your relationship.* Couples often need some outside intervention to stimulate discussions and change the way they typically operate. The checkup is one effective way to kick-start discussions and begin to implement positive change.

U—*Understand each other.* Checkup results may surprise you when you learn how your partner responded to the statements. By sharing the results, you can gain a better understanding of each other's ideas and feelings.

P—*Proactive versus reactive.* Too often couples wait for a problem to become more serious before they deal with the issue directly. The checkup can help you be proactive by giving you exercises to complete and encouraging you to resolve current issues.

The following are a few more positive reasons for taking the Couple Checkup:

- It's a simple, fun way to learn about yourself and your relationship.
- It's tailor-made to your relationship based on background questions.
- It's relevant to couples at various stages of their relationship— dating, engaged, married.
- It can be completed on a computer, tablet, or smart phone.
- It only takes about twenty to thirty minutes for each person to complete.
- It's completely confidential.
- It stimulates discussion about your relationship.
- It primes you for improving your relationship.

- It's an easy way to identify and explore your relationship strengths.
- It helps you to clarify and resolve problematic issues.
- The Checkup and Report are objective in nature.
- A detailed Couple Report goes directly back to you.
- It personalizes the couple program so it is more relevant to your relationship.

One of the first steps in your *Ready to Wed* experience is to go online at *www.FocusOnTheFamily.com/ReadyToWed* and take the Couple Checkup. To maximize the value and effectiveness of the *Ready to Wed* experience, the Couple Checkup and the *Ready to Wed* book have been fully integrated. They provide a comprehensive picture of the same twelve important areas of a couple's relationship.

This table illustrates the corresponding sections of the *Ready to Wed* book and the matching Couple Checkup categories.

Ready to Wed Chapters	Couple Checkup Category
2—Leaving Your Parents and Cleaving to Your Spouse	Family of Origin—page 12
5—Soul Mates: Building Spiritual Intimacy	Spiritual Beliefs—page 8
6—One Flesh: Sexual Intimacy in Marriage	Affection & Sexuality—page 7
7—Communication: The Language of Love	Communication—page 4
8—We Are So Different!	SCOPE Personality—pages 13–17
9—What Do You Expect?	Marriage Expectations—page 9
10—Fight Our Way to a Better Marriage	Conflict Resolution—page 5
11—Teammates: Ending the Chore Wars Before They Start	Relationship Roles—page 10
12—Our Money Relationship	Finances—page 6

Once you have both completed the assessment, you will be notified that your Couple Report (approximately twenty to twenty-five pages) is available for each of you to view, store, and/or print. It will be important to print at least one copy for your use as you go through the *Ready to Wed* experience. (Optional Guide: There is also a discussion guide, which contains about twenty couple exercises related to the various topic areas. This guide is in addition to the materials and ideas provided in this program. You can review the guide and selectively print out the relevant pages for each couple exercise.)

DAVID H. OLSON, PhD, is Professor Emeritus, Family Social Science, University of Minnesota, St. Paul, MN, and founder and CEO of PREPARE/ENRICH. He is the past president of the National Council on Family Relations and the Upper Midwest Association of Marital and Family Therapists. He has received over ten national awards for his contributions. He developed the PREPARE/ENRICH Program, which has been taken by nearly four million couples and has offices in thirteen countries (eight different languages). His most recent books include *The Couple Checkup* and *The Smart Stepfamily Marriage*. He has appeared numerous times on national television, including the *Today* show, *This Morning*, *Good Morning America*, and *The Oprah Winfrey Show*.

AMY K. OLSON, MA, MFT, is director of programs at PREPARE/ENRICH and has been with the company since 1996. She serves on the executive team and customer service team. She is coauthor of several books and group programs, including *The Couple Checkup*, *Empowering Couples*, and *PREPARE-ENRICH-INSPIRE* for youth. She is coauthor of numerous scientific and popular articles on the PREPARE/ENRICH Program.

APPENDIX B

THE LOGB PERSONAL STRENGTHS SURVEY

John Trent, PhD

DURING MY DOCTORAL PROGRAM, I studied many different tests that were created to help people see their strengths. However, I quickly discovered that while most were very helpful, almost all of them were extremely complicated to take, and even the results were hard to understand! For example, one popular personality tool uses 364 questions to assess a person's strengths and weaknesses—and you have to be certified to explain what your answers to those questions mean!

So I decided to create a tool that was accurate and easy to read and that someone could take in just three to five minutes. The goal of the assessment was to give people a picture of their unique, God-given strengths.

If you look at the survey we're asking you to take (at the end of this section), you'll see it has only four boxes—an L box, an O box, a G box, and a B box. And in each box, there are only fourteen words or short phrases in two lists, and then below those words, there is one phrase.

For example, if you'll look at the L box, you'll see a list of words in two columns beginning with "Takes charge." Underneath that list of fourteen words, you'll see the statement in italics, *"Let's do it now!"*

To complete this survey (not a test but a tool to help you see your strengths), all you need to do is think about how you naturally react when you're *at home* with your fiancé(e) or spouse. (Feel free to take this instrument later on to determine who you are when you're *at work*. Many of us tend to be one personality type when we're at home and someone very different when we're at work.)

For now, however, focus on identifying your strengths *at home*, with your fiancé(e) or spouse. Read through all four boxes (the L, O, G, and B boxes), and *circle* every word and phrase in each box that describes who you are as a person.

For example, start with the L box. Using a pen or pencil, read and circle *every word or phrase* in the list that sounds like you. If you are "assertive" when you're at home, circle it. If you tend to "take charge," then you'd circle those words. Be sure and circle the statement at the bottom of the L box—*"Let's do it now!"*—if it describes you as well.

That means there are fourteen words or phrases and one statement in each box you could choose to circle—or fifteen possible responses in each box. Feel free to circle all fifteen words or phrases in a box if all of them describe you. In some of the boxes, you might circle only a few words, or even none. Just be sure to circle every word and phrase that gives you an internal head nod that says, *Yep! That's me all right!*

After you've gone through each box circling every word and phrase that describes you, then do what it says at the bottom of each box, and "double the number circled."

For example, let's say in the L box you circled seven words and the statement "Let's do it now!" So that's eight total circles in the L box. Doubling the number circled would mean that your total score for the L box would be 16 (8 x 2 = 16).

What do you do with that number?

See the Strengths Assessment Chart below the four boxes? You'll notice that on the graph, there is an L line, an O line, a G line, and a B line. And over on the left, you'll see the numbers 0–30. Just take your total score from your L box (in the example above, 16 was the total score), and put a dot on L line just above the 15. (Note: Some of you might end up with a tie for the highest score, which is common.)

Now double the number circled in the O, G, and B boxes as well.

The last thing to do is *connect the dots*! That will give you a graph. That's it! Now you have a picture of your unique, God-given strengths!

L

Takes charge	Bold
Determined	Purposeful
Assertive	Decision maker
Firm	Leader
Enterprising	Goal-driven
Competitive	Self-reliant
Enjoys challenges	Adventurous

"Let's do it now!"

Double the number circled _____

O

Takes risks	Fun-loving
Visionary	Likes variety
Motivator	Enjoys change
Energetic	Creative
Very verbal	Group-oriented
Promoter	Mixes easily
Avoids details	Optimistic

"Trust me! It'll work out!"

Double the number circled _____

G

Loyal	Adaptable
Nondemanding	Sympathetic
Even keel	Thoughtful
Avoids conflict	Nurturing
Enjoys routine	Patient
Dislikes change	Tolerant
Deep relationships	Good listener

*"Let's keep things
the way they are."*

Double the number circled _____

B

Deliberate	Discerning
Controlled	Detailed
Reserved	Analytical
Predictable	Inquisitive
Practical	Precise
Orderly	Persistent
Factual	Scheduled

*"How was it done
in the past?"*

Double the number circled _____

Strengths Assessment Chart

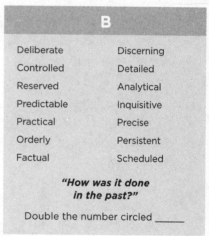

	L	O	G	B
30				
15				
0				

NOTES

INTRODUCTION

1. David Olson, Amy Olson-Sigg, and Peter J. Larson, *The Couple Checkup* (Nashville: Thomas Nelson, 2008), 6.
2. Ibid.
3. David H. Olson and Amy K. Olson, *Empowering Couples: Building on Your Strengths* (Minneapolis: Life Innovations, 2000).
4. Jason S. Carroll and William J. Doherty, "Evaluating the Effectiveness of Premarital Prevention Programs: A Meta-Analytic Review of Outcome Research," *Family Relations* 52, no. 2 (April 2003): 105–118.

CHAPTER 1: GOD'S DESIGN FOR MARRIAGE

1. John Eldredge and Stasi Eldredge, *Love and War* (New York: Doubleday, 2009), 18.
2. Reb Bradley, *Help for the Struggling Marriage*, quoted in "What Is God's Primary Purpose for Marriage?" http://www.familyministries.com/marriage_purpose.htm.
3. Tim Keller and Kathy Keller, *The Meaning of Marriage: Facing the Complexities of Commitment with the Wisdom of God* (New York: Riverhead Books, 2011), 112–113.
4. Gary Thomas, *Sacred Marriage: What If God Designed Marriage to Make Us Holy More Than to Make Us Happy?* (Grand Rapids: Zondervan, 2000), summarized in Wendy Connell, *Christian Book Summaries* 4, no. 25, http://www.christianbooksummaries.com/archive.php?v=4&i=25.

CHAPTER 4: HONORING YOU ALL THE DAYS OF MY LIFE

1. John Gottman, quoted in "Quotes on 'Communication and Conflict,'" *Marriage Missions International* (blog), accessed November 15, 2014, http://marriagemissions.com/about-us-2/quotes-on-communication-and-conflict/.
2. Quote by Scott Stanley, ibid.
3. Max Lucado, *3:16: The Numbers of Hope* (Nashville: Thomas Nelson, 2007), 28.

4. Doug Apple, "Marriage Key: Soften Your Heart," radio transcript, May 9, 2008, in *Apples of Gold* (blog), accessed November 21, 2014, http://dougapple.blogspot.com/2008/05/marriage-key-soften-your-heart-apples.html.

5. Susan Forward, *When Your Lover Is a Liar* (New York: HarperCollins, 1999), 92.

CHAPTER 5: SOUL MATES

1. Adapted from Lon Adams, "Do We Have to Pray Together?" in *Complete Guide to the First Five Years of Marriage* (Carol Stream, IL: Focus on the Family/Tyndale, 2006), 285–287.

2. Teri K. Reisser and Paul C. Reisser, *Your Spouse Isn't the Person You Married* (Carol Stream, IL: Focus on the Family/Tyndale, 2010), 29–30.

3. Tricia Goyer, in Ken Blanchard, Phil Hodges, and Tricia Goyer, *Lead Your Family Like Jesus* (Carol Stream, IL: Focus on the Family/Tyndale, 2013), 169.

CHAPTER 6: ONE FLESH

1. John Piper, *This Momentary Marriage: A Parable of Permanence* (Wheaton, IL: Crossway, 2009), 135.

CHAPTER 7: COMMUNICATION

1. John Gottman, *What Makes Love Last? How to Build Trust and Avoid Betrayal* (New York: Simon and Schuster, 2012), 47–48.

2. Ibid.

3. David Burns, *Feeling Good Together: The Secret to Making Troubled Relationships Work* (Bourbon, IN: Harmony, 2010).

4. Jason Headley, *It's Not About the Nail*, YouTube, accessed November 22, 2014, http://www.youtube.com/watch?v=-4EDhdAHrOg.

5. Adapted from Gary Smalley and John Trent, *Love Is a Decision* (Nashville, TN: Thomas Nelson, 2001).

6. Richard Swenson, *Margin: Restoring Emotional, Physical, Financial, and Time Reserves to Overloaded Lives* (Colorado Springs, CO: NavPress, 2004).

7. Based on examples in Brené Brown, *Daring Greatly: How the Courage to Be Vulnerable Transforms the Way We Live, Love, Parent, and Lead* (New York: Gotham Books, 2012).

CHAPTER 9: WHAT DO YOU EXPECT?

1. This concept originally appeared in Bill and Pam Farrel's book, *The Marriage Code* (Eugene, OR: Harvest House, 2009).

2. Discussion adapted from Bill Farrel and Pam Farrel, *Men Are like Waffles— Women Are like Spaghetti* (Eugene, OR: Harvest House, 2001), 11–13.

CHAPTER 10: FIGHT OUR WAY TO A BETTER MARRIAGE

1. Max Lucado, *When God Whispers Your Name* (Nashville: Thomas Nelson, 1999), 44.

2. Scott M. Stanley et al., "Strengthening Marriages and Preventing Divorce: New Directions in Prevention Research," *Family Relations* 44, no. 4 (October 1995):

392–401, http://content.csbs.utah.edu/~fan/fcs5400-6400/studentpresentation 2009/04DivorceReadingStanley.pdf.

3. John Gottman, *Why Marriages Succeed or Fail: And How to Make Yours Last* (New York: Simon and Schuster, 1994), 28.

4. Dallin H. Oaks, "World Peace," *Ensign* (May 1990): 71.

5. Sabrina Beasley McDonald, "10 Surprising Ways to Increase Romance," *FamilyLife*, 2008, accessed November 23, 2014, http://www.familylife.com /articles/topics/marriage/staying-married/romance-and-sex/10-surprising-ways -to-increase-romance#.UlNPKhaLN0U.

6. Posting by Adrian, "Don't Let Your 'Hot Buttons' Spoil Your Chances," Lifehack.org, accessed November 15, 2014, http://www.lifehack.org /articles/communication/don%e2%80%99t-let-your-%e2%80%9chot -buttons%e2%80%9d-spoil-your-chances.html.

7. Matthew D. Lieberman et al., "Subjective Responses to Emotional Stimuli During Labeling, Reappraisal, and Distraction," *Emotion* 11, no. 3 (2011): 468–480, http://www.scn.ucla.edu/pdf/Lieberman-Emotion(2011).pdf.

8. Adapted from Greg Smalley, *Fight Your Way to a Better Marriage* (New York: Howard Books, 2012), 233–234.

9. Gary Smalley, *Secrets to Lasting Love* (New York: Fireside, 2000), 94–95.

10. Gary Smalley, *Making Love Last Forever* (Nashville: Thomas Nelson, 1997), 230.

CHAPTER 11: TEAMMATES

1. Adapted from Dale Mathis and Susan Mathis, *Countdown for Couples: Preparing for the Adventure of Marriage* (Carol Stream, IL: Focus on the Family/Tyndale, 2008), 135.

CHAPTER 12: OUR MONEY RELATIONSHIP

1. Survey cited in Raina Kelley, "Expert Advice: Love by the Numbers: Your New Marriage Is Bliss—Until the Bickering over Finances Begins. How to Keep Money from Wrecking Your Home Life," *Newsweek*, April 9, 2007, 48.

2. Melanie Hicken, "How to Talk About Money Before Saying, 'I Do,'" CNN Money, June 13, 2013, http://money.cnn.com/2013/06/13/news/money -marriage/index.html.

CHAPTER 13: STORM SHELTER

1. Research cited in Benjamin Karney, "Stress Is Bad for Couples, Right?" National Council on Family Relations, NCFR.org, accessed November 15, 2014, https://www.ncfr.org/ncfr-report/focus/couples/stress-bad-couples-right.

2. "Stress Management—Topic Overview," Stress Management Health Center, WebMD.com, accessed November 15, 2014, http://www.webmd.com/balance /stress-management/stress-management-topic-overview.

3. Les Parrott and Leslie Parrot, "Busyness: The Modern Disease," eH Advice, eHarmony.com, accessed November 15, 2014, http://www.eharmony.com /dating-advice/about-you/busyness-the-modern-disease/#.VGgTcuktDIV.

4. Judy Ford, quoted in Margarita Tartakovsky, "How Couples Can Help Each Other De-Stress and Improve Their Relationship," PsychCentral.com, accessed November 15, 2014, http://psychcentral.com/lib/how-couples -can-help-each-other-de-stress-and-improve-their-relationship/0009691.

5. Lisa A. Neff and Benjamin R. Karney, "How Does Context Affect Intimate Relationships? Linking External Stress and Cognitive Processes Within Marriage," *Personality and Social Psychology Bulletin* 30, no. 2 (February 2004): 134–148, cited in Karney, "Stress Is Bad for Couples, Right?" https://www.ncfr.org/ncfr -report/focus/couples/stress-bad-couples-right.

6. Lisa A. Neff and Benjamin R. Karney "Stress and Reactivity to Daily Relationship Experiences: How Stress Hinders Adaptive Processes in Marriage," *Journal of Personality and Social Psychology* 97, no. 3 (2009): 435–450, cited in Karney, "Stress Is Bad for Couples, Right?" https://www.ncfr.org/ncfr-report/focus /couples/stress-bad-couples-right.

7. Neff and Karney, "Stress and Reactivity to Daily Relationship Experiences," 448.

8. Max Lucado, *3:16: The Number of Hope* (Nashville: Thomas Nelson, 2007), 28.

9. Judy Ford, quoted in Tartakovsky "How Couples Can Help Each Other De-Stress and Improve Their Relationship," http://psychcentral.com/lib/how-couples-can -help-each-other-de-stress-and-improve-their-relationship/0009691.

10. American Academy of Family Physicians, cited in "Learning to Relax," Stress Awareness Health Education Program, accessed November 15, 2014, http:// www.amerihealth.com/pdfs/custom/worksite_wellness/turnkey_programs /stress_awareness/stress_fact_sheet.pdf.

11. Robert Barron, *Heaven in Stone and Glass* (New York: Crossroad, 2002).

12. Karney, "Stress Is Bad for Couples, Right?" https://www.ncfr.org/ncfr-report /focus/couples/stress-bad-couples-right.

13. Lisa Neff, cited in Margaret Wheeler Johnson, "11 Ways to Keep Stress from Hurting Your Marriage," *Huffington Post*, August 19, 2013, http://www .huffingtonpost.com/2013/08/19/11-ways-to-keep-stress-from-hurting-your -marriage_n_3756436.html.

14. Lisa A. Neff and Elizabeth F. Broady, "Stress Resilience in Early Marriage: Can Practice Make Perfect?" *Journal of Personality and Social Psychology* 101, no. 5 (November 2011).

15. Dr. Larry Barlow, quoted in Becky Sweat, "How Can You Manage Marriage Stress in Troubling Times?" *Good News*, accessed November 15, 2014, http://www.ucg .org/relationships/how-can-you-manage-marriage-stress-troubling-times/.

APPENDIX A: COUPLE CHECKUP

1. US Census Bureau, *Statistical Abstracts of the United States*, 132th ed., (Washington, DC: Government Printing Office, 2012), www.census.gov.

2. Linda Waite and Maggie Gallagher, *The Case for Marriage: Why Married People Are Happier, Healthier, and Better off Financially* (Cambridge, MA: Harvard University Press, 2000).

3. Warren Buffett, interview by Mohnish Pabrai, 2007, quoted in Heather

Koerner, "Warren Buffet on Marriage," *Boundless Blog*, June 23, 2009, accessed November 25, 2014, https://community.focusonthefamily.com/b/boundless /archive/2009/06/23/warren-buffett-on-marriage.aspx.

4. David Brooks, "The Sandra Bullock Trade," Dallas News Opinion, *Dallas Morning News*, March 29, 2010, http://www.dallasnews.com/opinion/latest -columns/20100331-David-Brooks-The-Sandra-Bullock-7115.ece.

5. David Olson, Amy Olson-Sigg, and Peter J. Larson, *The Couple Checkup* (Nashville: Thomas Nelson, 2008).

6. Ibid.

The *Ready to Wed* Video Study Program

Finally—a complete, all-in-one program for pastors, marriage mentors, and counselors who long to help couples create a loving, healthy marriage that will last a lifetime! Featuring an engaging 10-session video series, useful online tools, and comprehensive couple's workbooks, this toolkit is the perfect companion to any premarital counseling program or church marriage ministry. For more information, visit FocusOnTheFamily.com/ReadyToWed. Available fall 2015.

More Resources to Help You Thrive in Marriage and Life

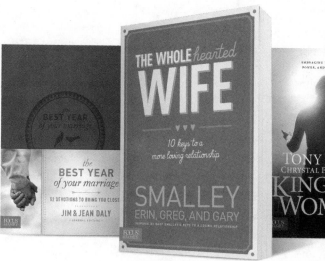

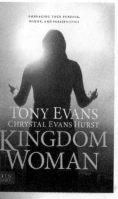

Starting now, this could be your best day, week, month, or year! Discover ways to express your needs, embrace your purpose, and love more fully. We offer life-transforming books, e-books, videos, devotionals, study guides, audiobooks, and audio dramas to equip you for God's calling on your life. Visit your favorite retailer, or go to FocusOnTheFamily.com/resources.